TRANSFORMING CONVERSATIONS

TRANSFORMING CONVERSATIONS

*Feminism and Education in Canada
since 1970*

Edited by Dawn Wallin and Janice Wallace

McGill-Queen's University Press
Montreal & Kingston • London • Chicago

© McGill-Queen's University Press 2018

ISBN 978-0-7735-5356-9 (cloth)
ISBN 978-0-7735-5357-6 (paper)
ISBN 978-0-7735-5431-3 (ePDF)
ISBN 978-0-7735-5432-0 (ePUB)

Legal deposit second quarter 2018
Bibliothèque nationale du Québec

Printed in Canada on acid-free paper that is 100% ancient forest free (100% post-consumer recycled), processed chlorine free.

This book has been published with the help of a grant from the Canadian Federation for the Humanities and Social Sciences, through the Awards to Scholarly Publications Program, using funds provided by the Social Sciences and Humanities Research Council of Canada. Funding has also been received from the University of Saskatchewan Publications Fund.

We acknowledge the support of the Canada Council for the Arts, which last year invested $153 million to bring the arts to Canadians throughout the country.

Nous remercions le Conseil des arts du Canada de son soutien. L'an dernier, le Conseil a investi 153 millions de dollars pour mettre de l'art dans la vie des Canadiennes et des Canadiens de tout le pays.

Library and Archives Canada Cataloguing in Publication

Transforming conversations : feminism and education in Canada since 1970 / edited by Dawn Wallin and Janice Wallace.

Includes bibliographical references and index.
Issued in print and electronic formats.
ISBN 978-0-7735-5356-9 (hardcover). – ISBN 978-0-7735-5357-6 (softcover). – ISBN 978-0-7735-5431-3 (ePDF). – ISBN 978-0-7735-5432-0 (ePUB)

1. Feminism and education – Canada. 2. Feminism and higher education – Canada. I. Wallin, Dawn C. (Dawn Colette), 1971–, editor II. Wallace, Janice, 1944–, editor

LC197.T73 2018   370.82   C2018-900596-3
                                       C2018-900597-1

This book was typeset by True to Type in 10.5/13 Sabon

Contents

INTRODUCTION

Transforming Conversations: Feminism and Education in Canada since 1970
Janice Wallace and Dawn Wallin 3

PART ONE DISCOURSES OF TEACHING: SPEAKING UP
Janice Wallace 17

1 Who Do You Think You Are? Feminist Change in Post-Secondary Education: An Uneven Record
Sharon Anne Cook 22

2 Feminist Reformers: Creating Pedagogical Change to Curriculum in Toronto Schools through Inclusive Content
Rose Fine-Meyer 42

3 Feminist Influence on Ontario Schools
Jean Hewitt 71

PART TWO DISCOURSES OF LEADERSHIP: SPEAKING OUT
Dawn Wallin 91

4 Rewriting Sisyphus: The Possibilities of Feminism in Educational Administration
Janice Wallace 98

5 Moths to the Flame Tend to Get Burned: Life on the Liminal
Dawn Wallin 120

6 Performing Boundaries: Feminism Entanglements in Educational Administration
Melody Viczko   144

PART THREE   DISRUPTING DISCOURSES: SPEAKING BACK TO FEMINISM
Janice Wallace   165

7 Lessons on Dismantling the Master's House: An Adult Educator's Reflections on Intersectional Feminism
Evelyn Hamdon   171

8 Indigenizing My Roots in Feminism
Marlene McKay   188

9 Visible Minority Teachers in Canada: Decolonizing the Knowledges of Euro-American Hegemony through Feminist Epistemologies and Ontologies
Thashika Pillay   210

CODA   ROUNDING OUT THE CONVERSATION
Janice Wallace   227

10 A Critical Feminist Exploration of Arts-Based Education in Canada: Embodied Teaching, Learning, and Research within an Equity Framework
Carol E. Harris   229

CONCLUSION

Moving On: An Invitation to Continue the Conversation
Dawn Wallin and Janice Wallace   259

Contributors   267

Index   269

TRANSFORMING CONVERSATIONS

INTRODUCTION

Transforming Conversations
Feminism and Education in Canada since 1970

JANICE WALLACE AND DAWN WALLIN

I have come to believe over and over again that what is most important to me must be spoken, made verbal and shared, even at the risk of having it bruised and misunderstood.

Lorde 1984, 40

This is a moment in feminism that is fraught with great risk and that tantalizes with promise: a time in which feminism has become a very public object of deeply divided and lively conversation. Feminism, it seems, has come out of the shadows as Canada's Prime Minister Trudeau[1] and pop culture icons from Beyoncé to Alicia Keys to Emma Watson have openly declared themselves as feminists. Yet, as Janell Hobson argues in the December edition of the *Ms. Magazine Blog*, "2016 was so feminist in its memes, shows, music, and other cultural moments that some have argued this political momentum created the backlash that led to Donald Trump's election to the presidency of the United States" (2016).

While the causal connection between the popularization of feminism and a growing movement toward populist right-wing politics characterized by what Fraser (2009) calls "reactionary chauvinism" (143) may be overstated, current events demonstrate the chasm between social and political positions in relation to feminism. On the one hand, in the United States, we have a demonstrably misogynist president elected in a country where legal gains for women are under attack or have been rolled back entirely; on the other hand, President Trump's inauguration was followed the next day by a women's march that was not only the largest in the history of the United States, but also international in scope, including in several locations across Canada.[2] The clear message of the Women's March was solidarity among feminist activists across feminisms for human rights in the face of misogynistic and increasingly racist and homophobic rhetoric and policy, and acts of violence by those emboldened by reactionary populist political movements epitomized by Trump's election.

The Women's March also revealed lively conversations and disagreements across feminisms deeply rooted in differing histories of race, class, sexual orientations and identities, and ableness.[3] The points of contention across feminisms are not new: nor are the solidarity and resistance to continued allocation of social, political, and economic advantage to men. The Royal Commission on the Status of Women (Canada 1970), commissioned in 1967 and tabled with the federal government in 1970, is a kind of case study of those conversations in Canada. The RCSW (Canada 1970) emerged out of the multiple voices of second-wave feminists in the 1960s. While their motivating theoretical positions were multiple – particularly critical and liberal feminism – the final iteration of the RCSW report represented the liberal feminist perspective that women could best achieve their goals for equality with men with the support of the state. The RCSW report was an important milestone, "[h]owever, apart from occasional references to First Nations women, even fewer allusions to 'immigrant women,' and the sporadic use of parallels between 'women' and 'minorities,' the REPORT renders invisible the social and political realities of racialized Canadians" (Williams 1990, 750).

Of course, now twenty-five years later, Williams's concerns might also be viewed as limited, in that they do not extend to sexual minority or disabled women. The absences demonstrate that change in "feminist theory ... is informed by social movements and historical contexts, in part due to the lack of explanatory power of earlier theories with regard to changing social, economic, and political conditions" (Blackmore 2016, 2). As feminist theories emerge in response to a changing social, political, and economic order, and the advocacy of suppressed voices, they do so in the context of the persistent demands of the capitalist state. The iteration of liberal feminism demonstrated by the RCSW was a practical politics that attempted to achieve its goals – as determined largely by white, middle-class, cisgender women – through claims upon the state: a state that critical feminists pointed out was patriarchal and that saw women's goals as "particularist"

(Canada 1970, 63–4). Thus, while the promise and subsequent gains of the RCSW were partially successful because of the strategic actions of feminist activists, they are also open to critique.

The RCSW (Canada 1970) "listed education as one of nine public policy areas 'particularly germane to the status of women'" (ix) (Coulter 1996, 434). Yet, as Williams (1990) notes, the report on education in chapter 3 of RCSW "addresses the 'special' educational needs of 'Native Women of the North'. Both rural and immigrant women are perceived to face problems of access to education and training and of adjustment to the lifestyles of Canadian urban environments. However, while the needs of rural women are to be met by governments, responsibility for delivering educational services to immigrant women is delegated to the voluntary sector. As for 'Native Women of the North', the Commission sympathizes with their alienation from the intrusion of Euro-Canadian education into their lives. But ultimately the REPORT holds First Nations women responsible for ensuring that their daughters receive 'proper' education" (746). Clearly, a liberal feminist perspective did little, if anything, to encourage the government to meet the educational needs of immigrant and Indigenous women, nor did the report name sexual minority, racialized, or disabled women as subjects of concern in its report on education.

More than fifteen years after the release of the RCSW, Jane Gaskell and Arlene Tigar McLaren published a co-edited collection of feminist papers that focused specifically on education entitled *Women and Education: A Canadian Perspective* (1987). They note in the introduction (5) that, although there had been substantial feminist policy and theoretical work produced about women and education in the United States and Britain, their book was the first of its kind in Canada. It is a remarkable experience to read their book now, thirty years after it was published, because the themes remain so familiar: critiques of theories of sex-role stereotyping, political and theoretical differences within feminism, the centrality of women to teaching and the devaluing and sex discrimination they have experienced, the implacability of sex-segregated work at home and the workplace, and the challenge of whose knowledge is represented in schools and classrooms. It is also the story of agency – of women who spoke out and engaged one another in conversations that led to action and change around gender issues in schools and school systems. However, it, like the RCSW, does not problematize the category of "woman," nor does it explore the intersectional experiences of women – Indigenous women, racialized women, sexual minority women, disabled women – in educational locations.

Thirty years after the Gaskell and McLaren book (1987), and almost fifty years after the Royal Commission on the Status of Women (Canada 1970) was published, we, the co-editors of this book, were talking with Sharon Cook, who has been a key supporter in this venture. We had what started out as a casual conversation about issues that were of significant importance to us: the effects on feminist scholarship and practice in education following the retirement of so many Canadian feminist scholars whose lives and careers have followed the trajectory of feminism in education since the Royal Commission, our own experiences in school systems and academe, the state of feminist scholarship, and the need for a reconsideration of the effects of feminism on education in Canada. That conversation led to many more, and to the decision to write a book that reflects our attempt to reinvigorate a critical conversation by providing an historical context for Canadian feminism in education subsequent to the 1970 report of the Royal Commission on the Status of Women. Our goal was to explore the development of feminist thought and action in education over the past fifty years, and the absences and possibilities in current feminist discourses that invite reimagining and supporting a more equitable educational future. Essentially, the book we imagined would explore the question: "What effect, if any, has feminism had on education in Canada since the Royal Commission on the Status of Women, and to what end?"

In order to address this question, then, it was important for us to consider the meaning of feminism – a task that is impossible in any fixed sense since, as already noted about feminist scholarship and activism, various feminist approaches have emerged in response to a wide range of complex social, political, and economic constructs in social institutions, including education. Most definitions have at their core an understanding of feminism as "a social movement whose basic goal is equality between men and women" (Lorber 2010). However, this core understanding is problematized by those who argue that sex is a spectrum rather than a binary construct (Connell 2009) and, therefore, the definition is exclusionary. Lorber suggests that a more productive way forward is to understand that there are multiple feminisms: for example, liberal, Marxist, socialist, postcolonial, Asian, radical, lesbian, psychoanalytic, standpoint, and others.

Given the plethora of possibilities, we have chosen to approach the question, "What is feminism?" by considering it in the context of predominant theoretical strands in feminist educational scholarship as well as the history of feminism's enactment by activist educators. For example, as the chapters in part 1 demonstrate, liberal feminism, premised on individualism and reliance on the state to implement social policy, was the predominant theoretical platform underpinning teacher activism in the 1970s, and continues to play a predominant role in the vestiges of feminist advocacy that remain in contemporary neo-liberal education bureaucracies. Liberal feminism has been a useful approach to resist and reconstruct social systems premised on false notions of meritocracy in hiring school and system administrators. For example, the Federation of Women Teachers' Association of Ontario (FWTAO) worked hard to change board hiring policies that favoured men, to set up workshops to encourage women to consider leadership roles and prepare them for interviews, and to advocate strongly for provincial equity policy that set goals for increasing the number of women in positions of authority.

The critique of liberal feminism, particularly from critical/neo-Marxist/socialist feminists (e.g., Eisenstein 1978; Marshall 1992; Blackmore 2016) was that this approach did nothing to challenge the social and political systems and institutional practices that held gender hegemony in place. Instead, they advocated for a feminist solidarity to end oppression and to challenge the ways in which capital and the means of production worked to privilege male teachers and administrators. bell hooks's (1984) critique extended this critical analysis by arguing that liberal feminism was premised on a false unity that negated the voices of Black, poor, and oppressed women within a capitalist patriarchal society. The validity of this critique is evident in part 1 as the authors explore liberal feminist reforms in education and reveal, by who speaks (and who does not), whose interests were served in schools and school systems (and whose were not) as a result of liberal feminist advocacy in Canadian educational contexts.

Radical feminists (Gilligan 1982; Belenky et al. 1986; Noddings 1992) critiqued both liberal and critical/neo-Marxist/socialist feminism for, among other things, the lack of differentiation between men's and women's social reality, ethics, ways of being and knowing, and the presumption that women were simply interchangeable, nonsexed ciphers in a workplace that was organized around male norms. They argued, instead, that women's experiences were informed by their embodied lives as women and that the political was very much the personal. Thus, they advocated for a woman-centred social order in which women's values and "ways of being" were central to both the public and private spheres of social and political engagement (Belenky et al. 1986). Rather than denying its existence in order to move into positions of authority, radical feminists celebrated women's ways of knowing and being, and considered emotionality and multiple forms of knowledge as strengths. Critical feminists countered with the argument that radical feminism was overly essentialist and arbitrary, and simply exchanged one set of constraints for another in limiting possibilities for women in a world dominated by patriarchal norms. Radical feminists in education responded with support for girls-only classes and schools in which girls could develop and learn in an environment that supported their "essential" feminine self without the need to respond to male dominance, oppression, and overt sexualization.

The emergence of postmodern/post-structural feminism (e.g., Cherryholmes 1988; Lather 1991), which informs many of the chapters in parts 2 and 3 of this book, was a response to essentialized claims in feminism and turned to the ways in which language structures how we construct meanings that are indeterminate and contextual. As Wallin (2001) suggests, postmodern feminism "accepts that knowledge is always provisional, open-ended, and relational. The contextual character of all knowledge and knowing suggests that there can be no finite and unitary truths; inherent in this framework is the centrality of subjectivity and context. Various postmodern feminists maintain an interest in signification, in power/knowledge relationships, in damage done by master-narratives, and in the way institutional structures are controlled. The postmodern feminist pedagogy therefore demands a critical examination of underlying assumptions" (28).

Post-structural feminism extends and is complementary to postmodern feminism in that it is situated in language and the formation of discourses that construct gendered subjectivities. It is an epistemology that questions universalizing constructs such as woman and man and, therefore, opens up possibilities for those who perform gender in non-normative ways. Post-structural feminism has been particularly helpful in challenging gendered assumptions that hide behind a mask of rationality (Rottmann 2006). For example, Rottmann argues that introducing queer theory to the study of educational administration provides an "implicit challenge to normative structures and its embodiment of the physical and emotional elements of schooling that are so often hidden by a mask of mandated rationality" (1). Similarly, post-structural men's studies (e.g., Atkinson and Kehler 2010) deconstruct notions of hegemonic masculinity and open up possibilities for performing a reconstructed masculinity that may occupy multiple locations on a gender spectrum.

While some theorists critique post-structural constructs, such as discourses of power and oppression, as lacking materiality (e.g., Fraser 1997), many postcolonial feminists have found that exploring intersections of gender, race, class, sexual identity, ethnicity, able-ness, and so on, opens up spaces that have been previously ignored in education. For example, Black/antiracist feminism has carved out significant theoretical space for the work of Black/racialized women in education (e.g., hooks 1994; Collins 2010; Mirza 2014). This work, as well as that of Indigenous feminists – rooted in critical, postmodern, and post/anticolonial feminism – makes significant epistemological approaches that inform the chapters in part 3. These approaches are long overdue and helpful for recognizing the experiences and devastating consequences of racism and colonialism among Canada's Indigenous peoples, as well as migrating populations who have settled in Canada from the Global South (Angod 2006). Post/anticolonial feminists have noted that much of feminist theorizing has valorized the experiences and knowledges of white, middle-class, heterosexual women. Instead, postcolonial/Indigenous feminism makes the experiences of those who have been colonized – and bear the effects of that history on their bodies, minds, and hearts – central to their research and analysis (e.g., Tuhiwai Smith 1997, Battiste 2013). Further, as Peden (2011) notes, "the potential strength of Indigenous feminist scholarship is that it provides the tools and methodologies that can be used to deconstruct, analyze, and reconstruct those bureaucratic structures that have typically marginalized those people who do not represent the mainstream in terms of color, ideology, sexual orientation, or ability. As such, this perspective supports the deconstruction of colonial practice" (58).

Despite the challenge to orthodox educational practices that feminist scholarship offers, however, the paradox remains; while education offers the potential for social change by deconstructing social norms, formal educational systems too often respond with deeply entrenched conservatism (O'Brien 1986). For example, the formal education system in Canada was seen by the RCSW (Canada 1970) as key to "bring[ing] dramatic improvements in the social and economic position of women in an astonishingly short time" (161). In some ways, their optimism about increased access to equal educational opportunities for girls and women was justified. Many women have taken advantage of increased educational opportunities in higher education by, for example, working to end quotas for women admitted to medicine and law faculties. However, problems persist in many of the same ways first outlined by the RCSW (although they would likely be taken up differently, both theoretically and practically, today), from prekindergarten to grade 12[4] and in universities and colleges. For example, while the formal education system prepares and credentials graduates seeking employment, career movement, and status in the workplace, evidence persists that women receive less remuneration, career flexibility, and status[5] in the workplace compared to men, despite wider access to educational opportunities. Further, despite formal citizenship education in contemporary democracies, girls and women continue to face barriers, exemplified by the persistent underrepresentation of women in formal political roles or positions of power in political organizations.[6] These observations are even more true for structurally disadvantaged women.

And so we return to the question that is at the core of this book – What effect, if any, has feminism had on Canadian education since the Royal Commission on the Status of Women, and to what end? – while recognizing that defining our question is as complex as the educational context with which we are engaging and as the meaning of feminism itself. As we turn to the inevitable and longstanding tension between feminisms and education that becomes evident in each chapter that follows, we recognize that it is impossible to present a fully encompassing text on the influence of feminism in Canadian education. Rather, we view this book as an invitation to a critical conversation that continues – and needs to continue until gender equity in education is achieved – and encourage others to add their own voices to this often difficult conversation.

We have organized the authors' contributions in this book into three sections followed by a coda and a concluding chapter. Each section begins with an introductory discussion that situates the contexts and issues of its chapters. Part 1, "Discourses of Teaching: Speaking Up," explores the historical context of feminists and female educators in Canadian education who spoke up for women's rights in formal education systems from the 1960s to the 1990s, particularly with regard to policy development, feminist activism, and feminist pedagogy. In doing so, these educators changed the shape of education systems in K–12 settings and university faculties of education. Part 2, "Discourses of Leadership: Speaking Out," discusses the impact of feminists speaking out through their academic work in research, teaching, and service in academe. The authors explore the experience of re/theorizing discourses of educational leadership, and the challenges faced by women who move into formal leadership roles in K–12 settings and higher education. Part 3, "Disrupting Discourses: Speaking Back to Feminism," gives voice to authors who trouble feminism by providing critiques and possibilities for feminist theory and activism in an education system that ostensibly has become more inclusive yet remains bounded within formal, Western, colonial, neo-liberal ideologies. These chapters reflect on the shifting terrains of educational inequity that are reflective of the intersectionalities that differentially affect women's voice, access, representation, and meaningful engagement. The last section is called "Coda: Rounding Out the Conversation." In music, the coda provides a conclusion to a long series of musical pieces and is connected to them but provides something additional and unique. The paper in our coda does just that as it revisits some of the themes already introduced in previous chapters but extends the discussion by exploring the possibilities and contribution of aesthetics and the arts to and through feminism and pedagogy.

We believe that the chapters in this text are representative of the kind of feminist theorizing and agency that have emerged in response to changing social, economic, and political conditions and have made an impact on Canadian education over the past fifty years. While the authors speak from different theoretical perspectives and Canadian locations, they cannot possibly represent every lived experience or educational context that exists in this vast country. For example, we recognize that many of these authors write from an Ontario perspective. This focus is not entirely surprising as Ontario's education system has the highest student enrolment and number of publicly funded schools, and its size has inevitably been overrepresented in framing educational practice and theory. Further, the influence of the FWTAO,[7] a powerful, extremely well-funded and longstanding organization that specifically supported the professional aspirations of women teachers, proved influential in initiating reforms that often spread to other provinces (Mawhinney 1997). However, this emphasis also needs to be recognized as a limitation in the text given the strong work of feminists in other parts of Canada. In particular, Quebec, Yukon, and the Northwest Territories are not represented in the perspectives offered. In addition, this text does not address, or does so only tangentially, a number of other scholarly foci in which feminist theorists have been active in Canadian education, including curriculum development, adult education contexts, and LGBTQIA (lesbian, gay, bisexual, transgender, queer, intersex, and ally) studies.

Ultimately, then, this text, like feminism itself, needs to be critiqued for what it excludes as much as for what it includes. However, our intent was not to focus on specific disciplines in education, but rather on how the influence of feminism is understood by and enlightens each author as she engages with her particular context and educational scholarship. To that end, the contexts, like the field of education itself, are disparate, and our efforts are not all-inclusive regarding the impact of various feminisms in Canadian education. We hope, instead, that the papers provided in this text, which are representative of the plethora of ways in which feminist conceptualizations of education have been taken up by scholars, will (re)inspire feminist conversations within the Canadian educational milieu.

Our final chapter takes up the discussion, initiated in each section of the book, on the effect, if any, feminism has had in various Canadian education contexts, and to what end. We conclude that, while feminism, from its many theoretical perspectives, has had a muted but evident effect on Canadian education, that effect has been uneven, painfully slow, and unrepresentative of structurally disadvantaged voices. However, the complexity of feminist thought and agency is becoming more inclusive as education in Canada reflects more diverse and complex perspectives and social locations. Finally, the discourse of feminism is itself becoming more nuanced as it is being reconstituted within the liminal spaces of varied lived educational experiences.

Contemporary feminists are venturing into shifting ideological territories and educational milieus that are both promising and daunting in the face of mounting social and political repression and reawakened activism. Our hope is that this text provides a sense of how past feminist pursuits have shaped the current state of education and will prompt further conversations toward the development and support of new and productive trajectories for feminist scholars and practitioners.

NOTES

1 Trudeau's self-proclaimed feminism has met with some critique. See, "Is Justin Trudeau Living Up to His Self-Proclaimed Feminist Ideals?" *The Guardian*, 16 March 2017, accessed 24 April 2017, https://www.theguardian.com/world/2017/mar/16/justin-trudeau-feminism-scorecard.
2 See "For Women's March on Washington Protesters, the Fight Is Far from Over," *Globe and Mail*, 16 March 2017, http://www.theglobeandmail.com/news/world/for-womens-march-on-washington-protesters-the-fight-is-far-fromover/article33700263/.
3 For a sense of the debates, see Karen Grigsby Bates, "Race and Feminism: Women's March Recalls the Touchy History," NPR Code Switch, 21 January 2017, accessed 25 April 2017, http://www.npr.org/sections/codeswitch/2017/01/21/510859909/race-and-feminism-womens-march-recalls-the-touchy-history.
4 We are using the grade designations most often used in the Canadian context.
5 See Canadian Women's Foundation, "The Facts about the Gender Wage Gap in Canada," http://www.canadianwomen.org/facts-about-the-gender-wage-gap-in-Canada, and Statistics Canada, "Women in Canada: A Gender-Based Statistical Report," last modified 30 November 2015, http://www.statscan.gc.ca/pub/89-503-x/89-503-x2010001-eng.htm, for further information.
6 According to Equal Voice (see https://www.equalvoice.ca/facts.cfm), currently women occupy 25 per cent of the seats in the federal government – an historic high. Given that women are slightly more than 50 per cent of the Canada's population, this represents an improvement but leaves much room for improvement.
7 FWTAO was amalgamated with the Ontario Public School Men Teachers' Federation in 1998 and is now called the Elementary Teachers' Federation of Ontario (ETFO).

REFERENCES

Angod, L. 2006. "From Post-Colonial Thought to Anti-Colonial Politics: Difference, Knowledge and R. v. R.D.S." In *Anti-Colonialism and Education: The Politics of Resistance*, edited by G. Dei and A. Kempf, 158–74. Rotterdam: Sense Publications.

Atkinson, M., and M. Kehler. 2010. *Boys' Bodies: Speaking the Unspoken*. New York: Peter Lang.

Battiste, M. 2013. *Decolonizing Education: Nourishing the Learning Spirit*. Saskatoon, SK: Purich Press.

Belenky, M., B. Clinchy, N. Goldberger, and J. Tarule. 1986. *Women's Ways of Knowing in Development of Self, Voice, and Mind*. New York: Basic Books.

Blackmore, J. 2016. *Educational Leadership and Nancy Fraser*. London: Routledge.

Canada. 1970. *Report of the Royal Commission on the Status of Women*. Ottawa: Queen's Printer.

Cherryholmes, C. 1988. *Power and Criticism: Poststructural Investigations in Education*. New York: Teachers' College Press.

Collins, P.H. 2010. *Another Kind of Public Education: Race, Schools, the Media, and Democratic Possibilities*. Boston, MA: Beacon Press.

Connell, R. 2009. *Gender in World Perspective*. 2nd ed. Cambridge, UK: Polity Press.

Coulter, R. 1996. "Gender Equity and Schooling." *Canadian Journal of Education* 21 (4): 433–52. doi:10.2307/1494895.

Eisenstein, Z., ed. 1978. *Capitalist Patriarchy and the Case for Socialist Feminism*. New York: Monthly Review Press.

Fraser, N. 1997. *Justice Interruptus: Critical Reflections on the 'Postsocialist' Condition*. New York: Routledge.

– 2009. *Scales of Justice: Reimagining Political Space in a Globalizing World*. New York: Columbia University Press.

Gaskell, J., and A.T. McLaren, eds. 1987. *Women and Education: A Canadian Perspective*. Calgary: Detselig.

Gilligan, C. 1982. *In a Different Voice*. Cambridge: Harvard University Press.

Hobson, J. 2016. "The Top 10 Feminist Moments in Pop Culture from 2016." *Ms. Blog*, 27 December. msmagazine.com/blog/2016/12/27/feminist-moments-popular-culture-year-review/.

hooks, b. 1994. *Teaching to Transgress: Education as a Practice of Freedom*. New York: Routledge.

Lather, P. 1991. *Getting Smart: Feminist Research and Pedagogy within the Post-Modern*. New York: Routledge.

Lorber, J. 2010. *Gender Inequality: Feminist Theories and Politics*. 4th ed. New York: Oxford University Press.

Lorde, A. 1984. *Sister Outsider: Essays and Speeches*. Trumansville, NY: Crossing Press.

Marshall, C. ed., 1992. *The New Politics of Race and Gender: The 1992 Yearbook of the Politics of Education Association*. Washington, DC: Falmer Press.

Mawhinney, H. 1997. "Institutionalizing Women's Voices, Not Their Echoes, through Feminist Policy Analysis of Difference." In *Feminist Critical Policy Analysis I: A Perspective from Primary and Secondary Schooling*, edited by C. Marshall, 216–29. London: Falmer Press.

Mirza, H.S. 2014/15. "Decolonizing Higher Education: Black Feminism and the Intersectionality of Race and Gender." *Journal of Feminist Scholarship* 7 (8): 1–12.

Noddings, N. 1992. *The Challenge to Care in Schools: An Alternative Approach to Education*. New York: Teachers' College Press.

O'Brien, M. 1986. "Feminism and the Politics of Education." *Interchange* 17 (2): 91–105. doi:10.1007/BF01807471.

Peden, S. 2011. "Dancing with the Elephant: Teacher Education for the Inclusion of First Nations, Métis and Inuit Histories, Worldviews and Pedagogies." PhD diss., University of Manitoba.

Rottmann, C. 2006. "Queering Educational Leadership from the Inside Out." *International Journal of Leadership in Education* 9 (1): 1–20. doi:10.1080/13603120500389507.

Tuhiwai Smith, L. 1997. "Maori Women: Discourses, Projects and Mana Wahine." In *Women and Education in Aotearoa*, ed. Sue Middleton and Alison Jones, 32–50. Auckland, NZ: Auckland University Press.

Wallin, D. 2001. "Postmodern Feminism and Educational Policy Development." *McGill Journal of Education* 36 (1): 27–43.

Williams, T. 1990. "Re-forming 'Women's' Truth: A Critique of the Royal Commission on the Status of Women in Canada." *Ottawa Law Review* 2 (23): 725–60.

PART ONE

Discourses of Teaching: Speaking Up

JANICE WALLACE

The mandate given to the Royal Commission on the Status of Women (RCSW) in 1967 was to "inquire into and report upon the status of women in Canada, and to recommend what steps might be taken by the federal government to ensure for women equal opportunities with men in all aspects of Canadian society" (Canada 1970). The result was a report made public in 1970 that was replete with 167 recommendations – many created to improve educational opportunities for girls. Since that time, and bolstered by the activism of female teachers across Canada, policies have been introduced, and opportunities for girls and women in education have improved. Yet, the full realization of the mandate of the RCSW continues to remain elusive.

The authors in part 1 explore the period of time both immediately before and after release of the RCSW when, arguably, the influence of feminism in education was most visible and the belief in the possibility of change was most hopeful. The authors draw on the experiences of female educators, scholars, and activists who spoke up with a feminist consciousness to reveal how second-wave feminist educators strategized together for pay equity and career opportunities, for representation in learning opportunities, and for the equitable organization of work in boards of education and teacher education.

The tenets of liberal feminism held that "female subordination is rooted in a set of customary and legal constraints that blocks women's entrance to and success in the so-called public world"

(Tong 2014). The state, from this perspective, is seen as an ally in formally supporting the rights of women through policy provisions such as pay equity, child care, family leave, and so on in order for men and women to enjoy equal autonomy and choice in realizing their potential. Liberal feminists in education, therefore, saw instruments of the state, such as formal systems of schooling, as allies in ensuring that "girls and boys would be encouraged to see one another as equals" (Enslin 2003, 73) through provision of, for example, non-discriminatory texts and inclusive curriculum. The RCSW was particularly concerned about the socialized sex-role stereotyping that was reinforced in the formal and informal curriculum. They questioned, for example, why "little girls in elementary texts played with dolls while their brothers played baseball; mothers wore aprons and baked cookies, while fathers drove off to work" (Gaskell and McLaren 1987, 8). Sex-role stereotyping was also pointed out in the informal practices of schools, such as "having separate playgrounds and line-ups for girls and boys, allocating different chores for boys and for girls ... [as well as] teachers' expectations about the capacities and interests of males and females" (8).

Bolstered by public policy, funding, and the energy that came from the public acknowledgement of the need for change that the RCSW provided, feminist teachers were the frontrunners in working toward gender equity in schools. They worked on school practices and pedagogical innovation through social activism and persistent advocacy within school systems. The optimism and agency in the voices of many of the participants quoted in the chapters in this section are palpable, as is the weariness and cautious optimism that accompanied their efforts, which were resisted, sometimes vehemently.

Resistance to gender reform in education increased with the advent of conservative reforms of the Klein government in Alberta, the conservative reforms of the Harris government in Ontario, and the liberal Campbell government's reforms in British Columbia. By the mid-1990s, three of the largest provinces in Canada were firmly in the grip of neo-liberal government reforms. Characterized by a drive for efficiency, fiscal conservatism, and accountability, education funding was cut and school districts were rationalized into larger, more entrepreneurial and competitive units whose primary goal was to enable the students to serve an economy that was able to compete successfully in a global economy (Wallace 2004).

As the authors in part 1, "Discourses of Teaching: Speaking Up," acknowledge, these neo-liberal reforms were gendered and highly detrimental to feminist goals. Ontario, for example, where hard-fought equity policy had been enacted to support the movement of women into positions of authority in educational organizations, saw that policy work almost immediately wiped out following the election of a majority Harris government. In Alberta and British Columbia, where no formal equity policy existed, the work continued through teacher organizations, such as the British Columbia Teachers' Federation. Ontario saw the amalgamation of the Federation of Women Teachers' Association of Ontario (FWTAO) with its male counterpart, Ontario Public School Men Teachers' Federation (OPSMTF), into a new organization, the Elementary Teachers' Federation of Ontario (ETFO), that arguably weakened the unique position that FWTAO had occupied on behalf of women for almost a century. Clearly, liberal feminist reform that was dependent on the will of the state – a state rooted in what Pateman (1997) calls fraternal patriarchal capitalism that became all too visible with the emergence of neo-liberal reforms – was not a dependable partner.

Within this political context, the authors in part 1, "Discourses of Teaching: Speaking Up," provide a historical exploration of various forms of advocacy that had mixed success in building pathways to gender equity in educational organizations. Sharon Cook's chapter, "Who Do You Think You Are? Feminist Change in Post-Secondary Education: An Uneven Record," explores the context for the preparation of a teacher – the faculties of education that replaced teachers' college and "normal" school. She uses a historical analysis of the effects of feminism to address how gender organizes privilege in faculties of education that prepare teachers for an equally gendered work environment in schools and school systems. Her chapter demonstrates how gendered privilege was systemically reproduced as power shifted when teacher education was folded into university structures. Given the tensions she reveals, she considers the crucial question: How can we explain the agonizingly slow integration of feminist principles and insights into Canadian faculties of education?

Rose Fine-Meyer's chapter, "Feminist Reformers: Creating Pedagogical Change to Curriculum in Toronto Schools through Inclusive Content," provides an historical exploration of the work of activist teachers. This paper begins with a brief examination of gender equity policies passed in Ontario in the 1970s and 1980s, and then provides a set of oral histories with retired history teachers who were teaching when gender equity policies were first implemented. These interviews provide a lens into the linkages between policy and practice, and demonstrate just how difficult the work of gender equity was, especially as the full effects of neo-liberalism became evident in hierarchical educational systems. However, the evidence also reveals that teachers can and did act independently to counter inequality within the curriculum by insisting on playing a larger role in decisions related to resource materials and pedagogy. Fine-Meyer concludes with an examination of government policies that have the possibility of enhancing or detracting from the independent equity work of teachers who wish to ensure a diverse and equitable curriculum in the future.

Jean Hewitt draws extensively on her life history and insider knowledge – as a school teacher, principal, senior administrator at both the Board and Ministry of Education level, activist, and historian – to explore links between the phases of change in Ontario schools as feminist beliefs and activism were brought to bear on the existing practices within the educational bureaucracy. Her paper, "Feminist Influence on Ontario Schools," also considers some of the underlying reasons why the hopes for fundamental institutional change on the part of feminist writers and activists in the late twentieth century were not realized.

All three authors in this section provide an analysis of the ways in which feminist educators spoke up and resisted inequitable practices in faculties of education, school systems, and classrooms. They forged new pathways to equity that were often challenging, sometimes led nowhere, and at other times provided new insights and possibilities for educators and the students they taught. Importantly, however, they kept speaking up on behalf of their students, their colleagues, and their communities. As noted in the introduction, however, while the authors' research and lived experience reveals the results of educators' persistent agency in the significant gains of liberal feminism throughout the 1970s and 1980s, it also demonstrates the tenuousness of early second-wave feminists' dependence on the state to support feminist initiatives as political ideologies shifted, and the absence of Other voices in their feminist efforts that advocated largely for white, middle-class, cisgender women.

REFERENCES

Canada. 1970. *Report of the Royal Commission on the Status of Women*. Ottawa: Queen's Printer. Canada. www.swc-cfc.gc.ca/rc-cr/roycom/index-en.html.

Enslin, P. 2003. "Liberal Feminism, Diversity and Education." *Theory and Research in Education* 1 (1): 73–87. doi:10.1177/1477878503001001005.

Gaskell, J., and A.T. McLaren, eds. 1987. *Women and Education: A Canadian Perspective*. Calgary: Detselig.

Pateman, C. 1997. *The Sexual Contract*. 6th ed. Cambridge, UK: Polity Press.

Tong, R. 2014. "Introduction." In *Feminist Thought: A More Comprehensive Introduction*, ed. R. Tong. Boulder, CO: Westview Press. doi: 10.1142/9789814566582_0016.

Wallace, J. 2004. "Educational Purposes Economicus: Globalization and the Reshaping of Educational Purpose in Three Canadian Provinces." *Canadian and International Education. Education Canadienne et Internationale* 33 (1): 99–117.

1

Who Do You Think You Are?

*Feminist Change in Post-Secondary Education:
An Uneven Record*

SHARON ANNE COOK

One of Canada's national treasures, author Alice Munro, invites us to recognize the long reach of retrogressive assumptions about women: her short stories are full of female characters who are "too full of themselves," who insist on a life of their own instead of endlessly serving others, whose horizons are limited by the disparagement of others. From her earliest works, including *Who Do You Think You Are?* (1978), to her most recent *Dear Life* (2012), Munro demonstrates that views of women's incompetence, although officially discounted and vigorously denied, live on in the twenty-first century through the power of social networks, familial expectations, and personal insecurities. Munro's lifelike fiction has encouraged me to ask similar questions about the post-secondary education system in this country: To what degree has the academy become open to women's opinions, agency, and authority? Why did feminism become absorbed into some parts of the academy so much more quickly than others? More specifically, how can we explain the agonizingly slow integration of feminist principles and insights into Canadian faculties of education?

To address these questions, this paper uses a conventional definition for feminism: "a social movement whose basic goal is equality between women and men" (Lorber 2010, 1). That is, feminism's aims include defining, establishing, and defending equal political, social, and economic rights for women in education. Access to education at the post-secondary level was one of the earliest goals of first-wave feminism (from about 1875 to the 1920s). Demands included women having the right to register as undergraduates in professional programs like medicine (Millar and Gidney 1999), dentistry (Adams in Millar, Heap, and Gidney 2005), and law (Leiper 2005) as well as the institutionalization of education for women in professions like elementary school teaching (Prentice 1977) and social work (James 2005). Second-wave feminists (from the 1960s to the 1990s) extended the task of challenging inequality in all educational settings as experienced by students, instructors, and administrators. Feminist scholars have explored subjects like women's work as elementary school teachers (many of whom in the nineteenth century successfully organized and maintained one-room schoolhouses that also served as community centres [Neatby 2001; Prentice 1977]), patriarchal assumptions and practices in the formal and informal curriculum (Dagg and Thompson 1988), accreditation of new fields (Wallace 2005), and the norms for employment as tenured faculty (Caplan 1994). Since the 1990s, "feminist solidarity politics [have] ... no longer [been] persuasive as class, race, ethnicity, and sexuality provided for a more complicated, disrupted view of women and women's experiences" (Kohli 2012, 23). This third wave of feminism extended demands for women's equality by focusing on women further disadvantaged by the intersections of race, ethnicity, class, or sexuality, and in both national and transnational settings. A fourth wave of feminism continues as researchers explore women's complex relationship with education, highlighting women's educational experiences as personal identities are filtered through social media and digitization to create new societal priorities (Cook 2012, 2001).

Within the academic context then, how can we explain this relatively late arrival of feminism to Canadian faculties of education? Further, how can we assess the impact of feminism on the academy generally? In exploring these questions, I begin by surveying the number of female students and faculty currently in faculties of education compared to the number in the humanities and, particularly, departments of history. I extend the comparison by assessing the impact of two associations that arose to represent women's scholarship and social needs: the Canadian Committee on Women's History (CCWH), and the Canadian Association for the Study of Women in Education (CASWE). I conclude the paper with some general explanations of why feminism's reach was delayed in faculties of education.

One measure of the effect of feminism on the academy is the number of women enrolled as faculty members or as students in a given area. In 2013–14, the Canadian Association of University Teachers'

(CAUT) Almanac indicated that 55 per cent of all teaching positions in faculties of education were occupied by women (CAUT/ACPPU Almanac 2013–14, 31), down from 58.47 per cent in 2010–11 (CAUT/ACPPU Almanac 2010–11, 14). Female students had taken more than half of the positions in education faculties for some years. For example, in 1990 when female students in engineering faculties across Canada occupied only 13 per cent of student places, women comprised more than 70 per cent of the student population in faculties of education (Peters 2013, A4). By 2010–11, the percentage of women in education faculties had grown further to 76.4 per cent for undergraduate enrolments, and 72.3 per cent for graduate degrees across Canada, according to the latest available statistics (CAUT/ACPPU Almanac 2013–14, 42–3). In that same year, the percentage of women enrolled in doctoral programs in faculties of education was the highest of any discipline in the academy at 69.7 per cent (CAUT/ACPPU 2013–14, 44). Similarly, a high proportion of women actually attained a doctorate at 62.9 per cent in 2010–11 (CAUT/ACPPU Almanac 2013–14, 48), especially when compared with other faculties.

These rates are higher than in many faculties, not just engineering. The humanities, for example, lag far behind education in the percentage of female students and instructors. In 2010–11, female undergraduates comprised 60.5 per cent of student places in the humanities (CAUT/ACPPU Almanac 2013–14, 42), while 56 per cent of students at the graduate level in the humanities were women (43). Only 49.5 per cent of doctoral candidates were women (CAUT/ACPPU Almanac 2013–14, 44), while a higher rate, 56.1 per cent of those awarded a doctoral degree in the humanities, were women (48).

Elsewhere in the educational system, women also dominate. For example, according to the 2006 Census, women are 83.6 per cent of elementary school teachers across Canada, 57.3 per cent of secondary school teachers and 52.9 per cent of school principals and administrators in elementary and secondary schools (*CTF Bulletin* 2013). And yet, as Ken Osborne observes, the school system has long featured economic, social, and intellectual disparity concerning the gender of its teachers. The very structures of teacher certification across Canada for many years typically required a university degree of male teachers, who then were qualified to teach in the secondary schools, while female teachers held a variety of certificates from normal schools and taught at the elementary level for lower pay than their male colleagues (Osborne 1999, 94–8). Hence, having numerical predominance did not, nor does it now, guarantee women either economic or professional advantages. In fact, the greater numbers of women in teaching might have foretold their subservience to men.

Does this robust representation of both students and instructors in faculties of education, and in the school system where those graduates often find employment, suggest that such sites were and are supportive of feminism? Of course not. In addition to female representation, we must consider a range of other factors, such as the breakdown of representation by rank; the orientation of curriculum to admit women's needs and contributions; institutional supports and/or disincentives for female undergraduates; graduate students and professors; leadership figures and groups; official policies, such as maternity leave and its integration into promotion procedures; and the less quantifiable culture of institutions that enables or suppresses scholarship by and for women (Cook 2004).

Female students outnumbering male students, whether undergraduate or graduate, does not offer convincing evidence that women have exerted influence at the policy level in that institution. More women need to have attained the highest ranks of the professoriate, and leadership by that group must be consciously exercised on behalf of women generally. Statistics Canada figures show that, for the academy as a whole, the prospect of more women in powerful positions is even less likely than it was a few years ago. The most recent figures demonstrate that the higher the university rank, the lower the percentage of women. In the 2010–11 Statistics Canada figures, for example, women comprised only 22.8 per cent of full professor positions in Canadian universities, 38 per cent of associate professor ranks, 46.4 per cent of those at the assistant level and 53.1 per cent of lecturers (CAUT/ACPPU Almanac 2013–14, 28). Except for the last category, which is the lowest ranked and least stable, these figures represented a decline from 2008–09 (Council of Canadian Academies 2012). With these declining numbers come reduced possibilities of influencing the culture of their respective departments and faculties.

However, the percentage of women in higher ranks of education faculties far exceeds those in other faculties, including the humanities. Here, we directly contrast the figures from the teacher education department in faculties of education and the history department in humanities' faculties. In 2010–11, teacher education had 56.5 per cent female full professors versus 23.6 per cent female full professors in history; teacher education had 65.5 per cent female associate professors, while history had only 43 per cent who were women. And 63.2 per cent of assistant professors in teacher education were women versus 42.9 per cent in history. Finally, while 71.4 per cent of teacher education lecturers were women, only 38.9 per cent of history lecturers were women (CAUT/ACPPU Almanac 2013–14, 24–5). While most of these figures are positive for those interested in women's promotion rates in faculties of education, the numbers of women as lecturers – traditionally the lowest paid of all ranks and usually untenured – indicate that women are part of a persistent underclass in education. However, aside from this embarrassing figure, education seems to have done well in the employment sweepstakes, suggesting that the culture must have been more amenable to feminist ideas than was the case in other departments, like history, where the departments hired fewer women in higher-ranked positions.

To test this assumption, we can consider the founding of women-centric academic organizations in education and history. The evidence garnered from the histories of CCWH and the CASWE shows that even though education faculties consistently had more women than men at all levels of the academy, the culture of faculties of education was less supportive of those women and of women generally.

The CCWH was established in 1974 to promote teaching and research in the field of Canadian women's history: to disseminate information about sources, current research, and publications; to encourage the preservation of archival sources in women's history; while monitoring the status of women in the historical profession and working to raise that status (CCWH-CCHF n.d.). To fulfill its mandate, the CCWH continues to compile, publish, and distribute a newsletter and directory; to adjudicate the Hilda Neatby Prize (for the best article in women's history each year in Canada); to promote meetings and conferences at local and regional levels; and to sponsor sessions on women's history at the annual meeting of the Canadian Historical Association (CHA) at the Congress of the Humanities and Social Sciences.

The CCWH was one of the earliest Canadian feminist pressure groups in the academy. It continues to be a major force in the parent historical association – the CHA. The CCWH provided a number of presidents to the CHA, complete with their feminist sensibilities, scholarship, and energy. The CCWH at the national level is reinforced by provincial associations (for example, the Ontario Women's History Network) and often by local book clubs or other groupings of women (for example, the Marion Dewar National Capital Region Women's Book Club in Ottawa) who have maintained their association for forty years or more.

Nationally, the CCWH and some provincial women's history groups have been supported through grants from Status of Women Canada. Very importantly, these provincial and local groups have consciously maintained the feminist networks in which they have long been a part, regularly reporting their achievements in newsletters and, in the process, reminding themselves of their responsibilities to the local, provincial, national, and international sisterhood. In all of these ways, the CCWH demonstrates that there is a high level of consciousness about the culture of feminism, as well as the necessity to contribute to knowledge about historical feminist praxis and theory.

Women's history and the significance of feminism in the academy was spurred by early scholarship that explored the salience of gender as a category of analysis. Joan Scott's germinal 1986 article, "Gender: A Useful Category of Historical Analysis," became a touchstone for feminist analysis by women's historians over several decades. Canadian scholars, such as Natalie Zemon Davis (1975) and Deborah Gorham (1979), added to Scott's analysis by publishing their own research and by taking leadership roles in the academy to support a new generation of feminist historians. This is not to argue that feminism has been embraced by departments of history or is well represented in course materials for students. However, feminism has found a home in historical scholarship to a degree that education cannot claim.

The parallel group is CASWE. It was established considerably after the CCWH in 1993 (Epp 1999, 139), although it had existed from 1991 as the Women's Issues Committee/Comité d'étude sur le statut des femmes as a component of the Canadian Society for the Study of Education (CSSE).

Operating with a similar mandate as the CCWH, the educationalists through CASWE have mounted preconference events every second year prior to the yearly meetings of CSSE. CASWE has aimed to provide social and networking activities to new and established scholars in the field, and sent a representative to serve on the parent organization's (CSSE) board of directors to defend and promote women's research and those who practise it. Its formal mandate is as follows: to advise the CSSE on policies affecting women and education; to make recommendations to the Board of Directors of CSSE on matters related to women and education; to promote exchanges of information about feminist scholarship and pedagogy within the CSSE; to develop forums within the CSSE for social and political action related to women and education; to participate actively in program development for and by women at the annual conference of the CSSE; and to assist in promoting the status of women at all faculties of education in Canadian universities.

Never as large or robust as the women's historians' association, and competing with many other associations related to educational research, CASWE has nevertheless attempted to serve most of the same functions as its historical sister organization. But unlike the women's historians' group, CASWE has operated without the resources offered by federal government agencies like Status of Women Canada. Furthermore, no provincial or local CASWE-like associations support the national group. In addition, because of the structure of its parent organization, the CSSE, most CASWE members have a second membership in one of the other associations along with their commitment to CASWE. The educational group is therefore more diffuse, with members' loyalties divided and, as a result, it is also less effective than the CCWH, which enjoys a more focused emphasis. But CASWE's pale comparison to the CCWH stems from more than structural concerns. CASWE has been unable to alter the prevailing culture of either faculties of education or mainstream educational scholarship to the same degree as has been achieved by female historians.

Even in the second decade of the twenty-first century, faculties of education have made only limited progress toward those goals identified as characteristic of feminism. One can readily see that, until the mid-1990s, such faculties of education offered only limited equal opportunities for women to be hired into tenure-track positions, rather than short-term teaching contracts, and distinctly limited access to the upper ranks of the professoriate (Caplan 1994). Women frequently complained of feeling invisible in the academy, of being overloaded with committee responsibilities at the expense of forwarding their own careers, and of pernicious role conflict (Caplan 1994, especially chap. 1). Sandra Acker (1999) has documented the effects of "relational feminism" where female academics have emphasized caring and connectedness in their teaching, but, the hard work attendant on this approach has been obscured because, too often, they have been assumed to be expressions of women's natural tendencies.

The curricula of all branches of education faculties were slow in accepting a social constructivist approach that included the study of the importance of gender in schooling (Cook and Riley 1990). Jane Gaskell, Myra Novogrodsky, and Arlene McLaren issued a powerful clarion call to educationalists (Gaskell, McLaren, and Novogrodsky 1989) to take gender into account in the curricular and care-giving domains and at all levels of the educational enterprise. This call was not quickly acted upon in faculties of education; it remains slow to this day in many settings, with a scattering of courses or themes in courses taking up that challenge, mostly as a component of educational foundations courses. Here, students are often exposed to feminism, among other "isms," and frequently as a companion study to the unacknowledged effects of pernicious racism in education. But there is inconsistency in how much course time is offered, the degree to which feminism is credited with historic significance, or whether feminism is merely presented as one more approach to unpacking our understanding of education. Currently, there are few systemic, permanent organizational changes that take gender into account in faculties of education in Canada. Thus, we must conclude that feminism's place in faculties of education is uncertain and fragile.

Why have faculties of education been so slow to accept gender as an organizing principle, women as policy leaders, and other fundamental principles of gender equality? A documentary analysis of women's experiences in faculties of education from 1980 to 2010, and a review of the selected secondary literature at that time, reveal that a number of factors account for the slow acceptance of feminism in faculties of education across Canada until the mid-1990s. These factors include the disparity of power at administrative levels of the new faculties of education, a limited pool of experienced women, the distractions to the feminist cause created by other liberating initiatives in education and in society at large, and limited external supports, including national leadership.

It is important to acknowledge that not all of the following factors were of equal importance in any one setting. As well, by no means did all of them apply in all sites. Finally, some factors not mentioned here influenced the culture of certain places. However, the documentary record indicates that all of the above had some bearing on the general disinclination of faculties of education to take up feminist notions of equity and fairness, while disciplines like history and their departments across Canada more enthusiastically embraced feminist research and researchers.

THE INCORPORATION OF TEACHERS' COLLEGES INTO UNIVERSITIES

In Eastern Canada, the folding of teachers' colleges into the university structure during the late 1960s and 1970s meant that the energies of faculty of education administrators were devoted primarily to questions of professional and academic status within the new university setting, rather than to issues of equity. In Western Canada, the pattern differed. Faculties of education were established in the main provincial universities at their founding at the turn of the twentieth century, but with limited authority because of other competing teacher-training institutions in prairie centres by the mid-twentieth century. For example, the fledgling University of Calgary received the right to present a two-year, teacher-training course in 1946–47 and the first three years of a four-year bachelor's of education degree (BEd) in industrial arts in 1948–49, dispersing teacher education throughout the province and away from the University of Alberta (University of Alberta Centenary 2008). In addition, whether in the east or west, faculties of education struggled for status in competition with other university faculties everywhere across Canada.

Just as professional teacher education was being folded into the university, the university itself was in the midst of a "revolutionary transformation" from liberal arts colleges to the complex and large institutions with which we are now familiar (Gidney 2005, 26). This meant that universities were most concerned with their own growing reputations, and with the need to supplement their funding through partnerships with private groups. The most advantageous partnerships would be offered to faculties or research collectives with the most impressive reputations. Advancing women in the academy did not figure in any of these calculations for status.

In their early years, at the same time as second-wave feminism was being shaped and defined, faculties of education reproduced the power structures of the traditional teachers' colleges that existed until the late 1960s. This was true in both English and French institutions, (Desjarlais 1998, 14) where women had very limited opportunities to teach beyond the areas of domestic science, foreign languages, and physical culture or physical education (for women). Women also served as librarians and deans of women as well as office secretaries, both in the teachers' colleges and in universities from early in the twentieth century. But whatever the setting, until very recently, women had limited institutional authority, particularly in matters of policy.

By the late 1980s, just as sizable numbers of newly minted female (and often feminist) doctoral graduates moved into faculties of education, the former power brokers in pre-service sectors – mostly male "master teachers" from teachers' colleges whose authority was waning after fifteen or twenty years in the university community – identified these feminist academics as the source of their power loss. Hence, feminism became coded as dangerous, both to the old-guard professors who stood to be supplanted (and in fairly short order, were replaced), but also to the institutions they sought to restructure (Acker 1999).

To take but one example, the Ottawa Teachers' College was fully incorporated into the faculty of education at the University of Ottawa by 1974. The former employees of the Ottawa Teachers' College were assigned an academic rank within the university. Of the twenty-eight faculty members absorbed in that year, only two were given the rank of assistant professor, with the other twenty-six identified as lecturers (Desjarlais 1998, 92). Four of the twenty-eight were women, and none of these received a rank above lecturer. Few additional faculty members were added in succeeding years as the old staff negotiated the new university hierarchy. In the 1980s, enrolments began to climb dramatically at the University of Ottawa for a variety of reasons and new academically oriented faculty members were needed. The old system of seconding teachers from local school boards was cut back in an attempt to elevate the faculty's reputation within the university and to save money. Far more candidates with doctorates were now available for these positions, and in the late 1980s, a number of professors with PhDs and school-based experience joined the faculty, almost all of whom were women. The tension between the new and old guard was palpable: it was expressed through program and curricular planning, leadership styles, and in the relationship between teacher education and graduate studies in education where these new doctoral instructors were invited to teach, but from which the old master teachers were shut out. The energy required to contest alternate models of academic and professional practice – conventional male models versus relational feminism, for example (Acker 1999, 278) – meant that feminist practice was not on the official or even the unofficial agenda. Furthermore, situations like this one at the University of Ottawa demonized feminism for significant portions of the academic staff, particularly by those who found themselves vulnerable with the new heightened standards of certification.

In addition to power struggles, there were distinct differences in organizational authority and institutional power within faculties of education. Graduate studies departments, with their emphasis on research and writing, possessed far more institutional power than did either the professional development or teacher preparation branches. This pattern played out internationally as well as nationally – emerging in Australia, the United Kingdom, and the United States – as a characteristic of the new faculty of education model within the university (Gardiner, O'Donoghue, and O'Neill 2011, chap. 2; Labaree 2004). The early incarnations of graduate studies departments were male-dominated and male-oriented, while teacher preparation divisions and those offering professional development had stronger female representation in the instructional cohort. This pattern generally paralleled that in the school system where women clustered in teaching positions with little bureaucratic control (Coulter and Harper 2005, 138–9).

The much-debated "Cinderella Complex" of faculties of education where "master teachers" from the normal schools and teachers' colleges felt academically inadequate and even fraudulent in this new context and where the demands of engaging in empirical research were daunting, meant that controversial feminist approaches would not likely be welcomed in education faculties. This overt hostility resulted in a "chilly climate" for female faculty members, and even more so for racialized non-white women. Hostility was expressed both socially and academically to female scholars of all races and sexual orientations (Chilly Editorial Collective 1995). In her ground-breaking book, Paula Caplan lists the many disincentives to be a female academic in the 1980s: "The effects that the maleness and heterosexism of the environment have on women academics range from mild irritation to complete devastation. They include interfering with their ability to concentrate, hampering their freedom to work, and destroying or thwarting the creation of a supportive environment, as well as using up women students' energies in conflict, anger and self-doubt" (Caplan 1994, 32).

Beyond individual institutions, newly minted academics with feminist inclinations also found it difficult to have their proposals accepted at national conferences (Caplan 1994), experiencing a classic "chilly climate" in that setting as well. Teacher preparation and professional development programs, in which most women were clustered in this era, were subject to external licensing agencies in the form of provincial ministries of education or colleges. Even if these agencies had not been hostile to feminist revisions of programs, their power over these programs intimidated academic administrative teams. This further blunted feminist initiatives.

THE LIMITED INFLUENCE OF TENURED FEMALE PROFESSORS

Despite the large percentage of female students in faculties of education during a period of feminist consciousness in the 1970s and 1980s, the percentage of *tenured* female professors and the number of women in positions of administrative responsibility remained relatively low until the 1990s (Epp 1995). Numbers of women in educational administration departments remained low well after 1995 (Reynolds 1995; Reynolds and Young 1995, chap. 1). Because of this, women in these settings felt less able to demand feminist-inspired change (Acker 1999). Ruth Rees reports that in 1994, for example, while 26 per cent of full-time faculty members at her university were women, only sixteen women of 126 faculty or 13 per cent were in middle management positions, and three female faculty members out of fifteen (20 per cent) were in upper-level management positions. In contrast, 69 per cent of the undergraduates and 71 per cent of the graduate students were women (Rees 1995, 35) – a significant disparity with the few women faculty and administrators. Yet, there were very limited numbers of women in doctoral programs in this period, and of those few, many tended to avoid the study of educational administration, which is a natural corollary to serving in administrative positions (Epp 1995, 19–20), thus perpetuating this disparity. Of course, not all women were feminists, so despite strong representation of female students, feminist sensibilities were muted in policy (Gaskell, McLaren, and Novogrodsky 1989).

As well, the perception remained for years that there were too few women with appropriate experience to take on powerful administrative roles, particularly in post-secondary institutions. This factor was exacerbated by the typical pattern of female employment in faculties of education where far more women than men were employed in part-time positions. Sandra Acker's research on the gendered experiences of female elementary school teachers and academics demonstrates high levels of stress experienced by women in the educational workplace as they struggled to be caring professionals at the same time as they yearned for some time for themselves. The academics reported putting in long hours on committees, supervising many graduate students' theses, while still producing the required publications for tenure, all in the face of unyielding norms in faculties of education that seemed arrayed against them (Acker 1999). Ruth Rees's research confirmed this pattern and further identified discriminatory practices at the university level, including the use of exclusionary language, standards that discouraged women from applying for tenure and promotion, and persistent inequitable allocation of resources (Rees 1995, 36–41). Women struggling with the home-work balance and with the usual demands of early career productivity were not likely to be considered for administrative positions on whose behalf feminist policies could be implemented. And the authority gained from holding senior ranks was still in the future.

THE EFFECT OF OTHER EMANCIPATORY INITIATIVES ON FEMINISM

On an even broader societal level, feminist scholarship and organization in the 1970s and 1980s were overshadowed by other forms of liberation in education. By the mid-1960s, for example, youth culture was in full flower. Hippies made a broad range of demands on the post-secondary educational system and its professoriate for "relevance." Doug Owram reminds us that in 1965, half of the population of North America was under twenty-five years of age (Owram 1996, 192). At the other end of the scale, Rochdale College, the post-secondary educational experiment in Toronto, was finally closed down in 1964, showing the difficulty of recasting education in an era of so much flux, and so many drugs (Owram 1996, 185–6).

The civil rights movement, beginning in the early 1960s, drew idealistic young people to its cause with educational access defined as a primary human right. Distrust of political leaders took on new urgency in the later 1960s with protests against the war in Vietnam featured on most Canadian campuses. The poverty of Canada's Indigenous peoples also emerged as a cause in this period. And the thorny question of how to introduce more racialized non-white candidates into teacher education programs entered the debate as well. Thus, feminism was one of many components of the radicalism of the era, both competing with other causes and also drawing advocates to it through close association.

The radicalism of the 1960s found a number of educational expressions. Three influential provincial reports were presented in this period: the five-volume Parent *Report of the Royal Commission of Inquiry on Education in the Province of Quebec* between 1963 and 1966 (Quebec 1963), the Hall-Dennis 1969 report entitled *Living and Learning* (Hall and Dennis 1969) in Ontario, and the Worth Report in Alberta in 1972. All of these reports favoured dramatic departures from conventional schooling practices, including a curriculum with electives to meet students' individual interests, the end of streaming or tracks, the desire to realign civic and vocational education with goals of individual development, and a rejection of competition in favour of "collective solidarity" (Manzer 1994, 152). As the Worth Report expressed it, the goal of schooling should be "socially responsible individualization that helps set loose the creativity, inventiveness, and uniqueness of all individuals throughout their lives" (Manzer 1994, 154). Preparing teachers and administrators for this re-conceptualized system would tax the energies of all faculties of education. The interests of feminists were probably seen as a nuisance during a time of rapid change and even crisis. Education faculties were busy adapting to many changes and believed, therefore, that they had neither the time nor attention to also consider the primacy of gender.

LIMITED EXTERNAL SUPPORT AND FEMINIST LEADERSHIP

The scarcity of women in administrative positions at the national or university level, combined with few women in faculties of education in senior positions, meant that feminist women in post-secondary educational institutions had few mentors from whom to draw inspiration. There were exceptions to this situation, most notably at OISE/UT and UBC, where luminaries like Alison Prentice (1977), Jane Gaskell, and Arlene McLaren (Gaskell, McLaren, and Novogrodsky 1989) all took up feminist topics, and produced an impressive body of work that acted as beacons for the next generation of scholars. Nevertheless, their work, important as it was, did not often become integrated into educational scholarship as their feminist historian sisters' work had been in an earlier era. In addition, most of these women did not choose to take up administrative positions, either at their own universities or nationally, as the historians before them had done. As a case in point, none of these capable and forthright feminist educators involved themselves in CASWE, while virtually all of the prominent feminist historians were active in the CCWH. In the 1980s and 1990s, the result was few academic mentors in senior positions or national organizations devoted to women's research.

In the instance of women's historians, the situation was very different. A strong *esprit de corps* among feminist historians was supported by, indeed initiated by, an ever-enlarging group of talented, socially conscious feminist researchers, an increasing number of whom were males. As pioneering and now well-known historians like Veronica Strong-Boag (1976), Wendy Mitchinson et al. (1988), Linda Kealey (1979), Margaret Conrad (1988), and Constance Backhouse (1979) became established in tenure-track positions and took an active role in many organizations, including the CCWH, they facilitated networking among feminist historians, mentorships, and moved as a group into political positions of power, both within their own departments and also within the parent group, the Canadian Historical Association.

As feminist leaders from that period recall, the success experienced by women's historians in their classrooms and in publishing houses served to redirect energy to history from the feminist community in other faculties, like education (oral interview). Further, beyond history's tendency to draw feminists into its orbit, international conferences in women's history, especially the Berkshire Conferences, provided bracing experiences. These demanding conferences both terrified and sustained Canadian women historians, demonstrating the latest in cutting-edge scholarship. Their effect was galvanizing. One noted: "Those conferences were magnets for all of us. We met there, we drove there together, we socialized together, we were in awe of the breadth and depth of the panel presentations, we were inspired by the sheer number of us in one place. It gave us heart to challenge the 'canon' and the 'fathers' in the history departments" (anonymous oral interview). Feminist researchers in faculties of education had none of these supports, save the American Educational Research Association (AERA), where Canadian feminist researchers did not seem to create space for themselves, thus leaving them to forge on with their lonely battle.

CONCLUSIONS

Reinforcing the explanations for feminism's slow acceptance into faculties of education, as have been discussed here – the reorganization of teachers' colleges into the university framework; placing pressures on a waning elite of "master teachers" as they struggled to retain power; the relatively few women in tenured faculty positions or in senior administrative posts; and the influence of other emancipatory programs, such as the civil rights movement – is the truism that education is a conservative endeavour. Necessarily trailing in vanguard movements, education in all its guises must convince the public of the merit of any change in policy or attitude, as citizens pay for this service through taxes. Faculties of education are accredited as teacher-training institutions by external bodies, further blunting any tendency to initiate, rather than reflect, social change. One can see the value of reports like the Hall-Dennis Commission as expert publicity devices for a new educational blueprint. But the views expressed in that report, or in the Parent or Worth Commission reports, were a long time in gestation. And as revolutionary as they were at the time, and as formative as they were for the shape of modern education at all levels, they did not admit to gender inequity as a primary failure of the old system. It would take at least two more decades for feminism's effect to be felt in faculties of education.

Are current faculties of education reformed institutions that now accept women's contributions and feminist principles? It seems not. In their recent book, Blackmore and Sachs (2007) note that "the 'problem' of the under-representation of women in educational leadership is not about women's lack, whether of ambition or capacities, but rather, it is the consequence of the limited opportunities created by the systemically gendered cultural, social, and structural arrangements that inform women educators' choices and possibilities *relative* to their male colleagues" (12–13). Until the academy can honestly engage these systemic inequities, we cannot claim that faculties of education are much more open to feminism and feminists.

REFERENCES

Acker, S. 1999. "Caring as Work for Women Educators." In *Challenging Professions: Historical and Contemporary Perspectives on Women's Professional Work*, ed. E. Smyth, S. Acker, P. Bourne, and A. Prentice, 277–95. Toronto: University of Toronto Press.

Adams, T.L. 2005. "Education and the Quest for Professional Status: The Case of Ontario's Dental Hygienists." In *Learning to Practise: Professional*

Education in Historical and Contemporary Perspective, ed. R. Heap, W. Millar, and E. Smyth, 265–90. Ottawa: University of Ottawa Press.

Backhouse, C. 1979. *The Secret Oppression: Sexual Harassment of Working Women*. Toronto: Macmillan.

Blackmore, J., and J. Sachs. 2007. *Performing and Reforming Leaders: Gender, Educational Restructuring, and Organizational Change*. New York: SUNY Press.

Canadian Teachers' Federation (CTF) Bulletin. 2017. Accessed 1 December. https://www.ctf-fce.ca/Research-Library/HumanRightsEducation_WEB.pdf.

Caplan, P.J. 1994. *Lifting a Ton of Feathers: A Woman's Guide to Surviving in the Academic World*. Toronto: University of Toronto Press.

CAUT/ACPPU Almanac of Post-Secondary Education in Canada 2010/11. Accessed 1 December 2017. https://search-proquest-com.ezproxy.library.uvic.ca/docview/756045738?pq-origsite=summon&accountid=14846.

CAUT/ACPPU Almanac of Post-Secondary Education in Canada 2013/14. Accessed 24 October 2017. www.caut.ca/latest/publications/almanac.

CCWH-CCHF (Canadian Committee on Women's History – Comité canadien de l'histoire des femmes). 2017. "About Us." Accessed 24 October. http://ccwh-cchf.ca/.

Chilly Editorial Collective. 1995. *Breaking Anonymity: The Chilly Climate for Women Faculty*. Waterloo, ON: Wilfrid Laurier Press.

Conrad, M., T. Laidlaw, and D. Smyth. 1988. *No Place Like Home: The Diaries and Letters of Nova Scotia Women*. Halifax, NS: Formac.

Cook, S.A. 2004. "A Case Study of Teacher Education: Rethinking Feminist Leadership." *Canadian Journal of Education/Revue canadienne de l'éducation* 26(4): 419–35.

– 2012. *Sex, Lies and Cigarettes: Canadian Women, Smoking, and Visual Culture, 1880–2000*. Montreal and Kingston: McGill-Queen's University Press.

Cook, S.A., L.R. McLean, and K. O'Rourke, eds. 2001. *Framing Our Past: Canadian Women's History in the Twentieth Century*. Montreal and Kingston: McGill-Queen's University Press.

Cook, S.A., and J. Riley. 1990. "The Case for a Gender Issues Course in Teacher Education." *Education Canada* 32 (3): 2–3.

Coulter, R.P., and H. Harper. 2005. *History Is Hers: Women Educators in Twentieth Century Ontario*. Calgary: Detselig.

Council of Canadian Academies. 2012. "Strengthening Canada's Research Capacity: The Gender Dimension." The expert panel on women in university research. 40.

Dagg, A.I., and P.J. Thompson. 1988. *Women and Canadian Universities.* Toronto: OISE Press.

Davis, N.Z. 1975. "'Women's History' in Transition: The European Case." *Feminist Studies* 3 (3): 83–103.

Desjarlais, L. 1998. *The History of the Faculty of Education at the University of Ottawa.* Ottawa: University of Ottawa.

Epp, J.R. 1995. "Insidious Deterrents: When Educational Administration Students Are Women." In *Women in Leadership in Canadian Education*, ed. C. Reynolds and B. Young, 19–32. Calgary: Detselig.

– 1999. "Where Are We Coming From? The Birth of the Canadian Association for the Study of Women and Education." Accessed 15 December 2015. http://www.csse-scee.ca/acefe_fem/Archives/WhereComeFrom.htm (no longer available).

Gardiner, D., T. O'Donoghue, and M. O'Neill. 2011. *Constructing the Field of Education as a Liberal Art and as Teacher Preparation at Five Western Australian Universities: An Historical Analysis.* Lewiston, NY: Edwin Mellen Press.

Gaskell, J., A. McLaren, and M. Novogrodsky. 1989. *Claiming an Education: Feminism and Schools.* Toronto: Our Schools/Our Selves Education Foundation.

Gidney, B. 2005. "Learning to Practise in Historical Perspective." In *Professional Education in Historical and Contemporary Perspective*, ed. R. Heap, W. Millar, and E. Smyth, 13–42. Ottawa: University of Ottawa.

Gorham, D. 1979. "Flora MacDonald Denison: Canadian Feminist." In *A Not Unreasonable Claim: Women and Reform in Canada, 1880s–1920s*, ed. L. Kealey, 47–70. Toronto: The Women's Press.

Hall, E.M., and L.A. Dennis. 1969. *Living and Learning: The Report of the Provincial Committee on Aims and Objectives of Education in the Schools of Ontario.* www.connexions.org/CxLibrary/Docs/CX5636-HallDennis.htm.

James, C. 2005. "Professional Enactments: Practical Training and the Education of Social Workers in Toronto, 1914–1929." In *Learning to Practise: Professional Education in Historical and Contemporary Perspective*, ed. R. Heap, W. Millar, and E. Smyth, 69–92. Ottawa: University of Ottawa Press.

Kealey, L., ed. 1979. *A Not Unreasonable Claim: Women and Reform in Canada, 1880s–1920s.* Toronto: Canadian Women's Educational Press.

Kohli, W. 2012. *Feminism and Educational Research.* New York: Rowman and Littlefield.

Labaree, D. 2004. *The Trouble with Education Schools.* New Haven, CT: Yale University Press.

Leiper, J.W. 2005. "Gender, Class, and Legal Education: Standing in the

Shadow of the Learned Gentleman." In *Learning to Practise: Professional Education in Historical and Contemporary Perspective*, ed. R. Heap, W. Millar, and E. Smyth, 239–64. Ottawa: University of Ottawa Press.

Lorber, J. 2010. *Gender Inequality: Feminist Theories and Politics*. New York: Oxford University Press.

Manzer, R. 1994. *Public Schools and Political Ideas: Canadian Educational Policy in Historical Perspective*. Toronto: University of Toronto Press.

Millar, W.P.J., and R.D. Gidney. 1999. "'Medettes': Thriving or Just Surviving? Women Students in the Faculty of Medicine, University of Toronto, 1910–1951." In *Challenging Professions: Historical and Contemporary Perspectives on Women's Professional Work*, ed. E. Smyth, S. Acker, P. Bourne, and A. Prentice, 215–33. Toronto: University of Toronto Press.

Millar, W.P.J., R. Heap, and B. Gidney. 2005. "Degrees of Difference: The Students in Three Professional Schools at the University of Toronto, 1910 to the 1950s." In *Learning to Practise: Professional Education in Historical and Contemporary Perspective*, ed. R. Heap, W. Millar, and E. Smyth, 155–88. Ottawa: University of Ottawa Press.

Mitchinson, W., A. Prentice, P. Bourne, G.C. Brandt, B. Light, and N. Black. 1988. *Canadian Women: A History*. Toronto: Harcourt Brace, Jovanovich.

Munro, Alice. 1978. "The Moons of Jupiter." *The New Yorker*, 22 May.

– 2012. *Dear Life*. Toronto: McLelland & Stewart.

Neatby, N. 2001. "Introduction: Teaching and Learning." In *Framing Our Past: Canadian Women's History in the Twentieth Century*, edited by S. Cook, L. McLean, and K. O'Rourke, 149–55. Montreal and Kingston: McGill-Queen's University Press.

Oral History Interview. 2015. University of Ottawa.

Osborne, K. 1999. *Education: A Guide to the Canadian School Debate – Or, Who Wants What and Why?* Toronto: Penguin.

Owram, D. 1996. *Born at the Right Time: A History of the Baby Boom Generation*. Toronto: University of Toronto Press.

Peters, W. 2013. "Too Little Learned since Montréal Massacre." *CAUT/ACPPU Bulletin* 59(9): A4.

Prentice, A. 1977. "The Feminization of Teaching in British North America and Canada, 1845–1975." In *The Neglected Majority: Essays in Canadian Women's History*, ed. A. Prentice and S. Trofimenkoff, 5–20. Toronto: McLelland and Stewart.

Quebec. 1963. *Report of Royal Commission of Inquiry on Education in the Province of Quebec*. Montreal, QC: Province of Quebec.

Rees, R. 1995. "Systemic Discrimination in a University." In *Women and*

Leadership in Canadian Education, ed. C. Reynolds and B. Young, 33–44. Calgary: Detselig.

Reynolds, C. 1995. "Feminist Frameworks for the Study of Administration and Leadership in Educational Organizations." In *Women and Leadership in Canadian Education*, ed. C. Reynolds and B. Young, 3–18. Calgary: Detselig.

Reynolds, C., and B. Young, eds. 1995. *Women and Leadership in Canadian Education*. Calgary: Detselig.

Scott, Joan. 1986. "Gender: A Useful Category of Historical Analysis." *American Historical Review* 91 (5): 1053–75.

Strong-Boag, V. 1976. *The Parliament of Women: The National Council of Women of Canada, 1893–1929*. Ottawa: National Museum.

University of Alberta Centenary. 2008. "History: Expansion (1950–1959)." Accessed 12 December 2017. http://wayback.archive-it.org/1830/20140930 191927/http://www.ualbertacentennial.ca/history/expansion/index.html.

Wallace, J. 2005. "Assuming Leadership: Women Superintendents in 20th Century Ontario." In *History Is Hers: Women Teachers in Twentieth Century Ontario*, ed. R. Coulter and H. Harper, 137–60. Calgary: Detselig.

2

Feminist Reformers

Creating Pedagogical Change to Curriculum in Toronto Schools through Inclusive Content

ROSE FINE-MEYER

Teachers in Ontario have historically been entrusted with the task of delivering curriculum. This task allows for pedagogical decisions that address schools, communities, and the individual learning needs of students. Although expected to follow official curriculum expectations, teachers have flexibility in the ways in which course materials are presented and are encouraged to adapt individual course studies to address specific student needs. Teachers' acceptance of the responsibility to shape the curriculum is demonstrated through their ability to alter their pedagogical practices and to seek out specific resources that support student learning. This chapter explores the ways in which teacher agency shaped the delivery of curriculum in classrooms and, in the 1970s and 1980s in Toronto, provided an important entry point for the inclusion of women's narratives into history course studies.

Toronto teachers working in the 1960s–1980s initiated the changing of pedagogy to address changes taking place within society. This was a period when social movement activism and the second-wave feminist movements affected the lives of Canadians, including the work of teachers across Ontario. The city of Toronto, with a population of over two million in the 1970s, and approximately 166 schools, contained a large and diverse population that supported a significant number of community advocacy groups whose concerns about schools and education in general were widely published through local papers.[1] As front-line educators, often in isolation within their own subject departments, a number of feminist teachers actively chose to alter curriculum and include the experiences and knowledges of women. The decision to include women in subject curricula, at a time when diverse resource materials within schools were generally unavailable, relied heavily on the personal commitment of individual teachers, and the support they received from feminist grassroots networks. This study[2] incorporates evidence from archival documents and a set of interviews. Oral history as a methodology can provide insight into individual experiences omitted or marginalized from formal archival documents and records. The interviews explored in this study, part of a larger research project, provide a deeper understanding into the ways some teachers, responding to societal changes, found gaps in the curriculum (Fine-Meyer 2012). Teachers in this study reflected on the ways in which they shaped their pedagogical practices to provide a more gender equitable curricula. Archival evidence was found at the Toronto District School Board Archives, the Archives of Ontario, the Canadian Women's Movement Archives at the University of Ottawa, the University of Toronto Archives, as well as private collections. These documents included letters, newsletters, committee reports, published course materials, and lists of resources and events.

Toronto teachers interested in reform came to see gender inequality in the curriculum as a problematic issue and this led to curricular changes within their classrooms. These teachers were actively reshaping and rewriting parts of the existing history and social science curriculum as well as developing new syllabi in order to integrate women's experiences within their pedagogy. The second part of this study explores how a lack of resources for teaching women's history was handled at an institutional and community level, and how feminist teachers responded. This chapter reveals that many educators took a leadership role in generating curricular change in schools because they felt personally motivated by social movement activism.

This chapter analyzes at a micro level the ways in which women's movement activism influenced educational changes, predominantly by providing a model of what could/should take place in classrooms (Robbins 2008; Kohli 2012).[3] This study, therefore, is about feminist teachers who challenged the status quo by bringing in material about women into their classrooms, and how 1970s feminism and women's social movements provided important networks of support for teachers that helped shape their perspectives on curricula (see Lieberman 2000; Day and Sachs 2004; McCormick 2011).

The term "feminist" used in this chapter reflects the conceptualizations of the working and retired teachers in this study. These teachers were focused on the early second-wave feminist's understandings of women's inequity, when feminist consciousness was manifested through action – in this case the action of individual teachers to alter curriculum resource materials (Bascia et al. 2014). But, as Nancy Cott has noted, the term feminism is "inadequate to capture the multifarious ways that women through the ages have protested male domination or attempted to redefine gender hierarchy" (Cott 1989). Judith Lorber also recognizes the broad changes over time, noting that 1970s second-wave feminism stressed the binary framework of male versus female, but that by the 1980s, many feminists were beginning to challenge earlier narratives that situated women in a unified category (Lorber 2010, 1–4). Wendy Kohli examines the range of positions feminists have taken over time, noting that the second-wave women's movement contained a political commitment to end oppression, which heavily influenced understandings of the term feminism (2012). These definitions were supported in this study, as teachers, both men and women, indicated a range of perspectives about how feminism was defined, yet shared a core understanding of women's inequalities. Only the female teachers referred to themselves as feminists: their voices are represented in the majority of the quotations in this chapter. Male teachers, often the heads of departments, were either supportive of or indifferent to including women's experiences within their lessons.

The influence that teachers have on curricular change has received limited attention. As Nina Bascia has suggested, teacher-driven curriculum development often "starts with a small number of teachers working independently on new content or pedagogical approaches." Examining their work provides an important lens into understanding the interplay of curricular work with "social, political and intellectual contexts over time" (Bascia et al. 2014, 228). Teacher-driven curriculum development was not unique to Toronto during the period of the 1970s and 1980s, as feminist teachers elsewhere were developing resources to bring the experiences of women into their classrooms (Goodson 1995, 2005). Feminist teachers were influenced by the growth in feminist scholarship and the introduction of women's studies and women's history courses within the universities (Robbins 2008, 112; Andersen 2010). Many of these resources were leaking into public school classrooms.

As curricula is state directed and politically driven, teachers – both nationally and internationally – have been in the middle of debates over content. As employees of state schools, teachers are often aware of the ways in which school systems, curricula, and pedagogical and organizational structures were constructed by gender. History teachers struggled, for example, with the state's notions of citizenship education that were central to curriculum documents and history textbook narratives (see Forman 1990; Prentice 1992; Llewellyn 2012). Keith Barton argues that history education can present particular challenges as "history is so culturally, politically and ideologically charged that it cannot be separated from wider social forces" (Barton and Levstik 2004, 188). Scholars and education stakeholders continue to debate about history context in schools. These debates reflect how state ideologies are both accepted and challenged in classrooms globally (Taylor and Guyver 2012; Davies 2011). The teachers in this study reflected upon the challenges of teaching histories that were centred on military and economic narratives, but that omitted the experiences of women. In acknowledging this omission, they felt it was necessary to expand course resources to include women's historical experiences.

The majority of educators included in this study shared a firm belief in the equality of women and the inclusion of women in course studies. Berger Gluck and Patai (1991), Armitage (2002), Janovicek (2006), Sangster (1994), and Llewellyn, Freund, and Reilly (2015) have noted that incorporating oral history into research provides opportunities to uncover alternative perspectives, particularly those of women. Feminist scholars have reflected on similar challenges in post-secondary institutions. Alison Prentice (1991), Margaret Conrad (2012), Joan Sangster (1994), and others have documented how feminist scholars worked to address gender inequities in university course options and studies. However, few feminist scholars have addressed this work at a secondary school level (see, e.g., Forman 1990; Parr and Rosenfeld 1996; Sanders 2000; Clark and Millard 1998; Frawley 2005; Hanson 2000; Smyth and Bourne 2006). The eighteen female and nine male secondary school teachers included in this study provide a unique understanding of how both female and male teachers responded to gender-imbalanced history curricula, and how their initiatives translated into specialized teaching practices that focused on altering course content.[4] Although feminist scholars have contributed to our understanding of the ways in which women have been challenged by educational institutions, it is less clear how teachers in public schools have been able to reconcile the often conflicting realities of teaching that must incorporate demands from ministries of education, local school boards, individual school subject departments, and their own professional practices. The oral histories in this chapter provide important insight (Prentice 1991; Martin 2011).

Understanding definitions of feminism as they relate specifically to education was also a central concern while conducting these oral histories. The teachers' commitment to feminist ideology reflected the paradox of working within inherently inequitable spaces. Mary O'Brien argues, "When we speak of feminism and education we are immediately confronted by a contradiction. On the one hand, education is seen as a necessary and important part of action directed toward social transformation. On the other hand, educational systems and school curricula are structured hierarchically and are profoundly conservative" (1986, 91). Scholars have argued that neo-liberal education systems, although publicly supportive of eliminating fundamental inequities, have also played a part in the maintenance of the status quo (Braedley and Luxton 2010; Solomon et al. 2011; Shubhra 2012). Liberal states, such as Ontario, have historically supported individual freedom and economic rights, but as O'Brien notes, "education is the structure in which all children are said to start equal. After that, they are on their own, and the state has done its duty" (95). Susan Russell argues that schools, as representative of the state, seek to maintain stability through support of existing hierarchical systems (Russell 1987, 230).

The challenges to liberal state systems brought forward by the women's movement placed feminist teachers in a difficult position – as both active participants in and resisters to state institutions. The Royal Commission on the Status of Women (Canada 1970) helped to articulate the links between gender and politics, and supported notions of resistance such as adding resource materials or altering state curriculum. At the organizational core of the women's movement was an understanding of the importance of women's networks as structures for social change. Women's organizations developed and broadened networks, created and published resources, and lobbied governments and institutions. This was not particular to Canada; it was representative of the ways in which women organized on a global scale (Carstairs and Janovicek 2013; Robbins 2008; Adamson, Briskin, and McPhail 1988; Dufour, Masson, and Caouette 2010; Ferree and Tripp 2006). For example, school board affirmative action committees, present in all schools in Toronto, networked with teachers' unions, the provincial Ontario Women's Directorate, and the National Action Committee on the Status of Women that pressed the federal government for change (Adamson 1988; Marsden 2012; Sangster 1995).[5] On a local level, women networked through meetings, conferences, workshops, and book and film clubs, which produced posters, newsletters, and pamphlets (Women's Education Resource Centre/WERC at Ontario Institute for Studies in Education/OISE).

Bringing women's experiences into the classroom was automatically seen by educators and administrators as a feminist act – a challenge to the status quo – not just a means by which to achieve gender equity. Based on the social and political context of the time, the participants in this study responded to feminism in a variety of ways that reflected their personal and professional positions: sometimes supportive and other times resistant. Their commitment to feminism, for example, reflected the complexities of the period when women faced challenges in their homes and workplaces. One teacher recalled, "I was a feminist in my own way – I just wasn't out there like some of the others – I probably became that later, but not at that time." But this same teacher also noted the excitement, commitment, and dedication during the early years of the women's movement, while she was a member of several women's groups. She recalled, "There was excitement – International Women's Year – there were exciting people around, Rosie Abella, Lorna Marsden, Joni Mitchell, Rita McNeal – there were people doing things!" (Teacher S 2010). Another teacher remembered, "In my teaching of Canadian history, right from the beginning, questions about how events impacted women and how women impacted events were there – because that was an outcome of who I was and certainly I came out of a feminist perspective in the 1960s, which was really about challenging the old history so that there was – very much – a revisionist paradigm that you brought to the classroom" (Teacher S 2010). The majority of the female teachers interviewed had proudly supported or were active members of women's organizations. Some of these organizations included women teachers' unions (FWTAO), women's history organizations (OWHN), women's political organizations (the Feminist Party of Canada, Liberal or New Democratic Party [NDP] women's caucuses), and women's arts organizations, such as the National Film Board (NFB) Studio D (Robbins 2008; Vanstone 2007). Many teachers agreed that women's organizations provided important opportunities to network with a common community and felt that their feminism and activism directly affected their work as teachers (Teacher K 2009). Examining the teachers' inclusion of women's experiences reveals the gaps between policy and practice, and suggests that previous studies that focused entirely on policy change did not reflect the educational experience in its entirety, often excluding the vital role individual teachers played and continue to play in sharing knowledge.

The Toronto Board of Education first established the position of affirmative action adviser in 1979 with double responsibilities for both race relations and women's issues.[6] In 1980, the school board divided the position into two, separating race and women's issues (McCaskell 2005). One teacher questioned this directive, arguing, "I don't think they're entirely separate issues, [race and gender equity] but they were treated as separate things – but we were looking at stereotyping people" (Teacher S 2010). Another teacher recognized this altering lens when she noted, "Materials about women just gradually got into history teaching. I included women when examining the Industrial Revolution and, of course, the Royal Commission on the Status of Women. I used material directly from the Commission. By the 1980s, we used material about race and so I included women in the Underground Railroad" (Teacher E 2009). The issues of race, gender, and identity entered policy discourse simultaneously, and many teachers responded by providing new content in their teaching to provide greater diversity. Several agendas were driving educational policy reform throughout the 1970s and early 1980s: a focus on Canadian identity and a focus on human rights and individual freedoms.[7] Implementation of these policies within schools was inconsistent. Teachers were left on their own to integrate continually changing policies within course studies, and were responsible for accessing their own resource materials to use in their teaching.

Gender and race policies were implemented within schools through a number of initiatives, including resource development and community networking. The majority of teachers in this study were active in the development of curricula through their own professionalism. For example, one teacher noted that her master's degree classes provided materials she used directly in her classes. She reflected on this experience, "I was teaching Modern Western Civilization and it was great because my students would say, 'Ms, you had class last night!' because I would come back having learned about Mary Wollstonecraft, and then would teach about her in my class" (Teacher K

2009). Another teacher recalled, "I got [resource] materials from the Women's Bookstore and from the OISE/UT library. I ran articles, and the copy machine was my best friend. I heard stories about people [at other school boards] having to secretly pass resources [about women] and materials around, but that was not the case in the Toronto Board of Education" (Teacher Q 2009). Many teachers demonstrated their deep understanding of the relationship between professional communities, supplementary resources, and good teaching by reaching out to a variety of women's communities. Important larger institutions and communities such as the Ontario Institute for Studies in Education (OISE), Women's Education Resource Centre (WERC), the Voice of Women (VOW), and the Toronto Women's Bookstore had strong ties to feminist activism, and they provided common spaces in which resources about women could be found.

The Ontario Ministry of Education and Toronto Board of Education equity policies were developed throughout the 1970s and 1980s and addressed affirmative action and sex-role stereotyping (see Ontario Ministry of Education 1986; Fine-Meyer 2012). Policies focused more on the lack of women in positions of responsibility and less on providing new resources for classroom use. Women's Committees at the Toronto Board of Education were formed to create a space for women to network and develop resources. However, school board events were attended by a limited number of teachers. Therefore, school board resource materials were not found in all schools. As a number of the teachers in this study noted, making women's resources mandatory in all course studies would have addressed issues of inequity head-on, but that was not implemented. Therefore, the work to create resources about women remained peripheral to the main curriculum expectations. Although the Ontario Ministry of Education and the Toronto Board of Education worked to create an awareness of the systemic gender inequalities within schools, they did not take bold steps to make substantial change to the curricula in all classrooms.[8] Integrating gender equity in course studies required the support and commitment of both teachers and administrators and the teacher interviews reveal they took steps to enhance their resources to include women's perspectives. Their advocacy for the inclusion of women and their willingness to share with each other altered curriculum in course studies across the city (Novogrodsky 1985, 34–5).[9]

Toronto Board of Education (TBE) affirmative action policies, developed during the 1970s and 1980s, were influential as a stimulus for equity, but they relied on voluntary action (TBE Report 1977; Fobert and Kincaid 1976; Foster 1983; Julien 1987; Ontario Ministry of Education 1986). In 1980, for example, the Toronto Board of Education mandated that affirmative action representatives be appointed to every school. Interested teachers volunteered for this position, but equity implementation was erratic and dependent on the commitment of administrators in each school. It took until 1988 for mandatory measures to be formally implemented (Sheffield 1992).[10] Even by the 1990s, mandatory measures were slow to produce major results, despite the introduction of specific goals and targets (see Batcher, Winter, and Wright 1987; Labatt 1993).[11] In practice, government policies acted only as guidelines. Schools and teachers made independent decisions about how best to implement policies in their own classrooms. A lack of clarity by the school board to define how affirmative action policies directly affected curriculum resulted in inconsistent implementation within schools, and this was reflected in the teachers' comments, providing evidence that policy is not always reflected in practice. Pat Kincaid, who was hired in 1975 to a full-time position at the Toronto Board of Education as a women's studies consultant, noted: "I applied to the [Toronto] school board office because of issues of discrimination – the omission of women in so many parts of the curriculum was critical" (Kincaid 2010).

The participants' interviews provide insights into the daily practices of female history teachers who struggled between two realities: on the one hand, women teachers encountered antagonistic, male-dominated departments, administrators, curriculum, and textbooks, and, on the other hand, they experienced supportive feminist networks and communities, usually outside of the school. In general, all teachers felt at times externally pressured to "add women" wherever possible to course studies. However, only a number of self-identified "radical" feminist teachers presented themselves as "women warriors" up against the system – namely, particular male colleagues and outdated resources that acted as a barrier to their work to include women (Casey 1993, viii).[12] The "radical" feminist teachers represented half the female teachers in this study.

Some of the female teachers noted professional experiences that had led them to view education within gender constructs. These included limited opportunities for curriculum writing, positions of responsibility, and course teaching. Historically, teaching had provided an acceptable employment for women, but women had less of a presence in secondary school history departments. Common history department practice in Toronto was to hire male history teachers and to focus on a history curriculum that emphasized the experiences of men (Pierson and Prentice 1982; Batcher, Winter, and Wright 1987).

Although all teachers in this study were aware of the women's movement's demands to alter curricula, the majority of the teachers felt unprepared to integrate women's experiences into established course studies. Teachers who felt an urgency to address the absence of women viewed their teaching as an extension of their support and involvement in social movement activism. Some of the female history teachers had returned to university, while teaching, to pursue graduate degrees. Many published course materials, some helped write textbooks or developed courses, and a few won awards for their work as teachers. The oral histories revealed that many teachers acted independently in delivering curricula and took on the responsibility of ensuring course studies addressed student needs – both male and female.

Most history teachers taught from textbooks, adding supplementary materials from their own collections, to fill gaps in the curriculum. History textbooks used in schools were costly and therefore replaced infrequently, so they tended to be outdated. In the period before the 1990s, all history textbooks concentrated on the experiences of white, politically connected men, most of whom had ties to the military or to industry (Kealey et al. 1992).[13] Male university history professors played a major part in the transfer of this discourse to secondary classrooms in Toronto.[14] The dominance of white, male history teachers in Toronto schools reflected the support they received from history professors. One teacher interviewee recalled that she spent most of her undergraduate years at the University of Toronto, in the late 1960s, trying to join the History Club only to discover that it was only open to male students. This teacher added, "History was a man's field – most of the teachers teaching history at that time (1968) were men – same as in math and science." She recalled a male department head's remark that she was a great teacher, then added, "'Too bad I'll never hire you.' I would never hear of any women hired for his department" (Teacher N 2010).

Other female teachers noted that male professors met with them only after seeing male students, and excluded them from special events. Male university history majors ended up running history departments in schools in Toronto and many brought these exclusionary attitudes with them. One teacher specifically recognized this, adding, "My department head and assistant head were male. The history profession in schools in those days [1970s] was overwhelmingly male" (Teacher U 2010).

Male historians and educators were also textbook authors and editors. A study, published in 1980 by OISE, examined which textbooks, resource books, and reference books were used in classrooms to teach Canadian studies. The researchers concluded that most Canadian history textbooks did not reflect changing educational standards (Robeson and Sylvester 1980). The authors were critical of the ways in which women were omitted from course materials (CWSE 1980, 131; see Wright 1976; Anderson, Ryan, and Shapiro 1989)[15] and argued that textbooks still had a tendency to present the role of women as "outside the mainstream of Canadian history" (Robeson and Sylvester 1980, vii). Another study, published in 1989 and supported by the Ontario Ministry of Education, surveyed approved history textbooks and found that none of the books met gender equity policy expectations (Light, Staton, and Bourne 1989).[16] Equity policies had done little to alter formal curricula. A 1970 history textbook, representative of many, noted, "Women of Canada, because of their part in the war effort, intensified their drive for political, economic and social equality ... In their work they could count on help from prominent men in Canada." Thus, even when textbooks added women, they did so in terms of their links to the actions of men (Herstein, Hughes, and Kirbyson 1970, 324). One teacher acknowledged, "There was no integration of Canadian women and their contributions in any textbook that I can recall using" (Teacher L 2010). Another teacher confirmed this by stating, "To consider how they responded to gender inclusively makes a mockery of the reality. [Textbook] writers only began to 'throw in' bits of gender as the publishers kept up with general societal trends. The two basic Canadian history textbooks remained visually male and only marginally responsive to gender issues" (Teacher O 2009; see also Conrad 2012; Osborne 2012).

Teachers noted that women's history narratives were viewed by many as too political, and some colleagues felt the narratives did not hold the same weight. The Ontario provincial curriculum did not demand that women's narratives be included and therefore, left as a personal choice for individual teachers, they were viewed as less important. Many history teachers had resources that they were comfortable using, and were reluctant to change. Feminist teachers were required to employ a variety of strategies to include women's experiences within their tool kit of resources. These strategies included networking, attending feminist functions, shopping at the Toronto Women's Bookstore, or attending lectures or classes.

Most of the teachers spoke of their employer, the former Toronto Board of Education, as a place where they could find communities of like-minded female educators. These communities gave the teachers opportunities to develop and access curriculum resources, and a place where they could publicly articulate shared beliefs in social justice. The teachers viewed changes to curricula as the product of their hard work and dedication. They were, in fact, correct. The archival records, now held at the Toronto District School Board Archives, reveal how these women, and many others, were extremely active participants. They sat on school board committees, initiated workshops and events, developed and organized conferences, networked with one another, wrote and published newsletters, and took on leadership positions. The women teachers referred to this period as "the golden years." It was golden in terms of the many auxiliary outlets available for them to network, share, and organize common projects and initiatives. Many teachers, both male and female, indicated that the Toronto school board held regular evening events that featured "women's topics" (Teacher P 2009).[17] One teacher represented the position of many when she recalled, "I was on the [school] board's women's committee. We met once a month at the board office and there was a sub-committee. I was one of three who helped write the board policy and I ran workshops at schools for sexual harassment policy. There were things happening in the city – a general awareness of women and racial minorities. In the 1970s, the board power structure was the old boys but things were changing – they were changing dramatically, especially in the 1980s with the appointment of women" (Teacher K 2009).

Another teacher observed, "I was very active in the Women's Liaison Committee and on the Status of Women Committee, and the Bias Review in Education Committee. I worked on lots of curriculum documents such as curriculum documents about classrooms and girls. I did workshops on women and I worked on a lot of projects for the board. I did summer writing projects. When I started at the Toronto Board in 1974 there were lots of younger teachers and lots of women. People were open to new ideas – people who wanted to work on things had an opportunity. I liked to develop curriculum and was interested in women's issues" (Teacher N 2010).

Rebecca Coulter argues that history teachers in particular were called upon to either support or challenge state narratives (Coulter 2002; Coulter and Harper 2005). Feminist history teachers were often caught between their responsibilities as state employees and their desire to incorporate social change. Some teachers used the new focus on social history as a means to integrate women, as it broadened the historical lens. Moving away from grand narratives, social historians focused on the lives of ordinary people, and this allowed for women's lived experiences to be featured. As Veronica Strong-Boag noted in 1978, women's history had been "fortunate in finding in the 'new social history'– particularly historians studying labour and committed to recovering the past 'from the bottom up' – an ally in the reconstruction of historical scholarship in this country" (1978). Culture, race, labour, and class were part of the discourse for social historians and for committed teachers as well. One teacher explained, "Social history was a prevailing methodology by which to study the Canadian story. After mid-1980s, new history textbooks began to include specific chapters on suffrage" (Teacher O 2009). Teachers recalled that women appeared in defined spaces – as nuns, or wives of prime ministers – or in examinations of suffrage, but were absent in areas such as the arts. Working-class histories, covering themes such as factory work, suffrage, and families, lent themselves to including women. By the 1990s, women were appearing in history resources in increasing spaces as social history became an accepted part of course curricula.[18] Another teacher remarked, "I think that one of the problems was that, and it's the way that textbooks were set up, that you'll have a little section on women. The women's stuff was not part of political history or economic history. In some ways, because of the way that I argue that the entire curriculum is set up, that you are supposed to look at what the impact of economic and political structures are on daily life. That dilutes the importance of social history. I found my big challenge was getting enough original source documents. Not just to supplement the text, but to actually go beyond the text" (Teacher Y 2012). Social histories helped teachers expand the history narratives used in classrooms by placing a greater emphasis on those people who were frequently marginalized in textbooks. One teacher remarked, "I would say that I approached history as social history. It was about dealing with groups that were marginalized in history in texts" (Teacher K 2009).[19] It seems that many teachers looked for documents that provided more equitable course content. One teacher recalled, "The courses that I developed were labour history courses – and women were in there. We looked at major strikes in history – what was the issue – the economy, and the strike was an entry point" (Teacher M 2009).

Teachers noted that the increase in available published supplementary materials made the textbook less central to their teaching and opened the door for more class resources about women. One teacher noted, "When I look back 35 years, there are two things: one, that the textbook became less and less important, and two ... they did a poorer and poorer job in providing insight into history" (Teacher K 2009). Teachers were aware of textbook limitations and welcomed the increased availability of additional resources. The question remains as to why the Toronto school board continued to purchase textbooks that were not representative of their own equity policies or the evolving state of history. The policies implemented by the Ontario provincial government to demonstrate a commitment to women's equality required minimal change in course curricula. In response, interested teachers supplemented gaps in the curriculum and, in some cases, took the highly committed step to develop their own courses. One could argue that their work as teachers was more effective in changing history education to include women than were government policies. One teacher (Teacher L 2010) summed up what the majority noted in this study: "My greatest textbooks and resources were not on Circular 14" (the Ontario Ministry of Education approved textbook list). As independent professionals, teachers were aware of their vital role in accessing materials for their classes. One teacher argued, "The only effective way by which to provide for a fair overview of the role of women in our shared history was through supplementary materials. This was the stuff of history material" (Teacher O 2009).

Since teachers were left on their own to access materials about women, forms of communication were important. Few teachers were accessing resources and information from the internet until the mid-1990s. Instead, they relied on the materials they received in their school mailboxes or through department leaders. Newsletters played a central role in keeping Toronto Board of Education employees informed, and those that reflected the work of various women's committees played a significant role as a networking tool for women educators.[20] Supplementary materials used in classrooms were varied and included journal articles that teachers photocopied, filmstrips, as well as films and books that teachers borrowed or purchased. Some teachers displayed student projects about women on the walls of their classrooms or schools, and women's voices were uncovered as a result of independent research work by students.[21] Teachers and students turned to university libraries, public libraries, bookstores, and a variety of local venues. As one teacher explained, "Most of our resources were home-grown, self-made, and invented on site." He recalled, "Field studies in history in Toronto were easy. There was always a focus on the achievement of women. The early labour movement had female leadership and the health movement was dependent on women. The stories were available outside the classroom. Independent studies were designed to allow students to highlight women's narratives" (Teacher O 2009). Teachers used academic articles found through various publications. Like the women's resource centres, teachers had filing cabinets where they stored articles for independent research projects about Canadian women.[22]

All history teachers in this study noted the importance of films in their teaching of history. Films were easily available through school boards, the Toronto Public Library, and audiovisual departments. Films could be recorded from TV or purchased, and many titles were available to teachers through the National Film Board (NFB), which had offices in Toronto (Teacher L 2010). Teachers found time to access resource materials on professional development days. One teacher shared, "I shouldn't say this probably, but you know when we had those PD days? We never went. We went to the OISE Library and spent our day there finding things to use in our classes. There was also a lot of good stuff on public television, channel 17 at that time, and we taped everything" (Teacher D 2011). Other teachers noted that they accessed films about women from the Toronto Board of Education Women's Resource Centre, which was run by women volunteers. Pat Staton, who volunteered at the centre, got lists of topics from teachers and provided a variety of resources (Teacher Q 2009). Many history departments also had their own film collections; some were quite substantial and teachers spoke about their expertise in taping videos from TVO and PBS. Films provided one way in which to include women's experiences (Teacher L 2010; Teacher O 2009).[23] A number of films about women were available through the NFB's Studio D.[24] One teacher shared, "I am a film person. One of the reasons why I liked to show things is that it created a common ground for all the kids. There was this wonderful NFB film about a woman who wanted to start a union in Toronto in the garment district" (Teacher D 2011). This teacher included historical narratives that were relevant to all her students.

A number of teachers developed their own materials that focused on women (Forman 1990; Bourne and Centre for Womens' Studies in Education, Ontario Institute for Studies in Education 1994).[25] Janet Ray, a retired teacher/librarian in Toronto, published a number of books (1978, 1981) that examined the lives of individual Canadian women, including one on Emily Stowe. As well, some teachers were able to obtain positions on curriculum-writing teams where they argued for and demanded the inclusion of women. One teacher recalled, "One summer we developed a unit of material on women's suffrage and made links to labour studies and women's unions. All teachers got binders" (Teacher N 2010).[26] Teachers took pride in accessing and developing supplementary materials to support a more inclusive curriculum, and sought out opportunities where they could advocate for the inclusion of women's experiences.

In the mid-1970s, preliminary discussions began at the Toronto Board of Education about the possibility of introducing women's studies courses and about the development of resources for those teachers who taught stand-alone courses. Feminist teachers within the board did not wait for board approval. With the support of school principals, students, and parents, they developed and offered stand-alone women's studies courses at their schools. Many of these courses had women's history units within the course syllabus and were often the only course offered in which women's history was included. One teacher recognized that her women's history/studies course was one of the first secondary school courses about women (1980). She still has a copy of the original syllabus for this course, and her response to my inquiry about the course indicated a strong commitment to social justice. She asserted, "I taught *Man and Society* and one year, there were huge numbers of girls in the course. Students asked why it is called *Man and Society*. They argued that there should be a course with materials about women. In fact, in those days I could have just taught it – guidelines allowed you to alter the materials and still give the credit – but we didn't. I wanted to create this course – it was part of a political act. We wanted to make a statement that this should be there. Those women are not in the curriculum and we wanted a course called *Women and Society*" (Teacher M 2009).

Most teachers recalled the ways in which girls in their classes demanded materials about women. One teacher shared that research topics were "always feminized by an activist group of female students" (Teacher O 2009). Locally developed courses were permitted by the Toronto school board to address particular school needs. Permission was based on principal support. One teacher, who developed a course on women's history in the late 1970s, noted, "My principal was a feminist and a mover and a groover. There was an initiative at that time to develop experimental courses. I went to her about a course on women's studies and she supported beginning the course the next year. The course was called *The Canadian Women*. There were four separate classes the first year and that was a big thing" (Teacher Q 2009).[27] Many of these courses grew out of established women's studies course units, available through universities and colleges, and those developed by feminist organizations, school board women's committees, and other interested teachers. Teacher Jan Coomber, who wrote a Canadian women's history unit for the grade 10 Canadian history course entitled "The Role of Canadian Women in the Second World War," argued that "to integrate women's history and the feminine perspective into the curriculum can be a liberating experience for both girls and boys" (1986).

Teachers who wrote curriculum units or stand-alone courses recognized that "units" were viewed by administrators as an acceptable form of integration. They also understood that stand-alone courses reflected the government's way to address curricular change by setting women apart from the main curricula. Viewed as a "safe response" to feminist demands, governments could avoid making major overhauls to the curricula. This might explain why changes to curricula continued to focus on units and stand-alone courses, rather than fundamental curricular change. School boards were able to demonstrate a concern for gender inequities and maintain the myth of schools as the "great equalizers" of a liberal society. However, the inclusion of stand-alone courses was also a reflection of the commitment of some teachers to find a space in which to feature the experiences of women.

A common narrative from the women teachers who participated in the study was about the ways in which they networked with other women. The chair of Women's Liaison Committee at the board sums up what many women teachers noted about their own activism:

> The whole organization was very important. We put it together – there were six of us who founded it – Women in Educational Administration Ontario (WEAO–1980/81). We created it because of

the lack of women in positions of responsibility in education – that was the clear focus for it. WEAO and FWTAO ran the most successful supervisory officers' groups in the province, and scared the living daylights out of a lot of other groups, men mostly. We were so successful that those of us who were teaching were invited to school boards to do sessions ... That was a great organization which, again, the excitement of it and all the things that were accomplished in terms of women getting together, women discussing things, like curriculum. (Teacher S 2010)

Teachers were successful in the development of equitable history in the classroom because they were personally interested, wanted to serve the needs of their students, and could depend on the support of feminist networks (Teacher O 2009). Toronto feminists mobilized on a number of issues: abortion, poverty, violence, and education. Feminist groups were wide-ranging, providing space for like-minded women.[28] However, a number of women teachers commented on the lack of support they received from male colleagues and administrators. According to one teacher, "In my department I was the only woman until the late 70s, then over time two others were hired. It was a typical curriculum – male focus that was the standard. But I didn't feel at all intimidated by that ... The head of the history department was old school and I think the role of women never crossed his head, but he was a gentleman and I could get into historical debates with others in the department and he wouldn't interfere" (Teacher K 2009). The hostility toward some of the women who were advocating for women was clearly part of their work experience. One male teacher recalled the divisive environment; "Male teachers had a blind spot when it came to women. It was hard for them to take women seriously, as both colleagues and as objects of historical study. They reacted to the extremes of the women's movement" (Teacher U 2010).[29]

Female teachers who later became administrators remembered that they continued to face hostile environments while fighting for gender equity and recognition. Their change in status – both financial and in terms of position – did not significantly alter gender equality challenges. Placing women together, despite differences in salary, status, race, or experience, was central to some interviewee narratives. In re-creating their past, the interviewees situated themselves as champions of gender equality and focused on how they continually worked to break down barriers and implement change. Recurrent narratives recounted how they faced ridicule and were often marginalized or dismissed within their workplaces (Teacher N 2010).[30] These kinds of challenges made women's groups even more important for those female teachers who worked toward gender equity in school board policies, school curriculum, and school practices.

While male history teachers in Toronto during the 1970s and 1980s outnumbered female teachers, many of the women teachers developed, advocated for, and were active in sharing women's history resources. They also used a wide range of strategies to bring women's narratives into their history classrooms in Toronto and provided a foundation for resources and strategies to develop in the future. Despite facing a number of barriers that are outlined in this chapter, they were united in their resolve to implement gender equity within traditional history curriculum.

Reflecting on changes over time, the majority of the teachers in this study felt that the Ontario school board amalgamation (in 1998) marked the end to any momentum in their work for gender equity (see McCaskell 2005; Gidney 1999, 237).[31] One principal remarked, "Gender equity was high on the list at my school. It was the energy of change – excitement about it – because we had support of the school board. Then when right-wing trustees entered with [the election of Ontario] Premier Mike Harris – amalgamation broke that up" (Teacher Q 2009). The Harris Conservative government's focus on "accountability" did not include gender equity education but rather included the measurement of improvements in literacy and numeracy. This focus on accountability hampered reforms taking place within many schools and classrooms. These reforms could well have resulted in systemic change, if the late 1990s had not produced a political shift in priorities. This political shift was also characterized by a focus on educational objectives, on developing a common curriculum, and on the expanded use of computers and technology. Amalgamation also resulted in a tightening of teachers' independent curriculum development, resources, pedagogy, and a loss of networking support.[32] One teacher reflected, "Now education is into evaluation and cost-saving. For younger women all the battles have been fought – the feeling today is that people don't realize what happened in the past" (Teacher N 2010).

In placing these oral histories within the context of the time period, I recognize that some of the teachers' feminist beliefs had intensified or diminished over time (see Feminist History Society of Canada website). However, teachers who identified themselves as feminist recalled active membership in women's organizations that played a role in providing important spaces for solidarity. What also remained central to their oral history accounts was that, as feminist educators, they faced numerous challenges in identifying themselves as gender equity advocates. Their feminist activism was expressed through their progress in making curricular change and, as such, they were at the forefront of fighting for equity within their schools.

Feminist historians have turned to oral history as part of their methodology to access "authentic" voices (see Rowbotham 1973). In accessing the voices of individual history teachers during the 1970s and 1980s, it is clear that feminist history teachers deliberately situated their work within the feminist communities in which they were active members. An oral history methodology allowed me to measure the impact of feminism differently: to recognize the centrality of lived experience beyond the rhetoric of policy, thus revealing feminist teachers' collective refusal to see challenges as a barrier to their teaching.

CONCLUSION

This chapter demonstrates that curricular change, in particular altering curricula to include women's historical experiences, emanated more from a community level rather than from an institutional level. The interviews revealed common concerns and a belief that feminism played a role in changing the delivery of curriculum in individual classrooms. Educators' accounts also demonstrated that each school and each teacher acted independently, revealing that teacher pedagogy reflects the philosophy of individual teachers and their belief in a responsibility to address student needs. This study found that women's activism had influenced all areas of society, including schools and course studies. However, study participants, because of the lack of a coordinated government initiative, had to rely on their own agency to address gender inequity within curricula. The personal commitment of individual feminist Toronto teachers working in urban schools during the 1970s and 1980s had a social impact and resulted in curricular change that integrated women's experiences. This may be particular to the city of Toronto as a number of factors were strongly in place: a relatively supportive board of education, a healthy climate of women's activism, and a broad range of available networks and resources. Toronto was a supportive place to do this work, and, although individual schools varied, women's networks were strong during this time period, as the city was a hub for social movement activism. Toronto teacher activism was instrumental in changing curricula and challenging entrenched notions of equity within the educational institutions in which they worked.

NOTES

1 Examples include *This Magazine Is about Schools*, a community paper, and *NOW*, a large local paper.
2 As part of my PhD thesis (University of Toronto, 2012), interviews, with mostly retired Toronto Board of Education teachers, took place between 2009 and 2011 in Toronto, Ontario, in various venues. Their names have been replaced with letters.
3 This study uses the term "women's movement" to specifically refer to the "second-wave" women's movement that began in the 1960s. The editors of *Minds of Our Own* argue "a movement is by definition plural and diverse. The women's movement is transhistorical, inter and transnational, large scale and amorphous and comprised of individuals, groups and organizations with the general goals of promoting change to improve women's situation" (Robbins 2008, 37). Wendy Kohli (2012) argues that although the history of feminism is often described in terms of first, second, and third "wave movements," it is not a term that all historians support, noting that many scholars see the continuity of narratives over time.
4 A wide range of educators were consulted for this study: some are identified and some are anonymous. All names have been removed in the teacher interviews. Educators who are identified either were administrators or had publications that referenced their educational work.
5 The federal government passed Bill C-62 on employment equity for women in 1985. Sangster explores the formation and work of the Women's Bureau, which she argues was created to win support from the growing female workforce and not to make major alterations to the existing sexual division of labour.
6 This study examines the former Toronto Board of Education. In 1998, The Toronto Board amalgamated with the six school boards that were part of Metropolitan Toronto to form the Toronto District School Board (TDSB).
7 See Provincial Committee on Aims and Objectives of Education in the Schools of Ontario, *Living and Learning: The Report of the ... Committee* (Toronto: Published for the Committee by the Newton Pub. Co., 1968).

8 See Toronto Board of Education Archives (TBEA), 17 March 1977: *Report of the Task Force on Affirmative Action*. The *Provincial Affirmative Action Report of 1985* noted that as of May 1985, women held 20.4 per cent and men 79.6 per cent of the vice-principal positions; principals comprised 9.6 per cent of the women and 90.4 per cent of the men. Sheffield notes in her examination of affirmative action policies that "at this rate it would take another 80 years for women to represent even 50% of principals in the province." She attributes the slow response to the fact that Ontario initially made employment equity voluntary (Sheffield 1992).

9 Novogrodsky outlines the Toronto school board's steps to support women's studies.

10 TBEA/File: Duplicates: Depts. – Equal Opportunities – Affirmative Action Fact Sheets. The Pay Equity Act (1988) required all public sector employees to establish pay equity plans by January 1990. For a full discussion on affirmative action see Sheffield (1992).

11 Support for women's organizations is visible in the FWTAO newsletters, affirmative action reports, and publications.

12 This supports work by M. Apple and K. Casey who suggest that in the case of female teachers, the "personal has always been political," in part because of the ways that female teachers have been regulated historically, and in part by the "patriarchal assumptions" embedded within school institutions.

13 Two popular history textbooks from the 1970s: J. Ricker et al., *The Modern Era* (Toronto: Clarke Irwin, 1965), and B. Cruxton, *Flashback Canada* (Oxford University Press, 1978). By the 1990s, most publications of new Canadian history textbooks included women.

14 See Duncan McArthur, *The History of Canada for High Schools*, first published in 1944, used in schools until the 1970s. By 1970, history textbooks were written by male secondary school history teachers with master's degrees. See, for example, H.H. Herstein, L.J. Hughes, and R.C. Kirbyson, *Challenge and Change: The History of Canada* (Toronto: Prentice Hall, 1970), written by three high school teachers from Winnipeg.

15 In evaluating a textbook published in 1975, the authors expressed disappointment re: a short chapter entitled "Profiles of Canadian Women" as its placement at the end of the book "made it appear as an afterthought."

16 The study revealed that the textbooks devoted 12.8 per cent of the written text to include women, and that included any reference to women, such as "Elizabeth Simcoe, who accompanied her husband to Canada."

17 The Women's Liaison Committee at the Toronto Board received a sizable grant to support school libraries in purchasing books that portrayed

women in more equitable ways, thus making resource materials available for teachers in schools.

18 See Wright et al, *About Face: Is Anybody Out There Listening?* The authors examined history textbooks popular in schools during the 1970s and noted that textbooks traced thousands of years of world history with little reference to women. In conclusion they wrote "women are excluded as individuals and as a force in history. Their accomplishments are downplayed and credited to men ... women students have no role models or heroes to emulate. A sense of pride is denied them for they are not taught the contributions women have made to world development."

19 This teacher developed a curriculum unit for the school board on how to integrate labour studies that used primary sources about women.

20 Examples included *Women in Education* (WIE), *The Toronto Women's Education News* (TWEN), and *Women in Leadership* (OWL). Academic journals included RFR/DRF.

21 One school had a long hall of photos and biographies of Canadian women displayed on the wall of the third floor of the school. Each photo was accompanied by an essay written by a student.

22 Several filing cabinets filled with articles about women remained (as of 2011) at the TDSB Fran Endicott Equity Resource Centre in Toronto. The cabinets are filled with a variety of articles, newspaper clippings, published journal articles, photos, and learning resource materials.

23 A number of teachers indicated they had hundreds of videos in their school. One teacher added, "Thank God for the NFB and the newly invented videotape and videotape recorder."

24 Pioneer work was published by the BC Teachers Federation (BCTF) and could be found in libraries in Ontario. For example, *Famous Canadian Women, Early Canadian Women, From Captivity to Choice: Native Women in Canadian Literature.* The Corrective Collective published *She Named It Canada: Because That's What It Was Called* (Vancouver: Press Gang Press, 1971). There were copies of this book at the Toronto Board of Education. See: NFB film discussion in *A Report on the NFB/Educators Forum on Women's Studies in Secondary Schools* National Film Board (1986) and Gail Vanstone (2007).

25 The CWSE at OISE published two collections that contained a number of articles written by Toronto feminist educators: Forman (1990) and Paula Bourne and the Centre for Women's Studies in Education, Ontario Institute for Studies in Education (1994).

26 This teacher was on the "Bias Committee" at the school board and said that new materials were vetted by committee to allow for "feminist perspectives."

27 This teacher recalled that her four classes attracted over one hundred students. She noted that the principal gave her considerable backing stating, "I'm going to be your department head – make sure you get the money and resources that you need – and so she deserves a lot of credit. I made up my materials for my part of the course – which was all contemporary stuff – and Sheila took most of the history material from a university course by Jill Conway (U of T)."
28 Traditionalists joined the YWCA, church groups, or the Canadian Federation of University Women; leftists joined the Toronto Women's Liberation Movement, the New Feminists, and the Feminist Action League.
29 This teacher added, "Back then it was 'These crazy bra martyrs what they need is a good man to straighten them out! They're all frustrated or lesbians.'"
30 This teacher recalled, "At the school where I worked, there was a group created by some men on staff called PLOT (Potential Leaders of Tomorrow) to challenge our already established group called OWL (Ontario Women in Leadership). They were not really a group – just created to challenge our work. But despite this, I felt that I was doing the right thing – it wasn't all smooth sailing."
31 Gidney concentrates on policy/institutions rather than classroom teachers.
32 Bob Rae's NDP government in 1990–95 expanded equity education in the Ministry of Education through the Anti-Racism and Ethnocultural Equity Branch and through the Equity Opportunity Office. See McCaskell (2005). The NDP labour government introduced initial steps toward a "common curriculum" that was expanded under the Harris Conservative government along with major cuts to education in Ontario.

REFERENCES

Adamson, N., L. Briskin, and M. McPhail. 1988. *Feminists Organizing for Change*. Toronto: Oxford University Press.

Andersen, Marguerite, ed. 2010. *Feminist Journeys/Voies féministes*. Ottawa: Feminist History Society.

Anderson, L.W., D.W. Ryan, and B.J. Shapiro, eds. 1989. *The IEA Classroom Environment Study*. Oxford: Pergamon Press.

Armitage, S.H., ed. 2002. *Women's Oral History: The Frontiers Reader*. Lincoln: University of Nebraska Press.

Barton, K., and L. Levstik. 2004. *Teaching History for the Common Good*. Mahwah, NJ: Lawrence Erlbaum.

Bascia, N., S. Carr-Harris, R. Fine-Meyer, and C. Zurzolo. 2014. "Teachers,

Curriculum Innovation, and Policy Formation." *Curriculum Inquiry* 44 (2): 228–48. doi:10.1111/curi.12044.

Batcher, E., A. Winter, and V. Wright. 1987. *The More Things Change – The More They Stay the Same*. Toronto: Federation of Women Teachers' Associations of Ontario.

Berger Gluck, S., and D. Patai, eds. 1991. *Women's Words: The Feminist Practice of Oral History*. New York: Routledge.

Bourne, P., and Centre for Women's Studies in Education, Ontario Institute for Studies in Education, eds. 1994. *Feminism and Education: A Canadian Perspective*. Vol. 2. Centre for Women's Studies in Education, Ontario Institute for Studies in Education.

Braedley, S., and M. Luxton. 2010. *Neoliberalism and Everyday Life*. Montreal and Kingston: McGill-Queen's University Press.

Canada. 1970. *Report on the Royal Commission on the Status of Women in Canada*. Ottawa: Queen's Printer.

Carstairs, C., and N. Janovicek, eds. 2013. *Feminist History in Canada*. Vancouver: UBC Press.

Casey, Kathleen. 1993. *I Answer with My Life: Life Histories of Women Teachers Working for Social Change*. New York: Routledge.

Clark, A., and E. Millard. 1998. *Gender in the Secondary Curriculum*. New York: Routledge.

Conrad, Margaret. 2012. "A Brief Survey of Canadian Historiography." In *New Possibilities for the Past*, ed. P. Clark, 33–54. Vancouver: UBC Press.

Coomber, Jan. 1986. Private Collection: Syllabus: The Role of Canadian Women in the Second World War (a unit from Integrating Women's History into Contemporary Canadian History at the grade 10 level).

The Corrective Collective. 1971. *Famous Canadian Women, Early Canadian Women, from Captivity to Choice: Native Women in Canadian Literature*. Published as *She Named It Canada: Because That's What It Was Called*. Vancouver: Press Gang Press.

Cott, Nancy F. 1989. "What's in a Name? The Limits of 'Social Feminism'; or, Expanding the Vocabulary of Women's History." *Journal of American History* 76 (3): 809–29. doi:10.2307/2936422.

Coulter, R.P. 2002. "Why We Teach History: A Contesting View." Introduction in *Encounters on Education* 3 (Fall): 1–3.

Coulter, R.P., and H. Harper, eds. 2005. *History Is Hers: Women Educators in Twentieth Century Ontario*. Calgary: Detselig.

Cruxton, B. 1978. *Flashback Canada*. Oxford University Press.

CWSE (Canadian Women's Studies in Education). 1980. *Study 131*. Toronto: OISE Press.

Davies, Ian, ed. 2011. *Debates in History Teaching*. London: Routledge.

Day, C., and J. Sachs, eds. 2004. *International Handbook on the Continuing Professional Development of Teachers*. Maidenhead: Open University Press.

Dehli, Kari. 1994. *Parent Activism and School Reform in Toronto*. Toronto: OISE.

Dufour, Pascale, Dominique Masson, and Dominique Caouette, eds. 2010. *Solidarities beyond Borders: Transnationalizing Women's Movements*. Vancouver: UBC Press.

Feminist History Society of Canada. Available at feministhistories.ca.

Ferree, M., and A. Tripp, eds. 2006. *Global Feminism: Transnational Women's Activism, Organizing and Human Rights*. New York: New York University Press.

Fine-Meyer, R. 2012. "Including Women: The Establishment and Integration of Canadian Women's History into Toronto Ontario Classrooms 1968–1993." PhD diss., University of Toronto.

Fobert, Rolly, and Pat Kincaid. 1976. "Explore and Develop: Integrating the Study of Women into the Curriculum." *Report of a Working Conference*.

Forman, Frieda, ed. 1990. *Feminism and Education: A Canadian Perspective*. Toronto: OISE.

Foster, Theodora C. 1983. *Sex-Role Stereotyping in the Canadian School System*. Ottawa: Canadian School Trustees' Association.

Frawley, T. 2005. "Gender Bias in the Classroom: Current Controversies and Implications for Teachers in Childhood Education." *Childhood Education* 81 (4): 221–7. doi:10.1080/00094056.2005.10522277.

Gidney, R.D. 1999. *From Hope to Harris: The Reshaping of Ontario's Schools*. Toronto: University of Toronto Press.

Goodson, I. 1995. *The Making of Curriculum*. 2nd ed. London: Falmer.

– 2005. *Learning, Curriculum and Life Politics; The Selected Works of Ivor F. Goodson*. London: Routledge.

Hall, E.M., and L.A. Dennis. 1968. *Living and Learning. The Report of the Provincial Committee on Aims and Objectives of Education in the Schools of Ontario (The Hall-Dennis Report)*. Toronto: Newton Publ. Co.

Hanson, K. 2000. "Does All Mean All? Education for Girls and Women." *Women's Studies Quarterly* 28 (3/4, Fall): 249–86.

Heap, R., and A. Prentice. 1991. *Gender and Education in Ontario*. Toronto: Canadian Scholars' Press.

Herstein, H.H., L.J. Hughes, and R.C. Kirbyson, eds. 1970. *Challenge and Survival: The History of Canada*. Toronto: Prentice Hall.

Janovicek, N. 2006. "Oral History and Ethical Practice towards Effective Policies and Procedures." *Journal of Academic Ethics* 4:1–4.

Julien, L. 1987. *Women's Issues in Education in Canada: A Survey of Policies and Practices at the Elementary and Secondary Levels.* Toronto, Canada: Council of Ministers of Education.

Kealey, L., R. Pierson, J. Sangster, and V. Strong-Boag. 1992. "Teaching Canadian History in the 1990s: Whose 'National History' Are We Lamenting?" *Journal of Canadian Studies* 27 (2 Summer): 123–31. doi:10.3138/jcs.27.2.129.

Kincaid, Pat. 2010. Interview by author. Toronto: 13 June.

Kohli, W., ed. 2012. *Feminisms and Educational Research.* New York: Rowman and Littlefield Publishers.

Labatt, Mary. 1993. *Always a Journey.* Toronto: FWTAO.

Lieberman, A. 2000. "Networks as Learning Communities." *Journal of Teacher Education* 51 (3): 221–7. doi:10.1177/0022487100051003010.

Light, B., P. Staton, and P. Bourne. 1982. "Sex-Equity Content in History Textbooks." *History and Social Science Teacher Journal* 25 (1, Fall): 18–21.

Llewellyn, K. 2012. *Democracy's Angels: The Work of Women Teachers.* Montreal and Kingston: McGill-Queen's University Press.

Llewellyn, K., A. Freund, and N. Reilly, eds. 2015. *The Canadian Oral History Reader.* Montreal and Kingston: McGill-Queen's University Press.

Lorber, Judith. 2010. *Gender Inequality: Feminist Theories and Politics.* 4th ed. New York: Oxford University Press.

Marsden, Lorna. 2012. *Canadian Women and the Struggle for Equality.* Toronto: Oxford University Press.

Martin, Jennifer, ed. 2011. *Women as Leaders in Education.* Vol. 2. Santa Barbara, CA: Praeger.

McCaskell, Tim. 2005. *Race to Equity.* Toronto: Between the Lines Press.

McCormick, R. 2011. *Researching and Understanding Educational Networks.* London: Routledge.

Miles, Angela. 1989. "Women's Challenge to Adult Education." *Canadian Journal for the Study of Adult Education* 3 (1): 1–16.

National Film Board. 1986. *A Report on the NFB/Educators Forum on Women's Studies in Secondary Schools.* Montreal: NFB.

Novogrodsky, Myra. 1985. "Generating Women's Studies Programs in the Public Schools." *Canadian Women's Studies* 6 (3): 34–5.

O'Brien, Mary. 1986. "Feminism and the Politics of Education." *Interchange* 17 (2/Summer): 91–105.

Ontario Ministry of Education. 1986. The Status of Women and Affirmative Action/Employment Equity in Ontario School Boards – Report to the Legislature.

Osborne, K. 2012. "Teaching Canadian History: A Century of Debate." In *New Possibilities for the Past*, ed. P. Clark, 55–80. Vancouver: UBC Press.
Parr, J., and M. Rosenfeld, eds. 1996. *Gender and History in Canada*. Toronto: Copp Clark.
Pierson, R., and A. Prentice. 1982. "Feminism and the Writing and Teaching of History." In *Feminism in Canada: from Pressure to Politics*, ed. A. Miles and G. Finn, 37–46. Montreal: Black Rose Books.
Prentice, Alison. 1991. "From Household to School House: The Emergence of the Teacher as Servant of the State." In *Gender and Education in Ontario*, ed. R. Heap and A. Prentice, 19–29. Toronto: Canadian Scholars' Press.
– 1992. *The History of Women and Education in Canada*. Toronto: Canadian Scholars Press.
Ray, Janet. 1978. *Emily Stowe*. Don Mills, ON: Fitzhenry and Whiteside.
– 1981. *Towards Women's Rights*. Toronto: Grolier.
Ricker, J.C. 1965. *The Modern Era*. Toronto: Clarke Irwin.
Robbins, Wendy, ed. 2008. *Minds of Our Own: Inventing Feminist Scholarship and Women's Studies in Canada and Quebec, 1966–76*. Waterloo, ON: Wilfrid Laurier University Press.
Robeson, V., and C. Sylvester. 1980. *Teaching Canadian Studies: An Evaluation of Print Materials Grade 1–13*. Curriculum Series/40. Toronto: OISE Press.
Rowbotham, S. 1973. *Hidden from History: 300 Years of Women's Oppression and the Fight against It*. London: Pluto Press.
Russell, Susan. 1987. "The Hidden Curriculum of School." In *Feminism and Political Economy: Women's Work, Women's Struggles*, edited by Meg Luxton and H.J. Maroney, 343–60. Toronto: Methuen.
Sanders, R. 2000. "Gender Equity in the Classroom: An Arena for Correspondence." *Women's Studies Quarterly* 28 (3/4 Fall): 182–93.
Sangster, Joan. 1995. "Women Workers, Employment Policy and the State: The Establishment of the Ontario Women's Bureau, 1963–1970." *Labour (Halifax)* 36 (Fall): 119–45. doi:10.2307/25143976.
– 1994. "Telling Our Stories: Feminist Debates and the Use of Oral History." *Women's History Review* 3 (1): 5–28. doi:10.1080/09612029400200046.
Sheffield, J.L. 1992. "From Barriers to Bridges: Selected Aspects of an Affirmative Action Policy of One Board of Education 1970–1990." Master's thesis, University of Toronto.
Shubhra, S. 2012. *Neoliberalism as Betrayal*. New York: Palgrave Macmillan.
Smyth, E., and P. Bourne, eds. 2006. *Women Teaching, Women Learning: Historical Perspectives*. Toronto: Inanna Publications and Education.
Solomon, P., J. Singer, A. Campbell, and A. Allen. 2011. *Brave New Teachers:*

Doing Social Justice Work in Neo-Liberal Times. Toronto: Canadian Scholars' Press.

Strong-Boag, Veronica. 1978. "Raising Clio Consciousness: Women's History and Archives in Canada." *Archivaria* 6 (Summer): 70–82.

Taylor, T., and R. Guyver. 2012. *History Wars and the Classroom, Global Perspectives*. Charlotte, NC: IAP.

Teacher D. 2011. (Retired teacher.) Interview by author. Toronto: 12 August.

Teacher E. 2009. (Retired teacher.) Interview by author. Toronto: 15 December.

Teacher K. 2009. (Retired teacher.) Interview by author. Toronto: 30 November.

Teacher L. 2010. (Retired teacher.) Interview by author. Toronto: 12 February.

Teacher M. 2009. (Retired teacher.) Interview by author. Toronto: November.

Teacher N. 2010. (Retired teacher.) Interview by author. Toronto: 8 April.

Teacher O. 2009. (Retired teacher and department head.) Email interview with author. Toronto: 18 November.

Teacher P. 2009. (Retired teacher.) Interview by author. Toronto: 28 October.

Teacher Q. 2009. (Retired teacher.) Interview by author. Ontario: 12 November.

Teacher S. 2010. (Retired teacher.) Interview by author. Toronto: 13 June.

Teacher U. 2010. (Retired teacher.) Interview by author. Toronto: 16 September.

Toronto Board of Education Archives (TBEA). 1977. *Report of the Task Force on Affirmative Action*. 17 March.

– 1988. File: Duplicates: Depts. "Equal Opportunities-Affirmative Action Fact Sheets." *The Pay Equity Act*.

Vanstone, Gail. 2007. *D Is for Daring: The Women behind the Films of Studio D*. Toronto: Sumach Press.

Wright, Susan. 1976. *About Face: Is Anybody Out There Listening?* Ottawa: Ontario Status of Women Council.

3

Feminist Influence on Ontario Schools

JEAN HEWITT

Any analysis of the influence of a belief system or a social movement on society is challenging. Changes in human behaviour and institutions occur over time, but determining precisely which particular factor or factors brought about these changes is not easy – especially when considering the influence of feminism on the school system in Ontario over the last fifty years. Much of what is included in this chapter, particularly when referencing historical events, is drawn from my own personal experiences as a teacher, school principal, senior administrator, and activist in various organizations, including the Federation of Women Teachers' Association of Ontario (FWTAO). I will focus primarily on observable changes in school board practices that occurred from 1960 to 1985 as a direct result of the actions of female teachers, followed by a discussion of more general changes that have taken place in Ontario schools since 1985 and the degree to which these changes may or may not have been influenced by feminism. Finally, in light of frequently expressed concerns in some feminist writings that the influence of women on institutions in general and education in particular has been minimal,[1] I will briefly explore the nature of bureaucratic structures such as those found in elementary and secondary schools, vis-à-vis the assumptions and expectations underlying feminist discourse of the late twentieth century.

The second wave of feminism[2] may be said to have begun with the founding of the Voice of Women in 1960. Although this was an antinuclear proliferation movement and the term "feminism" was not associated with it, it proved to be a wake-up call for women about their lack of political power, just as the temperance movement had been to first-wave feminists, many decades earlier (Delap, DiCenzo, and Ryan

2006, Part 12, xxxvii). By the early sixties, women across the country were challenging the inequities that faced them at all levels of society. They demanded and got the report of the Royal Commission on the Status of Women (RCSW) in Canada (Canada 1970), tabled in parliament in 1970.[3]

Elementary female teachers in Ontario took a particularly active role in the three years of hearings that preceded the tabling of the RCSW Report. In the 1960s, the public school system in Ontario was almost entirely run by men (Reynolds 1995). Women held 65 per cent of the classroom teaching positions and only 1 per cent of the administrative positions.[4] Servicemen who took advantage of the fast-track teacher training offered after the Second World War held the majority of senior positions as directors, superintendents, and assistant superintendents. It was rare to find a female principal or vice-principal, other than attached to a "special" school, and extremely rare to find a secondary school female teacher as a department head, other than in girls' physical education or domestic science.

The lack of women in positions of authority in Ontario schools of the 1960s is not surprising, as there was discrimination against women throughout the system. For example, in order to apply for an elementary vice-principal position, boards asked for experience in grades 7 and 8, but women seldom got a chance to teach in those grades because men were invariably given first preference. Also, as with entry into medical schools, there were unwritten quotas that discriminated against women seeking promotion in schools. Although a principal's course certification was necessary to become a principal, women received, on average, only 7 per cent of the positions available in these courses, regardless of their seniority or qualifications.[5]

The sexist attitudes that underpinned discrimination against female teachers affected students as well and were reflected in the routines and curricula of schools. Within many Ontario elementary schools, boys and girls were segregated on the schoolyard, or expected to enter by different doors. Girls took home economics and boys took shop. Studies of textbooks used during this period revealed that boys were represented as central characters and/or their pictures were shown three times as often as girls.[6] Young girls did get a break when it came to corporal punishment; record books in the offices of Ontario principals between 1940 and 1970 showed that boys were strapped considerably more often than girls (Hewitt 1980).[7]

In 1967, when the royal commission hearings began, the FWTAO was the most powerful and financially viable women's organization in North America. Founded in 1888 as a loose-knit coalition of local groups of women teachers, the organization had fought for and eventually won equal pay in 1951, and had steadily grown into a well-organized and respected federation of 35,000 members representing the needs of women in the elementary school system.[8] It is not surprising that FWTAO played an important part in persuading the government of Lester Pearson to set up the Royal Commission on the Status of Women, and in mobilizing its members to prepare briefs and attend commission hearings. In 1967, the federation headquarters on Bay Street in Toronto became a hive of activity. Leaders from other sectors of the female workforce met there, eager to take advantage of the organization's resources at a time when few women's groups had access to the funds needed to mobilize.[9] The briefs, petitions, and letters produced, addressing everything from maternity leave to family property law, poured into the commission. Once begun, the momentum created by these energetic women was unstoppable.

The provincial Status of Women Committee, set up by FWTAO in 1971, was central to the accomplishment of the great amount of work required following the publication of the *Royal Commission Report*. This committee, designed to oversee the dismantling of discriminatory practices in school boards, was responsible for creating a network of highly active regional and local Status of Women committees in every school district in Ontario. In many cases, local conveners of these committees met monthly with their regional counterparts.[10] The eight regional conveners attended either a conference or provincial meeting in Toronto every month – babysitting costs were covered by the federation. The Status of Women committees worked on feminist concerns that went beyond those falling strictly under the purview of education, including work on family law reform, abortion legislation reform, and the provision of more daycare places for young children. In addition, the local committee work groups often included women who were secondary school teachers, school secretaries, and custodians, all of whom felt they had no representation in their male-dominated unions.

The discourse in the early years of activity within the Status of Women groups in the Ontario school system was entirely action oriented. Indeed, what was commonly called feminism was defined almost totally in terms of achieving equity through the elimination of specific attitudes, policies, and practices within schools, and the bureaucracies that supported them. In the early seventies, it was those overt practices that discriminated against women in terms of dress, pregnancy, and fair access to promotion that were the first to be challenged. The elimination of a teacher dress code was a particularly interesting case study. The expectation that male teachers wear shirts and neckties, and female teachers wear skirts or dresses in the workplace was well entrenched. While not always written down as a policy at a board level, school principals were quite vigilant in enforcing the dress code for female staff, usually on the grounds that a skirt was more "professional looking" and "appropriate to the workplace." In an era of miniskirts, many teachers felt that the dress code expectations were hardly appropriate wear. Primary teachers did much of their work sitting on the floor or on low chairs, and those who taught adolescents had to make sure they walked up stairs behind students to avoid the leers of adolescent boys – but pantsuits were strictly forbidden.[11]

Local Status of Women committees repeatedly raised concerns about dress limitations with senior administrators with little success. In late 1971, women teachers in one particular Ontario school agreed to test the policy. They let the local newspaper know that all the female teachers working in their building would arrive at school in pantsuits the following Monday. The FWTAO president was on hand that day to explain to reporters why she considered pantsuits more professionally appropriate than miniskirts. This comment, coupled with a large picture in the next morning's paper and an item on the evening television news, caught the senior staff of the Board of Education by surprise. They had no rebuttal. The day was won.[12]

Protests of this type spread across the province as Status of Women conveners kept local groups informed of what was happening outside their district and gave them examples of the successful strategies being used by colleagues elsewhere. Although rarer, defiance was also used as an individual strategy. Shortly after the pantsuit protest, another woman in that district tested the requirement that female teachers take unpaid leave or resign as soon as they became "visibly" pregnant.[13] For decades, it had been the case in the majority of school boards that a female teacher had to leave her position as soon as her pregnancy was confirmed by a physician. By 1971, most boards had become more lenient, finding the rule hard to enforce. However, being obviously pregnant was another matter. Attitudes toward pregnant women in the workforce ranged between a paternalistic notion of female fragility during gestation to a Victorian prudery about displaying one's "condition." With the tacit agreement of her principal, a teacher chose to challenge these attitudes in 1972 by continuing to work until her due date in May of that year. She was a regional Status of Women convener for FWTAO and knew that she had the backing of the federation. Although her pregnancy grew ever more obvious, no pressure to resign came from the school inspector who represented the central administration at her school. His comment, when questioned by another teacher a few months later, was that this particular teacher was allowed to continue to teach because she was working in a program for gifted children whose parents were more "liberal" and would not complain. Regardless of this comment with its implication that this case had been an exception, increasing numbers of London women teachers in regular classrooms, and those elsewhere in the province, worked longer into their pregnancies.[14]

Most of the work done to redress the imbalance in power between males and females within the Ontario educational hierarchy was not as visible or daring as either the protest actions described above, or as the various marches that took place in the teacher strike of 1973.[15] In reality, most of the changes came slowly as a result of hundreds of hours of meetings after work and on weekends, preparing briefs, doing research, and working on draft documents dealing with everything from promotional interviews to maternity leaves. That this work was largely accomplished by women who had young children, were holding down full-time jobs, and were trying to survive in traditional marriages in which they continued to carry most of the household responsibilities was remarkable.

Frequently, in the quest for information by the Status of Women Committee members, support was solicited from within the male administrative ranks where there were some sympathetic voices. This type of inside support was essential to obtaining accurate information otherwise deemed confidential. As is frequently the case, discrimination occurred behind the closed doors of a board meeting or in an interview room, hidden in casual talk or in the wording of the forms and memos. My experience was that extremely well-qualified women who failed to get the promotions for which they applied were simply told that they did not score highly enough in the interview process. While the blank forms used in promotional competitions in school boards were usually available to the local Status of

Women committee members, it was the *completed* forms, invariably destroyed after the selection process was finalized, that really interested them. Anecdotal evidence, however, demonstrated how important it was to obtain such confidential materials from a sympathetic male official or a secretary.[16]

One typical example of built-in bias that came up time and again during the early 1970s involved scoring sheets commonly used in interviews for the positions of principal or vice-principal across the province. One such sheet, of which I was aware, allocated points to "overall impression" of candidates coming into the interview process using five categories: usually – appearance, voice quality, poise, interview readiness, and attitude. Each of these categories would be allocated five points for each candidate, to be determined by the interviewers. When female leaders were able to examine these forms,[17] the area that showed the most glaring discrimination consistently over time was appearance. Based on evidence that I was privy to, men rarely got less than a mark of five for appearance, whereas women seldom got a mark of five in this category: in fact, scores of two to three were the norm. Sometimes, the predominantly male interviewers wrote revealing comments beside their scores – "too much jewellery," "doesn't look good in red," "hair too long," and so forth. The second two categories in which women tended to be marked down were voice quality and poise. The effects of these biases were to give men a five- to eight-point advantage on average on this one element of the process.

Two other parts of the evaluation process for teachers seeking promotion were found to be problematic for the women: interview questions and the ranking of qualifications for the school leader role. During questioning, the evidence gathered revealed that candidates were not asked a common set of questions. Women were more frequently asked questions about their personal lives, their classroom teaching, and their concerns about school leadership. Men were more frequently asked questions about their extracurricular work at school, their ideas about leadership, and their positive contributions to the community, particularly their service club work.[18] When it came to ranking qualifications for the position, higher marks were given to community contributions, for example, than classroom teaching performance. These forms of systematic discrimination were found to be common across all fields of employment in which women competed with men for more senior positions. Once they were revealed, there was a steady effort made to bring in many new interviewing procedures, including having union representatives as monitors and requiring a set of common interview questions.

Although heavily committed to working systematically to change how females were treated, whether these women were in the public or private sectors, white- or blue-collar workers, married with children or single, the leaders in the second wave were also involved in a great deal of self-reflection. Women found time to meet in the newly formed women's centres or clubs, or in each other's homes, for various types of activities, such as consciousness-raising. They joined tea groups and awareness groups in order to share ideas with other women, and to explore their own forms of power, their sexuality, and their choices. In the seventies, these women were referred to in the media as "Women's Libbers" or, pejoratively, as "bra burners" or "man-haters." Ontario teachers were active in these external groups and brought many of the ideas discussed in them to the table as Status of Women issues. Some of these ideas led to spin-off committees and workshops. Concern about sex-role stereotyping in the schools was one such example. It led to at least three new areas of action among women in Ontario education: a review of textbooks used in classrooms in order to require the Ministry of Education to approve only those texts that met certain non-sexist criteria,[19] an opening up of the Ontario curriculum to allow both boys and girls to take home economics and industrial arts (shop),[20] and increased funding to girls' extracurricular sports activities at the secondary level.[21]

However, not all the initiatives generated by the school Status of Women committees would receive full approval from feminists today. While many of those actions did little to dislodge hegemonic male privilege and the social structures that hold it in place, they did address some of the issues already described. For example, the popular Dress for Success workshops were set up to counteract the ranking process used in interviews referred to earlier.[22] It was argued that women would score higher points if they looked more businesslike – wearing two-piece navy or black suits, keeping their hair cut short or tied back, eschewing purses for briefcases, and minimizing their jewellery. Workshops designed to help women lower the register of their voices or speak using more direct language, including more powerful verbs, flourished. Great efforts were made during this time to draw attention to the *similarities* between men and women and to play down any differences that could be used to justify sexist discrimination.

Ontario women teachers used the International Women's Year in 1975 as the impetus to accelerate the pace of change and to educate the general public about what women's liberation meant. Using its not insignificant financial resources, FWTAO funded conferences, speakers, projects, and a myriad of educational programs across the province. FWTAO commissioned a film, *The Visible Woman*, directed by award-winning director Beryl Fox, which traced the history of Canadian suffrage and articulated what second-wave feminists wanted. This film was shown to teachers and parent groups in all Ontario school districts. The message of documentaries such as *The Visible Woman*, alongside the powerful voices of Canadian feminists such as Laura Sabia, June Callwood, and Doris Anderson, gave an impetus to the countless briefs and policy recommendations that female teachers had been working on for over five years. During this same period, secondary school female teachers, who had made little progress toward equity up to this point, became more vocal, and formed more overt ties with their elementary school colleagues. This was a strategic move as they were fewer in number in proportion to male teachers, and lacked power in the male-dominated union to which they belonged.

One by one, many of the identified barriers to female teachers in Ontario began to fall: women were allowed equal access to professional courses; more generous maternity leave was instituted, funding for day-care centres increased, the interview practices were made fairer, and textbooks reflected more models for young girls to emulate. Concurrently, women began to be appointed to the roles of principal, superintendent, and even director of education, although the first women to achieve these positions were rarely those who had been openly involved in the struggle for equality. Not surprisingly, the first appointees tended to be women who were preferred by the male establishment: few were married, even fewer had children, and several adopted a masculinist administrative style, aligning themselves with male administrators and often not supportive of other women.[23]

As noted earlier, the discourse in these early years of feminist activity in the Ontario school system was largely about the equality of opportunity that comes when women are liberated from paternalistic and discriminatory practices. In fact, most female teachers of this time would not have used the term feminist to define themselves, if they were familiar with the term at all. The leaders of the movement spoke about "women's liberation," "personal choice," and "gender equity." However, in the late seventies, as some of the more blatant barriers began to crumble for the elementary female teachers, there was a period in which the front-line women activists in education expanded their discourse to include the broader issues of inclusion and respect for the value of the female perspective in key locations of power sharing. Time was spent looking more closely at such issues as female representation on decision-making committees, leadership styles, and the backroom games that occurred in most male-oriented bureaucracies. In effect, female teachers began to analyze more carefully how power was distributed within the administrative structures that had evolved to manage schools. The term feminism began to be used more frequently in their discussions.

By the 1980s, many of the female leaders who fought to raise the status of women in education were moving into administrative roles, usually by gathering more credentials than their male counterparts.[24] Unlike the earliest female appointees who, once through the door, sometimes coped with their almost entirely male work context by being "one of the boys" or found they were marginalized, these female leaders were less easy to ignore. They resisted attempts to be seen as meeting secretaries or coffee makers, they challenged sexist language, and they were aware in a way that the earlier appointees were not, of how the male game-playing worked. Most importantly, they gained strength from their increasing numbers and the supportive networks they had built. The influence of these women at this time was important in protecting rights that had already been gained, in closing loopholes that still existed in some policies, and in serving as models and mentors to the wave of female teachers who followed them into administration in the nineties. This is not to say that sexism had disappeared from the Ontario school system by the late 1980s; it had not. However, the balance of power had shifted for front-line female teachers. The actions of the neo-conservative government of Mike Harris that governed Ontario from 1995–2002 inadvertently abetted this shift in power when it increased the teachers' control of their unions by removing school administrators from them.[25] At the same time, it decreased the direct influence of supervisory personnel on teachers by amalgamating school boards into much larger units. The end result was a more flattened hierarchy in terms of influence and, if bureaucratic power and control underlie sexist behaviour (Jull 2002), arguably, opportunities for such behaviour diminished, too.

Some time in the 1980s, during the heady days of the rise of women's studies within universities and the proliferation of doctoral theses on feminist topics, attention appeared to shift somewhat from grassroots work on equity to making a case for feminism as a set of alternate ways of thinking politically and socially within institutions such as education. Much of the writing of this period was about the assumption that bureaucracies were patriarchal constructs against which feminists should take a stand. As Kathy Ferguson wrote in 1984, "The power structures of bureaucratic capitalist society are the primary source of the oppression of women and men" and there must be, "an elimination of such structures rather than their amelioration" (ix). She further suggested that women must look for "an alternative to the discursive and institutional practices of bureaucracy in the submerged and devalued experiences of women" (212). Along with the findings of academics like Ferguson about existing bureaucracies, there grew a strongly articulated belief that out of feminist research would come new theoretical constructs that could provide alternatives to the societal institutions and methodologies currently in place. As Ferguson argues, "A specifically feminist discourse can suggest a reformulation of some of the most central terms of political life: reason, power, community and freedom" (155).

While many practising teachers engaged in feminist discourse in postgraduate extension courses within university classrooms, by the 1990s there was an increasing disconnect between the dialogue on feminist theory and the practices female teachers saw happening inside their school bureaucracies. Many old organizational values and ideas that once held sway in Ontario schools had been swept away by the much freer society that emerged in the seventies and eighties. The brand of authoritarianism that supported using the strap on young children and sitting them in passive rows in the classroom had gone. Along with them went other forms of authoritarianism, such as the power of the principals and inspectors to impose certain types of sexist standards on female teachers, or to use a variety of forms of top-down command and control. Terms such as "collegiality" and "professional learning communities" were terms that emerged to describe preferred administrative relations and practices in schools during the early nineties. Education rhetoric had entered the days of "inviting schools" and collegial models of leadership.[26] Also, women began to equal or outnumber men in the ranks of department heads in some secondary schools and principals in elementary schools and, a decade later, began to enter the ranks of the superintendency in greater numbers.[27]

In contrast to the position that many women continued to occupy in other workplaces in Ontario, the gains made by female teachers during the latter half of the twentieth century were arguably exceptional in their scope and in the time frame within which they were achieved. A number of factors influenced this success. First and foremost was the existence of FWTAO, the powerful female union that had been working for almost eighty years to increase women's rights. This organization ensured that knowledge was shared in a systematic way so that female teachers were aware of every aspect of the progress being made to gain equity across the province. In addition, the elementary school female teachers had strength in numbers from the beginning of their struggle. They outnumbered their male counterparts by over three to one, increasing the force of their influence and the size of their collective coffers. In addition, the role of the classroom teacher is a relatively isolated and autonomous one. Arguably, then, female teachers were not exposed to the same kinds of social pressures found in workplaces where men and women work in proximity to each other and in more immediately dependent hierarchical relationships (e.g., manager and secretary).

It would be wrong to conclude that incidents of sexism did not still occur within schools and the central administrative bureaucracy during this period. Groups of female teachers in some Ontario school districts still felt the need to meet regularly to discuss equity issues.[28] These women were conscious that the gains that they had made were relatively new, and there was still a need to ensure that they were maintained. Today, these female teachers recognize that many of the same issues persist and that workshops and/or networking groups are still helpful in giving additional support to women as they move up in the hierarchy. At both the secondary school and college levels, young women still see issues that need to be addressed further, including sexual harassment and bias in curricula. The formation of the Miss G Project in 2005 by female students in Ontario secondary schools attests to this fact.[29] Women are still not well represented in the school curriculum, especially in history courses. The Miss G organizers lobbied for changes and in 2013, after eight years and a rigorous process that included expert and stakeholder consultation, feedback from the public, and piloting in classrooms, approval was given by the Ministry of Education for a gender studies elective course to be added to the social sciences and humanities curriculum as part of a suite of equity studies courses. Their status, however, continues to remain murky.

FEMINISM AND BUREAUCRACY

From my vantage point as a feminist who lived the history of feminist resistance, strategic action, and change in educational bureaucracies in Ontario from the 1960s to the present, I have been particularly interested in the feminist critique of the nature of bureaucracies and the nature of women. I have lived the reality that bureaucracies have stubbornly remained as the preferred organizational structure: hierarchical, compartmentalized, and dependent on a system of policies, procedures, and roles that are efficient, utilitarian, and pragmatic in expediting the work of complex human endeavours such as governments and institutions. However, this structure has not been hospitable to the goals and contributions of women. Certainly, changes have occurred; today's bureaucratic organizations are more flexible and less stratified, primarily because technology has taken away the need for some of the hierarchical layers and more liberal mores in Western societies have made internal relationships less formal.

Given that educational organizations generally accept that bureaucracies are practical structures designed to get a job done efficiently, it is not surprising that little changed in their day-to-day operations once women moved into positions of greater power within them. Indeed, does a female pilot fly a jet any differently than a male pilot? Like a bureaucracy, a jet has evolved over many years of steady changes to become an ever more efficient tool to accomplish a central purpose. As long as its central purpose – to transport people through the air to reach their destination – does not change, there is little reason to fundamentally change its structure. Likewise, when considering the impact of feminism on the school system, perhaps the central question should not be whether women have fundamentally altered the structure called a bureaucratic organization, but whether they have critically considered the central purpose or mission that the organization was set up to accomplish. One could argue that the nineteenth-century factory model of education, which clusters children of a certain age in classrooms to be taught a myriad of prescribed subjects and social expectations during a nine-month year, may not be an appropriate model in the twenty-first century. This discussion is surely critical to the discussion of the role of feminism in education.

Questions about the early feminist assumptions about organizations were being raised even as female teachers were achieving early victories in their struggle for equality. Many postmodern feminist writers argue that women's subordination has no single cause or single solution, and that the human experience is both created and interpreted through language. Thus, power is not about abstract concepts of control and coercion, but about the way in which language shapes discourses that both open up and restrict individual possibilities (Frug 1992, 1046).[30] These writers are more accepting of diversity, recognizing multiple truths in their rejection of essentialism (Lorber 2010; Olson 1996, 19).[31] There is no doubt that postmodern feminism has resulted in some interesting research through its use of discourse analysis. Indeed, some would say it has revitalized feminist theory by questioning many assumptions that were previously unexamined, and has created a wider space for an intersectional feminism that includes the broader experiences of structurally disadvantaged women. Yet discussion among female leaders within the Ontario school system today continues to demonstrate what is commonly called liberal feminism.[32] This is most clear in the wake of the consolidation of male teachers with female teachers in the Elementary Teachers' Federation of Ontario (ETFO),[33] where women continue to speak up to protect and extend the freedoms and rights won during the second wave of feminism.

CONCLUSIONS

The impact of feminism on practices and policies within the Ontario school system from 1960 to 1985 was substantial. Changes were made at every level of the system as a result of the particular actions taken by women who believed they were being discriminated against and marginalized within their workplaces and the larger society. However, the expectation frequently expressed by radical and critical feminist academics that women would fundamentally reject or transform bureaucratic organizations such as education when they gained power, did not materialize. Some have argued that change did not occur because women were co-opted into bureaucracies and uncritically accepted the ethos of these structures and the norms of their new leadership roles. However, perhaps it is as simple as women in leadership roles wanting and needing to "get on with it." Under current regimes, boards of education are required to manage complex, multi-layered systems as efficiently as possible within fairly inflexible, multi-million-dollar annual budgets with management tasks as varied as bus schedules and budgeting. Within this context, I contend that the work of the second-wave activists continues to have a role to play in education, but the work is not finished. In particular, there is much to do in jurisdictions in which equity for those women whose hopes and dreams were unrecognized by second-wave feminism are still unrealized.

NOTES

1 Numerous writers have expressed the belief that women have had only a minimal impact on social institutions such as education, and that these institutions are still primarily male-dominated and patriarchal. These include Ferguson (1984) and Marshall (1997).
2 Writers such as Kohli (2012) have suggested that the use of the term "wave" in connection with feminism is inappropriate in that it does not capture the continuity of the action toward gender equality that occurred over time. However, the galvanizing of human energy toward certain goals, followed by events such as war or economic instability that sap or redirect that energy, can be seen throughout history. This is not to suggest that nothing happened between these surges, but simply that waves did occur and marked historical periods in which much more was accomplished. Looking back, we can see two periods of rapid change for women in the years 1900–30 and 1960–85.
3 On 3 February 1967, after receiving pressure from Cabinet Minister Judy LaMarsh and activist Laura Sabia, Prime Minister Lester Pearson announced that his Liberal government had decided to establish a royal commission mandated to inquire into and report upon the status of women in Canada, and to recommend what steps might be taken by the federal government to ensure for women equal opportunities with men in all aspects of Canadian society, having regard for the distribution of legislative powers under the constitution of Canada, particularly with reference to federal statutes, regulations and policies that concern or affect the rights and activities of women. The report, tabled in late 1970, had a far-reaching impact on Canadian society.
4 Details on the composition of the Ontario teaching profession prior to 1975 are to be found in *High Button Bootstraps*, a history produced by FWTAO (no longer in print) and *ETFO Voice*, February 2007.
5 The percentage of women from public school boards allowed on principals' courses was remarkably consistent across the province, ranging between 6 per cent and 8 per cent until 1976.
6 Various local and provincial projects on sex-role stereotyping within the On-

tario K–8 curriculum and support materials took place between 1971 and 1980. They consistently demonstrated a significant bias toward males, their stories, and accomplishments, and a significant under-representation of female stories and accomplishments. By 1980, policy guidelines had been developed within the Ontario Ministry of Education to address stereotyping. Publishers wishing to have print or video materials approved for school purchase were obliged to follow the policies.

7 Until 1970, most Ontario Boards required principals to keep punishment books in which a record was made each time a student was strapped in the school. In her unpublished doctoral thesis, *Corporal Punishment: The Tip of the Authoritarian Iceberg* (1980), Jean Hewitt found that the ratio of boys to girls listed in these books averaged 18:1. However, in some schools, particularly rural areas, the difference was skewed even more in favour of girls.

8 Under the Teaching Profession Act of 1944, all elementary school teachers in the public school system in Ontario were required to be members of the FWTAO. This empowered the FWTAO to carry out its work.

9 In the mid-1960s, FWTAO began funding various affirmative action groups and projects, including some not directly connected to education. For example, a number of women lawyers used the FWTAO resources while working on the first drafts of the family law reform legislation.

10 The degree to which the Status of Women committees influenced the feminist agenda across Ontario cannot be underestimated. They were the primary vehicle for the dissemination of ideas and support materials from the urban centres to the smallest and most isolated school communities in Ontario.

11 For an interesting discussion around issues of dress, marital status, and sexuality, see Cavanagh (2007).

12 What was remarkable about this victory on dress code for women is how rapidly the old rule disappeared across the province. Within a few months, it was hard to find a school board in which female teachers were not wearing pantsuits or slacks and blazers. Once again, credit has to be given to the FWTAO Status of Women conveners who reacted to every small victory in one part of the province by bringing pressure to bear on the same issue in their own districts.

13 Strict social expectations of female teachers were strongly in place, even in 1965 when an FWTAO study found that women teachers were expected by parents not to smoke, place bets, run for political office, teach after marriage, or any of a number of other activities; there were strict expectations that they stop work if visibly pregnant.

14 While this was not the earliest case of a visibly pregnant woman teaching in

Ontario (there were a few others that flew under the radar), it was believed to be the first instance in which a teacher openly flouted the policy and taught to her due date. By mid-1973, the area's branch of the Women Teachers' Association had met with the senior administration and come to an agreement that its members would be allowed to continue to teach while visibly pregnant as long as they were in good health and could "do the duties expected of them." Later, in 1974, the province took a positive stand on workplace pregnancy.

15 In October 1973, when negotiations between seventeen local bargaining units and their boards broke down, teachers submitted letters of resignation, effective 31 December. The government tabled legislation (Bills 274 and 275) changing the effective date of the resignations to 31 August and mandating binding arbitration that excluded any right to strike. In December 1973, over 80,000 of the province's 105,000 teachers went on strike. Teachers' strike marches were held across the province and the legislation was withdrawn.

16 The promotion form was just one example of the materials used in interviews, teacher evaluations, recommendations for school moves, etc. that had built-in opportunities for bias in favour of male candidates.

17 I am basing my discussion here on personal knowledge as obtaining these confidential forms was a highly sensitive and private matter. Often the materials were provided for a few hours to an individual upon a promise of anonymity. The data were then laboriously hand copied and returned to the informant. Sources of information were jealously guarded and protected.

18 Male participation in service clubs such as Rotary International, the Kinsmen, Kiwanis, and societies such as the Masons and Knights of Columbus was widespread. Women were, of course, banned from such groups as these, as well as the clubs organized around golf, the militia, and political interaction. In a time when promotion was largely the result of being tapped on the shoulder, male teachers benefited greatly from their involvement in these clubs where they met with their superiors in a social context. Also, it was widely known that inside information was passed around in the club settings, leaving women very much out of the loop. Women's Clubs of the time, the Women's Institute being the most prominent, generally held meetings during the day and were not geared to working women.

19 Work on stereotyping in school texts was largely done by local board committees until 1977 when the Ontario Ministry of Education set up a regional committee to look at the issue. In 1978, the report of this committee led to a policy regarding those books allowed on Circular 14 (now called the Trillium List of approved texts).

20 Gender-based courses had been in place in Ontario schools since the late 1800s. By the 1960s, all Ontario grade 7 and 8 female students were required to take home economics while the boys did industrial arts. The low regard for "cookery" among the male leaders was made apparent as women began to petition the trustees to give intermediate students a choice of programs. One superintendent in charge of curriculum protested that he would never want his sons doing home economics: "They can already boil an egg!"

21 The large discrepancy in the funding allocated to sports for boys and girls in the secondary schools of Ontario became an issue in the late 1970s. Women in the physical education departments had worked hard to change the rules for sports such as girls' basketball and volleyball, and to increase the status of girls' teams within the school calendar. They then turned their attention to the lack of funding for girls' teams after finding that boys' sports ate up over 80–85 per cent of the school budget allocated to this area.

22 The term "dress for success" was first used by author John Malloy in the 1970s in his book by the same name. By the mid-1970s, female teachers who were intending to move up the leadership ladder flocked to courses in which they were told about the need to make over their image to fit the male business model.

23 Often referred to as Queen Bees, these women used their newfound status to distance themselves from other women and align themselves with men. In a number of documented cases, they blocked other women from promotion and actively worked to get rid of the Federation of Women Teachers. In 1977, FWTAO created a film about this phenomenon called *The Story of O*.

24 That female teachers were frequently more experienced and had higher professional qualifications than the male colleagues who competed against them for positions of additional responsibility was well-documented by FWTAO from 1970 onwards. Nevertheless, this did not significantly influence their chances of being promoted. However, in 1994, when the Ontario Ministry of Education made it a requirement to have teaching experience in three divisions in order to take Part II Principal Certification, female teachers had an advantage that could not be ignored.

25 Mike Harris made it clear at the beginning of his mandate that he had little respect for teachers. His years in office were marked by teacher protests and disruptions in school life. While it was his government's intent to decrease the power of the teachers' unions, Harris relied heavily for advice on his non-elected, young backroom staff on how to accomplish this. The result was a series of moves that actually *increased* the power of the unions in Ontario schools to the point that, arguably, they now have more control over many aspects of education than the Ministry of Education.

26 William Watson Purkey was one of a number of American motivational speakers who spoke extensively across Ontario in the 1990s about educational change. Long before he published his book on invitational education (2006), Purkey introduced teachers and school leaders to his four fundamental beliefs: students must be accepted and affirmed as valuable, capable, and responsible, and treated accordingly; teachers have the responsibility to create beneficial messages for themselves and students; all learners possess relatively untapped potential in all areas of learning and human development; finally, human potential is best realized by creating places, programs, policies, and processes intentionally designed to invite optimal development. There is no doubt that Purkey and education gurus like him tapped into the increasingly liberal and individualistic mindset of the 1990s, and the degree to which these ideas were embraced in Ontario's child-centred classrooms speaks to a readiness to move in that direction. Such thinking marked a significant shift in concepts of school leadership and staff collegiality.

27 Currently, women outnumber men on the senior administrations of many Ontario school districts: Thames Valley DSB has nine women to four men, Hamilton-Wentworth DSB has ten women to seven men, and Peel (the largest school board in the country) has eleven women to six men.

28 Most Status of Women groups did not survive the amalgamation of the elementary male and female teachers' unions in 1998. However, in a few districts such as Peel DSB, a status group still meets regularly.

29 The Miss G Project for Equity in Education (2005) is a grassroots feminist organization of young women working to combat all forms of oppression in and through education.

30 Mary Joe Frug in "A Post-Feminist Legal Manifesto" (1992) suggested that one principle of postmodernism is that human experience is located "inescapably within language."

31 Judith Lorber argues that women's voices are not unified but represent multiple hierarchies in which gender is linked with other forms of oppression. Hope Olson refers to multiple exclusions.

32 This includes sexual autonomy (Lehrman 1997, 23); freedom of expression – the right to appear in, publish, and consume pornography free of censorship (McElroy 1995; Strossen 2000); reproductive freedom – the right to use birth control, have an abortion (on the minority of pro-life libertarians see Tabarrok 2002, 157); freedom from interference with person and property also means that women have the right to engage in economic activity in a free market, entering contracts, and acquiring, controlling and transferring property free of sexist state limits (Epstein 1992; Kirp, Yudof, and Franks 1986, 204).

33 The Ontario Public School Men Teachers' Federation (OPSMTF) had made repeated attempts beginning in the late sixties to merge with the wealthier and more powerful women's federation, including three court challenges, but had been rebuffed. In 1994, a female principal led a complaint to the Ontario Human Rights Commission that the requirement that she be a member of FWTAO was discrimination. She won the case and in 1998, the two organizations moved into an uneasy alliance as the Elementary Teachers' Federation of Ontario (ETFO).

REFERENCES

Canada. 1970. *Report of the Royal Commission on the Status of Women*. Ottawa: Queen's Printer.

Cavanagh, S. 2007. "Female Teacher Gender and Sexuality in Twentieth-Century Ontario, Canada." *History Education Quarterly*, 45 (2): 247–73.

Delap, L., M. DiCenzo, and L. Ryan, eds. 2006. *Feminism and the Periodical Press*. London: Routledge.

Epstein, D. 1992. *A Dangerous Knowing: Sexuality, Pedagogy and Popular Culture*. London: Cassell.

Ferguson, K. 1984. *The Feminist Case against Bureaucracy*. Philadelphia: Temple University Press.

Frug, Mary Joe. 1992. "A Post-Feminist Legal Manifesto." *Harvard Law Review* 105 (5): 1045–75.

Hewitt, Jean. 1980. "Corporal Punishment: The Tip of the Authoritarian Iceberg." PhD diss., University of Toronto.

Jull, S. 2002. "Locating Gender Bias and Systemic Discrimination in Public Schooling Bureaucracy." *Alberta Journal of Educational Research* 48(1): 47–60.

Kirp, D., M. Yudof, and M. Franks Strong. 1986. *Gender Justice*. Chicago: Chicago University Press.

Kohli, W. 2012. *Feminism and Educational Research*. New York: Rowman and Littlefield.

Lehrman, K. 1997. *The Lipstick Proviso: Women, Sex and Power in the Real World*. New York: Doubleday.

Lorber, Judith. 2010. *Gender Inequality: Feminist Theories and Politics*. 4th ed. New York: Oxford University Press.

Marshall, C. 1997. *Feminist Critical Policy Analysis I: A Perspective from Primary and Secondary Schooling*. London: Falmer Press.

McElroy, W. 1995. *A Woman's Right to Pornography*. New York: St Martin's Press.

Olson, H. 1996. *The Power to Name: Marginalizations and Exclusions of Subject Representation in Library Catalogues.* Wisconsin: University of Wisconsin-Madison.

Purkey, W. 2006. *Teaching Class Clowns (and What They Can Teach Us).* Thousand Oaks, CA: Corwin.

Reynolds, C. 1995. "In the Right Place at the Right Time: Rules of Control and Woman's Place in Ontario Schools, 1940–1980." *Canadian Journal of Education/Révue Canadienne de l'Éducation* 20:129–45.

Strossen, N. 2000. *Defending Pornography: Free Speech and the Fight for Women's Rights.* New York: New York University Press.

Tabarrok, A. 2002. "Abortion and Liberty." In *Liberty for Women: Freedom and Feminism in the Twenty-First Century*, ed. W. McElroy. Chicago: Ivan R. Dee and the Independent Institute.

PART TWO

Discourses of Leadership: Speaking Out

DAWN WALLIN

Perhaps one of the most significant impacts of the advocacy and political work of second-wave feminists in Canadian education was the subsequent movement of more women into positions of formal authority and leadership. As part 1 of this book demonstrates, the advocacy of female teachers resulted in policies and practices that helped to create opportunities for women's access and representation in positions of formal power in education hierarchies. As Canadian feminist historians such as Rebecca Coulter (1979; 1996; 1998; 1999; Coulter and Harper 2005), Alison Prentice (1988; Heap and Prentice 1998; Houston and Prentice 1988; Prentice and Bourne 1988; Prentice and Theobald 1991), and Sharon Cook (2004; Cook and Riley 1990; O'Rourke, McLean, and Cook 2001) shed light on gender inequities in schooling, strategic action was taken up by teachers' organizations, Status of Women committees, and concerned educators. Doors began to open in the 1970s and 1980s for women to move into positions of formal leadership within and across school systems and the academy.

It was not until 1994, however, that Dr Beth Young from the University of Alberta reviewed the research on women studying educational administration. Her paper, "An Other Perspective on the Knowledge Base in Canadian Educational Administration," became one of the germinal pieces critiquing the absence of and revealing the possibilities of feminist studies in the field of educational administration in Canada. Young writes a cogent synthesis of the topical influences that gained credibility in the discourses of educational administration in Canada written by (primarily) white, middle-class, male faculty members who tended to be hired out of high-status formal administrative appointments in government or school systems. In her review of this Canadian research, she concluded that "women's experiences and feminist thought are only beginning to affect our knowledge base; they are, as yet, 'other' perspectives" (351). For example, she speaks to the impact of Thomas Greenfield in the mid-1970s, whose scholarship reshaped the epistemological possibilities of studying educational administration through his critique of positivism and power, yet whose work continued to reinforce the hegemonic privilege of male scholars and language use. She discusses the unrepresentative, but growing, numbers of women in positions within educational administration as well as the challenges they faced. In doing so, she acknowledged many of the "new" scholars of the time whose work on gender and equity ultimately laid the foundations for feminist scholarship in educational administration: Juanita Epp (1993), Hope-Arlene Fennell (1992), Jane Gaskell (1991), Barbara Gill (1993), Mary Nixon (1985; 1987; Nixon and Gue 1975), Ruth Rees (1990; 1991), Cecilia Reynolds (1987; 1988; 1991), and Ailsa Watkinson (1991).

Although the bulk of this scholarship focused on female educators and leaders in K–12 systems, there has also been a significant body of scholarship examining the "chilly climate" for women in post-secondary institutions (Hannah and Vethamany-Globus 2002; Chilly Collective 1995). A decade after *The Chilly Climate* was presented, the Council of Canadian Academies (2012) reviewed the effects of gender on research capacity in Canada, noting that women's rank is still disproportionately lower in comparison to their overall participation rates in higher education despite increases in representation in PhD programs and tenure-track positions (Council of Canadian Academies 2012). Some work also examines women in particular leadership positions in higher education, such as associate chairs, associate deans (Acker 2012; 2014), or deans (*Globe and Mail* 2010). The *Globe and Mail* story (2010) examined women's representation in positions of authority across social and economic sectors and reported that "In academia, one-quarter of deans at Canada's English-speaking universities were women, based on 2008 data – a quarter of them heading nursing and education faculties" (A16). Hewitt (in part 1) observed the positioning of early female school administrators in elementary schools – the location most attached to traditional female norms. So, too, are the few senior female administrators in higher education often located in the professional faculties that are most congruent with professions that reflect traditional notions of being female.

The literature suggests that power and authority in formal leadership positions in educational institutions are still not distributed proportionately, and the experiences of women who obtain those positions remain highly gendered. The movement of more women into positions of authority in educational systems does not necessarily equate with a feminist ideology being introduced. However, the resulting need to consider women's issues and contributions more explicitly has provided an opening for feminist principles to gain traction in what had previously been a "closed shop." The three chapters of this section speak to the ways in which the introduction of feminist thought into formal roles of leadership makes an impact on practice in educational institutions, and also takes a toll on the feminists who work to (re)shape them.

The three authors in this section of the book worked together on a SSHRC-funded project that explored the experiences and contributions of the first female faculty in departments of educational administration in Canada. The Viczko and Wallin chapters draw most directly on that research, while Wallace's chapter draws on it more tangentially. Janice Wallace opens part 2, "Discourses of Leadership: Speaking Out," with a chapter entitled "Rewriting Sisyphus: The Possibilities of Feminism in Educational Administration." Drawing on her own experience and research as well as the broader literature, she considers how the entry and movement of feminist scholars into educational administration programs caused disruptions and changes to the traditional discourses of this area of academic study. Her work affirms the influence of feminist theory on educational leadership discourses and practices, but also reveals the interpersonal and personal effects on feminist scholars who speak out and challenge the champions of the privileged discourses of educational administration. She also decentres herself as the privileged subject in an area of study where intersectional feminism is only now gaining ground.

Dawn Wallin's chapter, "Moths to the Flame Tend to Get Burned: Life on the Liminal," considers the tensions created in the liminal spaces in which female leaders find themselves when they come to understand themselves as feminists and begin to deconstruct the privileges and ideologies in which they are embedded as formal leaders. She reflects on how women learn to make sense of their subjective positions inherent in the hegemonic discourses surrounding educational leadership, and how they move forward with agency in the pursuit of more equitable educational environments.

Melody Viczko's chapter, "Performing Boundaries: Feminism Entanglements in Educational Administration," incorporates actor-network theory to make the case that feminism cannot be considered separately from women's practices of research and teaching in higher education. She illustrates her points through the perspectives of two of the first female academics in educational administration university programs. Their feminist work to achieve more equitable circumstances for women was imbricated in the ways in which they performed their academic roles and networked relationships.

The chapters of this section suggest that feminists have influenced the knowledge base, organizational practices, and leadership milieus within educational administration by speaking out about its masculinist epistemological roots and practices. Doing so has not been without personal and professional cost to the feminists who moved into this academic field of study – particularly those who took up leadership roles in the academy. However, while women have acted with agency in these roles, they have also been acted upon, as they have used feminist principles and ideas in their daily work and scholarship. As a consequence of feminists' persistence and strategic advocacy, educational environments and the people within them have benefited from their efforts to achieve greater equity in schools and post-secondary environments.

The authors are aware, however, that they occupy a privileged space as white, middle-class women – a demographic that, based on anecdotal evidence in a relatively small community of scholars, characterizes most of the women who are academics in educational administration in Canada. Their academic and personal journeys include a growing awareness of the need to work with women in and outside the academy who are structurally disadvantaged, and a willingness to step aside as "knower" (Blackmore 2010) and to recognize the power of Others' voices as they speak out against oppression in its many forms.

REFERENCES

Acker, S. 2012. "Chairing and Caring: Gendered Dimensions of Leadership in Academe." *Gender and Education* 24 (4): 411–28. doi:10.1080/09540253.2011.628927.
− 2014. "A Foot in the Revolving Door? Women Academics in Lower-Middle Management." *Higher Education Research & Development* 33 (1): 73–85. doi:10.1080/07294360.2013.864615.
Blackmore, J. 2010. "'The Other Within': Race/Gender Disruptions to the Professional Learning of White Educational Leaders." *International Journal of Leadership in Education* 13 (1): 45–61. doi:10.1080/13603120903242931.
Chilly Collective, The, ed. 1995. *Breaking Anonymity: The Chilly Climate for Women Faculty*. Waterloo, ON: Wilfrid Laurier University Press.
Cook, S.A. 2004. "A Case Study of Teacher Education: Rethinking Feminist Leadership." *Canadian Journal of Education/Révue canadienne de l'éducation* 26(4): 419–35.
Cook, S.A., and J. Riley. 1990. "The Case for a Gender Issues Course in Teacher Education." *Education Canada* 32 (3): 2–3.
Coulter, R.P. 1979. "Teachers and Political Action: Expanding the Arena." In *Educational Futures: Anticipations by the Next Generation of Canadian Scholars*, ed. K. Mazurek, 107–15. Edmonton: Faculty of Education, University of Alberta.
− 1996. "School Restructuring Ontario Style: A Gendered Agenda." In *Teacher Activism in the 1990s*, ed. S. Robertson and H. Smaller, 89–102. Toronto: James Lorimer.
− 1998. "'Us Guys in Suits Are Back': Women, Educational Work and the Market Economy in Canada." In *Education into the 21st Century: Dangerous Terrain for Women?*, ed. I. Elgqvist-Saltzman, A. Mackinnon, and A. Prentice, 107–17. London: Falmer Press.
− 1999. "'Doing Gender' in Canadian Schools: An Overview of the Policy and Practice Mélange." In *Gender Issues in International Education: Beyond Policy and Practice*, ed. S. Erskine and M. Wilson, 113–29. New York: Garland Press.
Coulter, R.P., and H. Harper, eds. 2005. *History Is Hers: Women Educators in Twentieth Century Ontario*. Calgary: Detselig.
Council of Canadian Academies. 2012. Strengthening Canada's Research Capacity: The Gender Dimension. http://www.scienceadvice.ca/uploads/eng/assessments%20and%20publications%20and%20news%20releases/women_university_research/wur_fullreporten.pdf.
Epp, J.R. 1993. "Women Students of Educational Administration." Paper pre-

sented at the annual meeting of the Canadian Society for the Study of Education, Carleton University, Ottawa, ON, June.

Fennell, H.A. 1992. "Leadership for Change: Two Cases from the Feminist Perspective." Paper presented at the annual meeting of the Canadian Society for the Study of Education, University of Prince Edward Island, Charlottetown, PEI, June.

Gaskell, J., and A. McLaren. 1991. *Women and Education*. 2nd ed. Calgary: Detselig.

Gill, B.A. 1993. "Breaking the Glass Ceiling or Sliding Back the Sunroof? Women in Educational Administration in New Brunswick." Paper presented at the annual meeting of the Canadian Society for the Study of Education, Carleton University, Ottawa, ON, June.

Globe and Mail. 2010. "Leaders Must Recruit Leaders." Editorial. 9 January. Accessed 21 August 2016. www.theglobeandmail.com/opinion/editorials/leaders-must-recruit-leaders/article4301503/.

Hannah, L.P., and S. Vethamany-Globus, eds. 2002. *Women in the Canadian Academic Tundra: Challenging the Chill*. Montreal and Kingston: McGill-Queen's University Press.

Heap, R., and A.L. Prentice. 1998. *Gender and Education in Ontario: An Historical Reader*. Toronto: Canadian Scholars' Press.

Houston, S., and A. Prentice. 1988. *Schooling and Scholars in Nineteenth-Century Ontario*. Toronto: University of Toronto Press. doi:10.3138/9781442679627.

Nixon, M. 1985. "Women in Administration: Is It Wishful Thinking?" *The ATA*. [Alberta Teachers Association magazine] May/June, 4–8.

– 1987. "Few Women in School Administration: Some Explanations." *Journal of Educational Thought* 21 (2): 63–70.

Nixon, M., and L.R. Gue. 1975. "Women Administrators and Women Teachers: A Comparative Study." *Alberta Journal of Educational Research* 21:196–206.

O'Rourke, K., L.R. McLean, and S.A. Cook. 2001. *Framing Our Past: Canadian Women's History in the Twentieth Century*. Montreal and Kingston: McGill-Queen's University Press.

Prentice, A. 1988. *The School Promoters: Education and Social Class in Mid-Nineteenth Century Upper Canada*. Toronto: McClelland and Stewart.

Prentice, A., and P. Bourne. 1988. *Canadian Women: A History*. Toronto: Harcourt Brace.

Prentice, A., and M.R. Theobald, ed. 1991. *Women Who Taught: Perspective on the History of Women and Teaching*. Toronto: University of Toronto Press. doi:10.3138/9781442683570.

Rees, R. 1990. *Women and Men in Education*. Toronto: Canadian Education Association.
– 1991. "The Ontario Principals' Qualifications Course: Towards Employment Equity?" *Journal of Educational Administration and Foundations* 6 (1): 37–52.
Reynolds, C. 1987. "Limited Liberation: A Policy on Married Women Teachers." In *Women Educators: Employees of Schools in Western Countries*, ed. P. Schmuck, 215–22. Albany: State University of New York Press.
– 1988. "Comparing the Experiences of Women and Men in Educational Administration." Paper presented at the annual meeting of the Canadian Society for the Study of Education, University of Windsor, Windsor, ON, June.
– 1991. "Integrating Feminist Scholarship into Teacher Education." Panel presentation at the annual meeting of the Canadian Society for the Study of Education, Kingston, ON, June.
Watkinson, A.M. 1991. "Equality, Empathy and Education." Paper presented at the annual meeting of the Canadian Society for the Study of Education, Kingston, ON, June.
Young, B. 1994. "An Other Perspective on the Knowledge Base in Canadian Educational Administration." *Canadian Journal of Education* 19 (4): 351. doi:10.2307/1495336.

4

Rewriting Sisyphus

The Possibilities of Feminism in Educational Administration

JANICE WALLACE

Freedom ought to be conceived of as an achievement within the concreteness of lived social situations rather than as a primordial or original possession. We might, for the moment, think of it as a distinctive way of orienting the self to the possible, of overcoming the determinate, of transcending or moving beyond in the full awareness that such overcoming can never be complete.

Maxine Greene 1988, 4–5

The Greek myth of Sisyphus tells the story of a man who was condemned to push a heavy rock up a hill every day. At the end of every day, it rolled back down, ready to be pushed up the hill again the next day ... and the next ... and the next. This story is the epitome of hard work that achieves no purpose, and it is tempting to think about the influence of feminism on education in this way. So many have worked so hard to change gendered policies and practices in educational institutions, and yet it sometimes feels like all that effort has produced little significant change. As I consider my feminist work over the past twenty-five years, I wonder if it has been worth it. On reflection, I believe it has, but not in some absolute sense; rather, it is a process that "can never be complete" (Greene 1988).

Perhaps it is time, then, to rewrite the story by acknowledging that the effort to achieve gender justice, while incomplete, leaves traces of increased awareness and greater freedom for many women and girls that felt almost impossible when I was a young woman. Orienting oneself to the possible, as Greene suggests (1988), may improve opportunities but also requires that we continue to "widen the lens and see/standing over the land myths of identity, new signals, processes" and, I would add, possibilities (Rukeyser 1938, cited in Greene 1995, 168) for feminism in education.

I have searched for the possibilities of feminism as located in the study and practice of educational administration.[1] I have attempted to widen my lens in considering these possibilities by including the mutually implicated perspectives of the personal and the political.[2] The personal is revealed in both my academic work in educational administration over the past twenty-five years and my prior teaching career in both the public and Indigenous education systems. Given the complex and fragile location of feminism in the field of educational administration, and the position of authority in education that graduates often occupy, the question that this book asks about the influence of feminism arguably takes on particular importance. In considering the "small p" political, I am taking a communitarian ethical stance toward politics (Brodie 2001, 76) and understand it to mean the processes by which social benefits are distributed in society equitably, given the intervening factors that Tilly (1998) refers to as "durable inequalities" – class, race, gender, minority gender identity, and ableness.

My critical approach to this paper is informed by two rich research traditions in feminist inquiry: feminist autoethnography (Allen and Piercy 2005) and institutional ethnography (Smith 1987, 2005). As Allen and Piercy note, "feminist autoethnography is a method of being, knowing, and doing that combines two concerns: telling the stories of those who are marginalized, and making good use of our own experience" (156). Institutional ethnography enables me to "make links between [my experience] and the policies and politics of various legislative and organizational contexts" (Reynolds and Young 1995, 363) as well as the academic field of educational administration. In the remainder of this paper, I begin each section with an autoethnographic account – recognizing both my marginalization and privilege – followed by an analysis of the "relations of ruling" (Smith 1987) that are evident in that account in order to consider this question: How has feminism influenced the study and practice of educational administration in highly gendered educational organizations in Canada, as revealed through my life experience and scholarly inquiry? The chapter is organized around the themes that emerge in my autoethnographic accounts below: What has been the effect of gender in deciding what knowledge is of most worth in the study of educational administration? How is feminist scholarship and advocacy taken up in the gendered opportunities for those seeking to become school administrators and in the ways that school administration is understood? And what is the role of an emergent intersectional feminism in enabling a more diverse heterogeneous vision of our schools and classrooms in educational administration?

COMING TO FEMINISM: LOSING AND FINDING MY VOICE

When I began graduate studies in 1992, I had already been a teacher for several years. As an elementary teacher, I was accustomed to primarily white, middle-class, female teaching colleagues and a male principal – supervised by a male inspector in the early years of my career – in every school in which I taught. My personal world was also organized around heteronormative social norms within religious traditions in which men led and women supported them. These gendered arrangements grated and made no sense to me, but I had no theoretical language to analyze what I felt to be wrong. I slowly came to an awareness of feminism through the work of feminist theologians during the early 1980s and, for the first time, I had a lens through which to make sense of the gendered arrangements I saw in schools, churches, my friends' personal lives – and my own.

Somehow, I expected a university environment to be more open to feminism and, sometimes, it was – but mostly it was not. Of the many undergraduate courses that I took in the arts, social sciences, and math throughout the late 1980s, all were taught by men. The only female professors I encountered were in two summer courses: one assistant professor, who shared that she was regularly mistaken for a university secretary, and a PhD sessional. As a graduate student and teaching assistant in a faculty of education, the gender distribution was more evenly divided in my learning and working environment overall, but the professors in the educational administration program were almost all male.[3] While the men in the faculty were supportive and encouraging, I began to notice how often they interrupted women in classes and meetings, repeated what women had already said, and seldom included female scholars' work in course syllabi.

In my classes, all the readings in my core educational administration courses and most of my option courses were written by men ... all but one Shakeshaft article (1987) at the end of one course. Two early theorists,

Mary Parker Follett and Lillian Gilbreth, were sometimes briefly mentioned, but the lectures quickly moved on to the "real" titans of educational administration theory – e.g., Mayo, Taylor, Weber, Barnard – most of whom were writing about the world of business. I might have despaired except that I also met a strong group of feminist scholars at the faculty where I was studying who encouraged me, introduced me to feminist authors, and taught me to think and act strategically. In them, I saw possibilities for feminist scholarship in educational administration, and those possibilities were fostered by their continued support.

I received support from male professors as well. For example, one of my male professors encouraged me to submit a paper I had written in his class to a national conference. I did and it was accepted. While at the conference, I noticed an advertisement for a book launch of an edited volume about women in educational administration in Canada. The editors – Cecilia Reynolds and Beth Young (1995) – and contributors were Canadian feminist scholars in educational administration. Given my experience up to this point, I was anxious to see for myself who was doing this kind of scholarship in Canada, but fully expected that I would be one of only a handful of people with an interest in this book. Imagine my surprise when I had to shoehorn myself into a spot in the back row of a large room full of people sitting in every available chair and standing in every other available square inch. In retrospect, that meeting was central to my scholarship from that moment on. The interest in their work from the broader academic community demonstrated that a community of feminist scholarship existed, that it had potential importance within the academy generally, and that it could inform the discipline of educational administration more specifically. I was hooked.

I returned to my studies with new enthusiasm for the many ways in which feminist scholarship opened up possibilities for studying "the woman question" in education. However, I learned very quickly that feminist scholarship was (and largely continues to be) seen as peripheral to the "real" questions of educational administration, and that the theoretical perspectives that feminist scholarship opened up – indeed required – were highly suspect. Interpretive, critical, post-structural, and psychoanalytic theories were relatively common in feminist curriculum studies, but positivist epistemology was still the dominant theoretical perspective well into the late 1990s in educational administration scholarship, despite Thom Greenfield's rigorous critique of positivism (Greenfield and Ribbins 1993). For my own work, I wished to use a critical hermeneutic[4] framework to explore the ways in which equity policy both mirrored, and had the possibility to resist, "durable inequalities"[5] in educational organizations.

As one of a small number of master's students writing a thesis, I was required to attend a non-credit class on Saturday mornings in which our emergent proposal was critiqued by two senior professors. My choice of a hermeneutic phenomenological approach to my research question – a precursor to my later feminist critical hermeneutical doctoral study – caused considerable angst, and so my carefully researched proposal was heavily interrogated. Not accustomed to such vigorous academic debate, I would go home after the seminar, cry, get mad, and then, in anticipation of next week's tutorial, head to the library to develop a stronger case for using what my professors perceived to be a suspect methodology. While this effort did make my work much stronger, the defensive rigour of this process was not required of any of the other students in the seminar who were all using more traditional methodologies.

By the late 1990s, however, although I met skeptics along the way, my male doctoral supervisor was very encouraging. A feminist committee member was particularly helpful as I wrote my PhD dissertation using a methodology that incorporated critical, hermeneutic, and feminist theories, and she encouraged me to submit my thesis for a national award. To my surprise, it won – the first explicitly feminist thesis to win the dissertation award for the national academic association in educational administration in Canada. A door seemed to be opening. However, my thesis topic – the ascendance, resistance to, and subsequent rescinding of gender equity policy in education organizations in Ontario – demonstrated a need for cautious optimism. Securing an academic position proved this point.

During my first interview, my feminist scholarship became a topic for discussion and some bewilderment. As one female participant on the panel noted, to knowing nods around the table, "There's already been a lot of work done about women in school leadership, so haven't the questions about women in education been answered?" I responded by noting, "There's been work done for millennia based on a masculinist understanding of the world, so I likely still have lots of work to do." I did not get the job. My second interview was at an institution in which I had studied, taught, and been involved in various committees and projects. The first question following my presentation from a future educational administration colleague was about my methodology: "How can you be sure of the reliability of your interview data – what makes your work any different than a newspaper reporter's?" A fair enough question, but it demonstrated that the quantitative/qualitative debate persisted in the world of "Ed Admin."

So, too, persisted questions around the connection of feminist work to educational administration. After I was hired, a senior scholar at a large and influential institution in Canada wrote and presented a paper at a national conference decrying the defiling of a more "pure" educational administration discipline. He used as one of his examples the fact that a feminist had recently been hired while another (male) scholar, a student of his, had not, despite the fact that his work dealt with the "real" questions of educational administration – bureaucracy, hierarchy, and the practical concerns of the field. Apparently he believed that feminist scholarship questioning forms of bureaucracy and institutional policies that maintained gendered relations of power did not consider "real" issues that were of sufficient importance for study or dissemination in the academy.

THE MISSING AND MUTED VOICES
IN EDUCATIONAL ADMINISTRATION SCHOLARSHIP

As my experience demonstrates, the canon of educational administration, while always contentious (see e.g., Donmoyer, Imber, and Scheurich 1995), has maintained a steadfastly male-dominated authorship. Mitchell (1998) addressed this phenomenon in a paper that she presented at the annual meeting of the Canadian Association for the Study of Women in Education (CASWE) (see "Who Do You Think You Are?" in part 1 for the important role of CASWE in feminist scholarship in Canada) in which she reported on her findings from an examination of texts used in core educational administration courses across Canada. By the time Mitchell wrote her paper, feminist scholarship was firmly embedded in education curriculum studies and was becoming more common in educational administration scholarship, yet Mitchell's study revealed that only two female-authored texts were listed on course syllabi – one required (by a feminist professor) and one recommended. One male author did "make extensive use of women's scholarship in text material and in the reference list" (Mitchell 1998, 3). Mitchell notes, "Women fared better on the suggested reading lists included in course outlines ... Gender issues or feminist critiques were listed as explicit course topics on six of the twenty-two course outlines" (3). She goes on to note that, at least as troubling as the absence of women scholars in syllabi and academic references in refereed journal articles, the contributions of female scholars "in the past have largely been written out of the knowledge base" (Mitchell 1998, 3). Lillian Gilbreth was entirely missing from any course outline, while Mary Parker Follett did appear on some suggested reading lists. More contemporary scholars – Carol Gilligan,

Rosabeth Moss Kanter, and Charol Shakeshaft – made appearances on the suggested readings lists: in other words, on the periphery of a male-dominated canon.

The absence of women's scholarship and feminist knowledge was arguably devastating to the academic study and practice of educational administration. As Mitchell (1998) notes, Gilbreth introduced psychology and Follett introduced sociology into organizational theory (4). In doing so, Gilbreth opened the possibility of studying "the psychology of management" while "Follett's work on conflict resolution and negotiation can be seen in popular administration books written in the past two decades, *but these two women are never credited with introducing the concepts*" (4, italics added). Instead, male authors, who reintroduced these topics much later, were credited with their introduction, in response to organizational studies premised on hierarchy, bureaucracy, and traditional relations of power. Things might have been different, as Mitchell explains: "Administrative and organizational theory could have been greatly enriched if the women's scholarship had been placed alongside the men's. Imagine what our organizations would have looked like if they had been founded on three pillars – the organization (bureaucracy), the individual (psychology), and the group (sociology) – rather than resting [primarily] on bureaucratic foundations" (4).

A reader, in considering these past absences, might be tempted to retort, "That was then; this is now!" but the story remains depressingly similar in more contemporary surveys of the academic literature in educational administration. Oplatka (2009), for example, does not reference any explicitly feminist paper in his historical overview of journal articles in educational administration from the 1960s to the present. In fact, the author does not note the significance of any of the social justice and feminist work done by several respected scholars – both women and men – in Canada and internationally. Instead, he delineates the continuing tension between theory/practice in educational administration scholarship as well as the fear that theoretical diversity will lead to disciplinary fragmentation and irrelevance. His study points to serious divisions within the academic field along the fissure lines between theory and practice that have worked to maintain exclusionary boundaries for feminist research and analysis as "too theoretical" and not sufficiently "practical."

However, the positional boundaries in organizations that were highly gendered in education organizations were exactly what informed the work of female academics. In our study of early female academics in educational administration, participants noted how often extant theories were not helpful in pursuing questions of interest to them (Wallace and Wallin 2015). This is not surprising given that, unlike their male colleagues, these women drew on life experiences that were largely outside the hierarchical line positions in educational organizations. Thus, while they were marked as outsiders, their positioning in their former careers and in departments of educational administration enabled them to blaze new trails of scholarship that were more congruent with their experiences in educational systems. In other words, their academic interests were informed by broad life experiences that were not dominated by formal organizational positions of power: a fact that raised different questions for them and their research. The following summary demonstrates the diversity of their research interests and the innovation that they brought to their field of scholarship:

> Two of the study participants edited, and several other participants contributed to, a collection of papers that mapped out the terrain of feminist and gender-based analysis of women in educational administration in Canada. Other participants looked outside the traditional hierarchical relations in educational organizations to explore a critical analysis of the political influences in educational organizations, including industrial relations and the professional development work of teacher federations/unions. Some participants explored aesthetics, emotions, and spirituality in leadership, which opened up fresh philosophical opportunities to think about educational administration in new ways. Others explored innovations in organizing schooling, including twinned principalships and year round schooling. (Wallace et al. 2014, 448)

Yet, while their research was well-received, especially among feminists internationally, many spoke with clear-eyed recognition that their work would likely have limited efficacy in shifting the scholarly field in the long term toward feminism. Like modern female versions of Sisyphus, they took their turn pushing the stone of feminist thought and analysis up the hill of educational administration, only to watch it roll, at least partially, back down for the next generation of feminist scholars to push up the hill again. Each generation did so within a context that was unique to them, and, yet, they all experienced resistance to the research that came out of and informed their experience, which is a phenomenon that is very familiar to generations of feminist scholars.

FEMINISMS' CONTRIBUTION TO EDUCATORS' UNDERSTANDING OF SCHOOL ADMINISTRATION

During my career in academe, I have enjoyed many opportunities but have also experienced many of the resistances that most women academics face (Wallace et al. 2014). I have seen, in my own faculty, the regular offering of a course on gender and educational administration as an options course – still on the periphery and definitely not required, but there; and, there are more tenured women faculty in educational administration. As neo-liberal policies, including severe cutbacks and increased measures of accountability, have become de rigueur in higher education (Giroux 2002), feminist work has been constrained by an increasingly competitive and individualistic model of meting out rewards on the basis of highly actuarial pseudo-scientific "merit" models. The academic "star" systems, such as the Canada Research Chairs, have skewed research to those areas that are more highly valued by the funding bodies and, despite vigorous critique, continue to award male scholars far more frequently than women (Side and Robbins 2007). Furthermore, because neo-liberal ideology has permeated education systems so thoroughly over the past two decades (Blackmore and Sachs 2007), the consciousness of many of the students we are teaching has been inevitably shaped by its ideals. A surprising number, however, when given the opportunity, remain committed to learning more about equity and practices that will increase educational opportunities for all students and educators in formal educational systems.

For example, students in a course I taught on gender and educational leadership advocated for and, in some cases, implemented policies and practices that would provide safe and accessible washroom facilities for transgender students; advocated for equitable leadership opportunities for women in rural schools; pointed out to the administration of their graduate program that working mothers were less able than male colleagues to leave their children behind in order to attend face-to-face, out-of-town summer courses; critiqued the under-identification of girls for special learning opportunities ... and the list goes on. In each case, their actions were prompted by feminist theory that questioned gender norms and encouraged thinking about more equitable practices.

Of course, feminist activism – whether named as such, or not – within schools, school systems, and the larger community has been a part of education history (e.g., Prentice and Theobald 1991), but not a part of the learning in most graduate educational administration courses. In one of my courses, I had assigned *The Feminist Case against Bureaucracy* (Ferguson 1984), which led to an interesting exchange with my students. Several of the men in the course met on Thursday nights to play basketball (gender implications noted) and apparently this text was the source of some tense discussion. The next morning, as the students came in one by one, there was some joking about what was to come and, finally, one of the men in the class said, "You know, Janice, we were talking about this book at the game and we all finally realized that we didn't know whether we should be worried about it or not since we have never taken any feminist courses and we really don't know what feminism means. So we decided to be open-minded about it." They were; they learned; and all students in the course challenged themselves to think about bureaucratic practices critically in order to encourage socially just practices. Regrettably, some in Ed Admin – both students and professors – are less open-minded and seldom include the rich possibilities of feminist scholarship in their own scholarship or syllabi.

Unfortunately, it is neither surprising nor unusual that many of my graduate students in educational administration, even at the doctoral level, have not been exposed to any feminist writers, texts, journal articles, or theories as they are taken up in most faculties of education rather quixotically, depending on the professor assigned or room in the program for optional courses. For example, very recently, one student asked me if it was really true that there were fewer women in school administration. For her, anecdotal evidence suggested that this was the case but, at the end of her program of studies, she, like most students, had never been exposed to any of the feminist literature that had explored this phenomenon for well over thirty years. Yet, there is a lively history of feminist scholarship and advocacy that has the potential to, and, in some cases, has been able to, benefit policies and practices in schools. Feminist scholars in educational administration have explored the particular ways in which gender acts to shape policies and practices in educational organizations. For example, feminist theories throw light on the gendered division of work in schools, deal more effectively with sexual harassment, provide curriculum support that recognizes the effects of gender norms on student results, and so on (Wallace 2004). Feminist theory illuminates the intersection between the personal and political (Blackmore 1989), reveals the ways in which power is organized around gender (Blackmore 1999; Brunner 2000) and the intersection of gender with class, race, minority sexual identity, ability, and Indigeneity (Fitzgerald 2003; Gaetane, Williams, and Sherman 2009; Lugg and Tooms 2010; Lee, Mansfield, and Welton 2016) and, importantly, takes up these questions in actively political ways (Marshall and Anderson 1995). That is, feminist theory enables practitioners to bring theory to action.

Unfortunately, policy initiatives, such as those that encourage more men to enter the teaching profession and more women to take on school leadership roles, often represent a naïve lack of awareness of the ways in which gender is performed (Connell 2009) through the power matrices of complex economic, social, political, and cultural arrangements in society. As a result of this lack of awareness, school leaders often do not question their own gendered/cultural practices or those embedded in institutional arrangements, and so these policies fail to achieve their stated goals. Ensuring that school leaders study and understand the complexity and intersectionality of gender, race, class, and sexual orientation on school practices creates the conditions that enable learners' and educators' needs to be met and the broader goals of education to be served more effectively (Blackmore 2010). Unfortunately, this has remained an elusive goal in educational administration.

However, all is not lost. Feminism is a theory for action and, despite significant resistance, the history of feminism in education provides some examples of possibilities for equity policy when theory meets practice. For example, liberal or rights feminism (Marshall and Anderson 1995) was the theoretical lens that was most frequently used by feminist scholars in history, sociology, and educational administration during the late 1980s and early 1990s. Liberal feminist ideology was taken up and acted upon by advocates within such organizations as the Federation of Women Teachers' Associations of Ontario (FWTAO). Their goal was equality for women in educational organizations, and their focus was on advocating for provincial policies to ensure that organizational practices would provide fair opportunities for women seeking positions of power, such as school principals and senior administrative positions at the board or ministry level. In many ways, their efforts were successful. Policies were passed that encouraged more equitable workplaces across differences around gender, visible minorities, Indigenous Peoples, and the disabled, such as *Bill 79: Em-*

ployment Equity Act that was passed in Ontario in 1993. By the mid-1990s, particularly in urban centres, female principals were no longer a total novelty in elementary schools, although the percentage of female administrators was much lower in secondary schools and senior administration at the board level.

While liberal feminists were successful in using the power of the state to improve employment equity for female educators, the weakness of such policy was that legislation could continue to be resisted through informal sexist organizational practices, and the state could – and did – withdraw its support. This is what happened in Ontario where the efforts of advocates for women's "rights" had a significant impact on provincial policy. Successive Liberal and New Democratic Party (NDP) governments passed legislation supporting goals for hiring in educational organizations that represented the population of the province, but informal and formal resistance continued.

My doctoral research (Wallace 2000) on equity officers[6] working in school boards in Ontario revealed that, while there was reluctant formal compliance with the letter of the law, the spirit of the law was regularly circumvented and resisted. One participant revealed, for example, that, while teachers' income for both men and women was equal on the pay grid, men were regularly tapped on the shoulder to take on consultative and support projects for the board that provided extra income, prestige, and network connections, but women were not. In addition, participants gave example after example of blatant sexism directed at them in formal and informal workshops on gender equity in the workplace, where anger about equity provisions was regularly directed at them in very personal ways. In other historical research on retired female administrators in Ontario (Wallace 2004, 2005) who gained their administrative positions following equity reforms, participants spoke about having to circumvent male networks of privilege and blatant resistance in order to be considered for an administrative role. In each scenario, a surface reading would suggest that gender equity was achieved in policy, but the spirit of the policy was ultimately resisted in very powerful ways, culminating in Ontario's very Conservative Harris government's first act to end *Bill 79* and replace it with *Bill 8: A Bill to Repeal Job Quotas and Restore Merit-based Employment in Ontario* (1995), which effectively rescinded all the provisions of *Bill 79: The Employment Equity Act*. Fraternal patriarchy (Pateman 1988) was very much alive and well, but so was the determination of feminist scholars and educators to improve educational and career opportunities for girls and women in schools and school systems. However, what feminism was not acknowledging was that its proponents and beneficiaries were predominantly white, heterosexual, middle-class women. Liberty was far from complete – inside feminism itself.

EXPANDING THE THEORETICAL BOUNDARIES

Most interesting and challenging for me (and for many others) who are products of second wave (liberal) feminism is the call for inclusion by the diverse voices of structurally disadvantaged students whose lived experience of gender is embedded in experiences of colonialism, racism, and globalized capitalism – none of whom are well represented in either the educational administration literature or in the feminist literature. Their charge that feminism has been focused on the problems of middle-class, white, heteronormative, able women while ignoring their significant issues has required a raising of consciousness that goes beyond reductionist bifurcations of us/them to more complex and challenging theoretical perspectives and practical engagements. Of the last several classes that I have taught, for example, one-third to two-thirds of my students were from the Global South, and most were international students, although some were students who had lived in Canada for most of their formative years. The rest, while born in Canada, had often done international work or taught many international students in their classrooms. Some students have chosen to declare their identification with a sexual minority group, while others argued for inclusion of readings about LGBTQIA issues in the community, schools, and classrooms.

To continue teaching without addressing the intersection of race, class, minority sexual identity, Indigeneity, cultural experience, and ableness with gender would have been a disservice to my students and in direct contravention of the tenets of equity and social justice that I have espoused and believe deeply. Thus began a learning process that continues. My privileged position as a white, middle-class, heterosexual instructor and scholar is now more complex – I am decentred – and this is not always a comfortable location. For example, how should I respond to a final paper that takes on the normative construction of my syllabus by a student from the Global South? Doing so requires abandoning my position of power as "knower" in order to assess fairly – and learn.

And so, as I retire, my feminist perspectives in educational administration continue to be challenging, uncomfortable, and resisted (sometimes by me). Based on my academic experience over twenty-five years, feminist theory has responded to legitimate critiques and moved toward a more inclusive and intersectional understanding of its possibilities, and yet the academic field of educational administration has returned to a more instrumental perspective (Heck and Hallinger 1999) that leaves less room for feminist perspectives (Blackmore 2013), and raises questions, yet again, about the influence of feminism in educational administration theory and practice in Canada. And so, we begin to move the stone up the hill again, but with a firmer and more inclusive notion of our goals and strategies for the work ahead.

As Giddens (1994) acknowledges, even as equity discourses were resisted, their residue remained and they were much more difficult to ignore. Therefore, even though equity policies that included women and minorities in Ontario were pushed back by pervasive sexist norms that were evident in neo-liberal reforms, it became more difficult to justify sexist, racist, ableist, and homophobic discourses in the public domain and in organizational practices. They certainly continued to exist but, in the absence of provincial policy, and at the urging of activist educators and their representative associations, many organizations wrote their own equity policies and, at least formally, acknowledged the need for more inclusive hiring and human resources practices. Others, informed by critical feminist scholarship (Coulter 1996), formed informal coalitions for action in formal educational organizations and pushed back against the systems of power that resisted feminist reforms.

Equity challenges persisted in academia as well. For example, while many more women were hired as professors in educational administration programs by 2000 in Canada, almost all were white, middle-class, able, and heterosexual.[7] I was one of them and brought my particular lived experience to my scholarship and my university classrooms. However, increasingly diverse students were mobilizing around issues of race, class, Indigeneity, ability, and minority sexual identity, and raised more complex issues that intersected with gender. Heterodoxical interests could not be satisfied any longer in classrooms that took up only dominant Western, white, middle-class, heterosexual feminist interests.

By the early 2000s in the academic field of educational administration, feminist theory began to open up to theoretical perspectives that called into question and deconstructed liberal or "rights" feminism. Critical, post-structural, postcolonial, and decolonial feminism decentred normative discourses and problematized dominant narratives that characterize women of the South as "victims of patriarchal cultures, oppression and power imbalances" (Spurlin 2010, cited in Mestry and Schmidt 2012, 541). Instead, picking up on scholars such as Bhabha (1998), Said (1978), Spivak (2000), and Bannerji (2000), intersectional feminists argued for a voice that speaks from a post/anticolonial space rather than the Global North interpreting and speaking for the Global South.

Post/anticolonial feminism and post-structural feminism have also been taken up by Indigenous feminists (see, e.g., McKay in this volume; Green 2007). This emergent scholarship takes on issues of oppression outside and within Indigenous communities, and provides the diverse voices of Indigenous women speaking to their issues, including "Inuit, Métis, First Nations, and non-status Indian women; some women were firmly located in Aboriginal communities and cultures, others had more urban or hybrid identities. It included women whose first language was their Aboriginal language, and who continued to speak it, and women who spoke only English. It included women with graduate and professional education, and women with basic in school education" (Green 2007, 16). Those who are white, middle-class, mostly heterosexual, Canadian-born females in academia have been called upon to question and deconstruct our own racist and sexist assumptions about the Other.

Blackmore (2010) describes the deconstruction of her positionality of whiteness – an understanding of privilege that became very visible when she attempted to "mentor" a female Indigenous colleague. She shares that "at our first official meeting, my new colleague quickly interjected, informing me she did not need a white middle-class feminist to mentor her, but rather someone who was not from the mainstream, the dominant, and from her culture." Blackmore continues:

> This critical incident confronted me with the invisibility of my whiteness that positioned me as the dominant in an institutional situation; one that I had imagined was between equals as women and unequal only with regard to gender within the male-dominated academy. It signaled to me how my location within the Western male-dominated academy, while marginal as a feminist academic, was culturally privileged within the Western (and patriarchal) value systems that subordinated [I]ndigenous cultural knowledge. *For me and my feminist colleagues, being female was what*

mattered most in terms of our positioning, never thinking how our whiteness provided a "public and psychological wage that advantaged us relative to our ethnic and [I]ndigenous sisters." (Frankenberg 1993, cited in Blackmore 2010, 46, italics added)

This critical incident points to the lack of reflexivity that I, most certainly, was guilty of, even as I took up questions of social justice around Indigenous and gender issues in educational leadership. Yet, a convergence of factors is calling for a much more informed analysis of the rising voices of Indigenous peoples for justice and inclusion: the "increased cultural diversity arising from the flows of immigrants and refugees into Western nation states" (Blackmore 2010, 48), the growing phenomenon of internationalization of education, and the commodification and marketing of Western curriculum internationally. In such a context, "'whiteness as a privileged signifier has become global' and English has become the lingua franca of knowledge capitalism" (Leonardo 2004, 117, cited in Blackmore 2010, 49). Unproblematized whiteness, then, becomes a colonizing force that is incompatible with the goals of feminism for fairness and emancipation for all and with the goals of a feminist educational administration that is concerned about equitable learning opportunities for all students within a working/teaching environment that effectively supports the work of all learners and educators.

My own critical incident, as noted already, came when I was teaching a course on women and educational administration in which about half the class was international students or students who had immigrated to Canada from the Global South. What immediately became clear to me was that my syllabus did not represent their experience of or concerns around educational leadership and that, even if my class roster had been predominantly white, middle-class students, I would have done them a disservice by not providing an opportunity to examine our positionality at the intersection of race, class, culture, and ableness: that is, as Kajner (2015) argues, to decolonize knowledge and our relationship to it. As mentioned already, one of my students chose to help me with this task by deconstructing the knowledge base represented in my syllabus in her final paper. It was embarrassing and instructive. This is tricky terrain, though, because I can carry my white privilege with me so easily with the best of intentions. Blackmore (2010) reminds us, however, that "white feminists have to challenge the 'trope of benevolence' within which white Western feminist cross-cultural praxis has historically been constructed" (51, citing Haggis and Schech 2000).

As some of my feminist colleagues and I take up the challenge, outlined by Blackmore (2010), by moving toward decolonizing our practices and learning from burgeoning Indigenous and international feminist voices, we must, as Gadamer (1992) suggests, be open to transformation by the Other. I would argue that this is particularly vital in educational administration, given our late start. We need to open spaces in our academic departments that are currently dominated by voices of the Global North. It also means that those of us who represent the dominant culture need to commit ourselves to learning to decolonize knowledge about the meaning of school administration so that we are able to bring together readings and resources that are meaningful to and with our students. And, despite the challenges of diminishing budgets, hiring freezes, and all of the other challenges of the commodified university, the diverse (feminist) voices of the Global South, Indigenous voices, LGBTQIA voices, differently abled voices are key to moving toward an intersectional feminism in re-theorizing educational administration.

There is no doubt that, within the conditions of neo-liberalism, the work of feminist advocacy, scholarship, and teaching in educational administration is challenging, and is particularly so around the intersectional and decolonizing feminist work that is necessary. However, in a climate where instrumental educational administration knowledge is privileged and critical analysis of the conditions in which knowledge is produced is not, feminist scholars, already marginalized, may feel a need to retreat to safer ground. But, "If we do not dare to analyse the very institutions in which we work and the ways in which we and our colleagues are implicated in the reproduction of racism and the propping up of whiteness, then, *how can we move beyond theory at its most hollow? How can we move toward transformation?*" (Fine et al. 2004, x, cited in Blackmore 2010, 58, italics added).

EPILOGUE – REWRITING SISYPHUS: ORIENTING TO POSSIBILITY

The hope of moving forward to transformation has enlivened my academic work in educational administration. During the past twenty-five years of active engagement in feminist scholarship in educational administration in Canada, I have often felt like Sisyphus must have – rolling that rock up the hill, only to watch it crest and then roll down the other side of the hill. However, in retrospect, perhaps the process that feminist scholars in educational administration have been engaged in has been much more like the persistent movement of water against an unyielding rock. Water is a patient but relentless force in carving out a path to its goal and so, too, has been feminism in educational administration in providing a pathway for women – and men – to recognize the possibilities of organizations and formal positions of power to "move forward to transformation." While the water may be slowed by obstacles and its path diverted, even the smallest rivulet eventually wears away resistance, all the time opening up new spaces and new opportunities.

As I retire and consider the question, "What has been the effect of feminism in educational administration?" I acknowledge that the effect has been limited. As we work toward transforming learning opportunities for all students, opening up career opportunities for all women, becoming mindful of our relationship to colonization and the need to disrupt and root out its harmful legacy, the task seems overwhelming, and it is difficult to be patient in the face of its urgency. From the perspective of time, however, I can see that, although feminism has not realized its full potential in the study of educational administration, it has etched new pathways that open up possibilities for small transformations at local sites. It has also allowed for larger transformations as better informed students participate in policy committees dealing with transgender issues and sexual harassment policy, serve on selection committees for new principals, consider discipline policy for diverse student populations, and welcome new refugee families to their schools. I watch and listen and remain cautiously optimistic that transformation will come even as new challenges present themselves, and I remain convinced that feminism will respond to those challenges with rigorous theory, thoughtful determination, and renewed vigour. I choose, as Greene (1995) advises, to orient myself to the possible.

NOTES

1 I am choosing to use the broader term "educational administration"; however, many scholars, journals, and departments have more recently identified themselves using the term "educational leadership." Generally speaking, both use the same core theories and scholarly canon.
2 Linda Napikoski, "The Personal Is Political: Where Did This Slogan of the Women's Movement Come From? What Does It Mean?" ThoughtCo, last

updated 31 December 2017, https://www.thoughtco.com/the-personal-is-political-slogan-origin-3528952.
3 Throughout, when I reference the gender of a person, I mean the gender identity by which they would identify. Gender identity was never discussed by any male professor, but all were white and middle class, although not all grew up in middle-class homes.
4 I recognize that there are significant issues in bringing together critical and interpretivist epistemologies; however, I argued in my thesis that doing so is possible and was necessary to my analysis. See Wallace 2000.
5 Here, I am referring to Charles Tilly's book, *Durable Inequalities* (1998), which explores the persistence of race, class, and gender as dominant categories of inequality in American society.
6 Equity officers were hired by many school boards in Ontario to help implement Bill 79.
7 I have not been able to locate any statistical evidence to support this claim, but the educational administration community is small and during the time cited, participants in conferences, those who were published, and other anecdotal evidence made it clear that faculty in educational administration were white, middle class, and most often male.

REFERENCES

Allen, K., and F. Piercy. 2005. "Feminist Autoethnography." In *Research Methods in Family Therapy*, 2nd ed., ed. D. Sprenkle and F. Piercy, 155–69. New York: Guilford Press.

Bannerji, H. 2000. *The Dark Side of the Nation: Essays on Multiculturalism, Nationalism and Gender*. Toronto: Canadian Scholars' Press.

Bhabha, H. 1998. "Cultures in Between." In *Multicultural States: Rethinking Difference and Identity*, ed. D. Bennett, 29–36. London, New York: Routledge.

Blackmore, J. 1989. "Educational Leadership: A Feminist Critique and Reconstruction." In *Critical Perspectives on Educational Leadership*, ed. J. Smyth, 63–87. London, New York: Falmer Press.

– 1999. *Troubling Women*. Philadelphia, PA: Open University Press.

– 2010. "'The Other Within': Race/Gender Disruptions to the Professional Learning of White Educational Leaders." *International Journal of Leadership in Education* 13 (1): 45–61. doi:10.1080/13603120903242931.

– 2013. "A Feminist Critical Perspective on Educational Leadership." *International Journal of Leadership in Education* 16 (2): 139–54. doi:10.1080/13603124.2012.754057.

Blackmore, J., and J. Sachs. 2007. *Performing and Reforming Leaders: Gender, Educational Restructuring and Organizational Change.* Albany, NY: SUNY Press.

Brodie, J. 2001. *Critical Concepts: An Introduction to Politics.* 2nd ed. Toronto: Prentice Hall.

Brunner, C.C. 2000. *Principles of Power: Women Superintendents and the Riddle of the Heart.* Albany, NY: SUNY Press.

Connell, R.W. 2009. *Gender in World Perspective.* 2nd ed. Cambridge, UK: Polity Press.

Coulter, R. 1996. "Gender Equity and Schooling." *Canadian Journal of Education* 21 (4): 433–52. doi:10.2307/1494895.

Donmoyer, R., M. Imber, and J.J. Scheurich, eds. 1995. *The Knowledge Base in Educational Administration: Multiple Perspectives.* New York: SUNY Press.

Ferguson, K. 1984. *The Feminist Case against Bureaucracy.* Philadelphia: Temple University Press.

Fine, M., L. Weis, P. Powell, and A. Burns, eds. 2004. *Off White.* London: Routledge.

Fitzgerald, T. 2003. "Changing the Deafening Silence of Indigenous Women's Voices in Educational Leadership." *Journal of Educational Administration* 41 (1): 9–23. doi:10.1108/09578230310457402.

Frankenberg, R. 1993. *White Women, Race Matters: The Social Construction of Whiteness.* Minneapolis, MN: University of Minnesota Press.

Gadamer, H.G. 1992. *Truth and Method.* Edited and translated by G. Barden and J. Cumming. New York: Crossroad. Original work published 1960.

Gaetane, J.-M., V. Williams, and S. Sherman. 2009. "Black Women's Leadership Experiences: Examining the Intersectionality of Race and Gender." *Advances in Developing Human Resources* 11 (5): 562–81. doi:10.1177/1523422309351836.

Giddens, A. 1994. *Beyond Left and Right: The Future of Radical Politics.* Paolo Alto, CA: Stanford University Press.

Giroux, H. 2002. "Neoliberalism, Corporate Culture, and the Promise of Higher Education: The University as a Democratic Public Sphere." *Harvard Educational Review* 72 (4): 425–63. doi:10.17763/haer.72.4.0515nr62324n71p1.

Green, J., ed. 2007. *Making Space for Indigenous Feminism.* Black Point, NS: Fernwood.

Greene, M. 1988. *The Dialectic of Freedom.* New York: Teachers' College Press.

– 1995. *Releasing the Imagination: Essays on Education, the Arts, and Social Change.* San Francisco: Jossey-Bass.

Greenfield, T., and P. Ribbins. 1993. *Greenfield on Educational Administration: Towards a Humane Science*. London: Routledge.

Haggis, J., and S. Schech. 2000. "Meaning Well and Global Good Manners: Reflections on White Women Feminist Cross Cultural Praxis." *Australian Feminist Studies* 15 (33): 387–99. doi:10.1080/713611987.

Heck, R., and P. Hallinger. 1999. "Next Generation Methods for the Study of Leadership and School Improvement." In *Handbook of Research on Educational Administration*, 2nd ed., ed. J. Murphy and K. Seashore Louis, 141–62. San Francisco, CA: Jossey-Bass.

Kajner, T. 2015. "Living Well with Others: Exploring Community-Engaged Scholarship in Canadian Higher Education." PhD diss., University of Alberta.

Lee, P.-L., K. Mansfield, and A. Welton. 2016. *Identity Intersectionalities, Mentoring and Work-Life (Im)balance: Educators (Re)negotiate the Personal, the Professional, and Political*. Charlotte, NC: Information Age Publishing.

Leonardo, Z. 2004. "The Worlds of White Folk: Critical Pedagogy, Whiteness Studies and Globalization Discourse." In *The RoutledgeFalmer Reader in Multicultural Education*, ed. G. Ladson-Billings and D. Gillborn, 117–36. London: RoutledgeFalmer.

Lugg, C.A., and A.K. Tooms. 2010. "A Shadow of Ourselves: Identity Erasure and the Politics of Queer Leadership." *School Leadership & Management* 30 (1): 77–91. doi:10.1080/13632430903509790.

Marshall, C., and G. Anderson. 1995. "Rethinking the Private and Public Spheres: Feminist and Cultural Studies Perspectives on the Politics of Education." In *The Study of Educational Politics*, ed. J. Scribner and D. Layton, 169–82. London: Falmer Press.

Mestry, R., and M. Schmidt. 2012. "A Feminist Postcolonial Examination of Female Principals' Experiences in South African Secondary Schools." *Gender and Education* 24 (5): 535–51. doi:10.1080/09540253.2011.628926.

Mitchell, C. 1998. "Women in the Educational Administration Canon: Reclaiming Lillian and Mary." In *Centering on the Margins: The Evaded Curriculum*, edited by J.R. Epp, 98–101. Proceedings of the biannual international summer institute of the Canadian Association for the Study of Women and Education, University of Ottawa, Ottawa, ON, Canada.

Oplatka, I. 2009. "The Field of Educational Administration: A Historical Overview of Scholarly Attempts to Recognize Epistemological Identities, Meanings and Boundaries from the 1960s Onwards." *Journal of Educational Administration* 47 (1): 8–35. doi:10.1108/09578230910928061.

Pateman, C. 1988. *The Sexual Contract*. Stanford: Stanford University Press.

Prentice, A., and M. Theobald, eds. 1991. *Women Who Taught: Perspectives on the History of Women and Teaching*. Toronto: University of Toronto Press. doi:10.3138/9781442683570.

Reynolds, C., and B. Young, eds. 1995. *Women and Educational Leadership in Canadian Education*. Calgary: Detselig.

Said, E. 1978. *Orientalism*. London: Penguin Press.

Shakeshaft, C. 1987. *Women in Educational Administration*. Beverly Hills, CA: Sage.

Side, K., and W. Robbins. 2007. "Institutionalizing Inequalities in Canadian Universities: The Canada Research Chairs Program." In *Special Issue: Women, Tenure, and Promotion. NWSA Journal* 19 (3): 163–81.

Smith, D. 1987. "Institutional Ethnography: A Feminist Research Strategy." In *The Everyday World as Problematic: A Feminist Sociology*, 151–79. Toronto, ON: University of Toronto Press.

– 2005. *Institutional Ethnography: A Sociology for People*. Walnut Creek, CA: Alta Mira Press.

Spivak, G.C. 2000. "Can the Subaltern Speak?" In *Postcolonialism: Critical Concepts*, ed. D. Brydon, 1427–77. London: Routledge.

Spurlin, W. 2010. "Resisting Heteronormativity/Resisting Recolonisation: Affective Bonds between Indigenous Women in Southern Africa and the Difference(s) of Postcolonial Feminist History." *Feminist Review* 95 (1): 10–26. doi:10.1057/fr.2009.56.

Tilly, C. 1998. *Durable Inequality*. Berkeley, CA: University of California Press.

Wallace, J. 2000. "En/Countering Resistance to Gender Equity in Educational Organizations." PhD diss., University of Toronto.

– 2004. "Learning to Lead: Women Administrators in Twentieth Century Ontario." *Oral History Forum/d'histoire orale* 24:87–106.

– 2005. "Assuming Leadership: Women Superintendents in 20th Century Ontario." In *History Is Hers: Women Teachers in Twentieth Century Ontario*, ed. R. Coulter and H. Harper, 137–60. Calgary: Detselig.

Wallace, J., and D. Wallin. 2015. "The Voice inside Herself: Transforming Gender Identities in Educational Administration." *Gender and Education* 27 (4): 412–29. doi:10.1080/09540253.2015.1019838.

Wallace, J., D. Wallin, M. Viczko, and H. Anderson. 2014. "The First Female Academics in Programs of Educational Administration in Canada: Riding waves of opportunity." *McGill Journal of Education* 49 (2): 437. http://mje.mcgill.ca/article/view/9016/6966 doi:10.7202/1029428ar.

5

Moths to the Flame Tend to Get Burned

Life on the Liminal

DAWN WALLIN

An old prairie saying I grew up with tells me that "Moths to the flame tend to get burned." As someone whose privilege provided me with an education that is often cloaked in a pompous presumption of "expertise" based on Euro-Canadian world views and credentialing, I can expound on how such sayings are riddled with Foucauldian (1995) understandings of the disciplinary society. However, as a rural woman whose life was highly engaged in experiential land-based learnings about the natural cycles of life, I cannot help but appreciate the organic simplicity of my elders' prophetic words. Even though my scholarship critiques the absence of women in Weber's (1978) work, and the discussion of women as heterosexist prizes in exchange for status in Mills's (2000) discussion of the power elite, these authors were trying to warn against a future of global ideological, economic, political, and militaristic convergence that we now call neo-liberalism (Blackmore 2006, 2013). Feminists the world over are resisting this neo-liberal structuring of society with rage, scholarship, and activism (Coulter 1996, 2007).

And yet, am I really a resistor? Or has my mindscape been shaped to crave the trappings of power and privilege that go along with formal leadership status? I enjoy administration, and I am fascinated with the study of educational leadership. I love using participatory and creative qualitative research and teaching methods, but I also get excited whenever I use an ANOVA to disentangle survey results. Have I become a co-opted conformist naively believing that my personal autonomy can make a difference within a dehumanizing system of power and privilege strategically designed to ensure the polity is rendered powerless?

One morning, I am a feminist raging against the policing of female bodies/sexuality reported in the *Winnipeg Free Press* (Giroday 2013) where school principals have banned leggings because they believe they are too revealing. That same afternoon, I am an acting department head policing attendance in the bachelor of education program with the potential to debar a woman who has chosen to attend her destination wedding rather than the administrative foundations of education course. Where does my feminism fit in this realm of educational administration? Perhaps I will forever be flirting within the liminal spaces of existence, not unlike a moth that is attracted to the flame – while at some point recognizing that to flirt with danger (note the sexualized connotations) means that I am likely to be burned. And yet, for Sinner (2012), liminal spaces "function as thresholds, transitions from one state to another, a space of ambiguity, a rite of passage, in which 'becoming' is a cultural shift where understood norms are disrupted and new cultural understandings and new social realities restructure identity and place (citing Cook-Sather 2006; Head 1992)" (603–4). What do women who profess to be feminist leaders make of their experiences? And who has the right to pin these beautiful creatures of light and darkness (second class to the butterflies but more courageous in their willingness to flirt with danger) to a cushion as specimens of examination?

This chapter is a personal narrative interspersed with findings from a study conducted by Dr Janice Wallace and me on the transformative experiences of the first female academics in educational administration programs in Canada. I acknowledge the complexities of women's experiences as educational leaders in systems dominated by hypermasculinized narratives that dehumanize and minimize the subjective experiences and positionalities found within each of us (Blackmore 2010). I consider how we move in and out of liminal spaces as we resist, yet are simultaneously embedded within the positions and institutions to which we commit. Regardless of our feminist "learnings, leadings and leanings," we fly into flames that we know are going to burn us. Sometimes we do so with purpose, strategy, and determination, while at other times we burn as we are distracted by whatever else is going on around us. Regardless of how it happens, feminist leaders emerge from the flames a bit scarred, somewhat disoriented, and forever changed. What is important is how women make sense out of those experiences and with what purpose they then move forward.

EMERGING FROM THE COCOON

Every woman in educational administration who calls herself a feminist has journeyed on a highly personal trajectory to her (re)clamation of feminist principles. Some have embraced feminism wholeheartedly based on early, direct life experiences with sexism. Others, like myself, were quite ambivalent about, or rejecting of, feminism as a consequence of unexamined privileges that facilitated our entry into leadership. For many women, there comes a time where we start to face resistance or differential treatment based as much on assumptions about women as about individual personality or work ethic. Without trying to homogenize sex or gender categories (Fitzgerald 2010), those assumptions can be held and enforced as deeply by women as they can be by men.

The rhetoric of enforced assumptions is couched in the appropriate professional language with a little bit of laughter to ease the sexism. Silencing brings with it attempts to shame so that redirection of behaviour can be accommodated. The attempts of female leaders to directly deal with such shenanigans are quickly sanctioned as career limiting moves (Wallace et al. 2014). I challenge any woman in an administrative position to suggest that she has not been subjected to a sexist comment or a sexual harassment event, has not been repeatedly (often through silence) compelled to assume the secretarial or homemaker tasks at meetings, has not been silenced by the group for something she said or did that was too aggressive or emotional, or has not had her ideas go unacknowledged but reified by a man who received credit for saying them. As one of our participants noted: "There is this classic case ... where we have a great idea and we speak it and the conversation goes on around us, and then 'Joe' says that and they are all electrified. I learned to say, 'Yes, I made that point five minutes ago. I hope you all realize that.' And then laugh, because ... when they're caught doing that, they know what has actually happened. But you have to tell them."

It is in the regularity and minutiae of these daily realities that we start to see the patterns of sexism running rampant in individual experience. Sexism is a "line of power/knowledge" (Foucault 1977) that has become embodied in our ways of being and knowing, and therefore often goes unrecognized. As Bell's (2012) description indicates, this line of power/knowledge holds us enraptured – almost like a moth to a flame: "whether and how a line of power/knowledge manages to form or reform a subject's sense of self depends on how it is able to capture her, to subtly hold her, to oblige her to organize her embodiment and, perhaps more accurately, her sense of inwardness, in accordance with its attentions. Without any recourse to a notion of ideological persuasion, this line of power becomes incorporated, embodied, or registered through arousal or sensation, be that conscious or unconscious, be it gratefully or ungratefully received" (109).

Because many of us do not want to see patterns of sexism in the institutions we support, we pretend they are the fault or failure of the individual rather than power/knowledge systems structuring the institutional patterns of leadership (Blackmore 2010). When these events happen to us, we may begin to internalize the possibility that there is fault or failure in ourselves. Rather than do this, as the "me too" response to sexual harassment and assault demonstrates very powerfully, we need to emerge from our cocoon of stupefaction and begin naming oppressive patterns for what they are (St Pierre 2000). Herein lies the first beacon toward the flames of danger for feminist leaders, because: "To call into question a regime of truth, where that regime of truth governs subjectivation, is to call into question the truth of myself and, indeed, to question my ability to tell the truth about myself, to give an account of myself" (Butler 2005, 27). Yet, it is only when we come to acknowledge power/knowledge systems that we can potentially resist and/or change them (St Pierre 2000).

In my case, "emerging from the cocoon" did not occur until after the completion of my dissertation. I was privileged to have Dr Beth Young as my external examiner, known as one of the first women to "write herself in" as a feminist "edadmin'er." I completed my entire PhD program not truly comprehending the significance of her contributions as a feminist scholar to educational administration in Canada. I look back on my dissertation with a sense of guilt for not doing more to turn my dissertation (focused on female rural leaders) into a truly feminist piece of work that could have had tremendous significance for female leaders. Rather, I resisted/minimized the feminist aspect of the work. My own privilege stopped me from seeing that my experience of early entry into educational administration in the K–12 public school system was not representative of all women's experiences and did not mean that gender equity was alive and well. My entry was as much due to my support of the reigning ideologies of the system as it was due to my abilities as a leader. And yet ... was my entry into educational administration all about access to privilege? How much was it about inherent personality characteristics? How much was it about accommodation to gender scripts? How complicit have I been in silencing or marginalizing others? These are difficult questions that feminist leaders lay awake at night pondering when they emerge from their cocoon.

Direct answers to these ambiguities are never forthcoming, but the fact that we ask them makes feminism important to our work. As Asher (2010) writes: "If I were simply to accept and shrug off philosophically my own implicatedness, then I would reduce myself to paying mere lip service toward the task of maintaining and strengthening integrity. Therefore, the most productive way for me to participate as a leader within the institutional context is actually to let myself be troubled by the dilemmas I encounter and work with each in a self-reflexive, recursive, rigorous way" (71). The ambiguity that develops when we trouble our leadership practice and become more self-reflexive "can be seen as a phenomenon that creates liminal, interstitial spaces, or indefinite spaces 'in between'... Ambiguity disrupts the social hierarchy by inhibiting the social 'sorting and grouping' that maintains the status quo and is therefore a critical site for social change and social justice" (Hudson 2012, 171). To that end, self-reflection on the ambiguities we sense in our embodied leadership experiences can become primary sites for social change.

In our research study, we asked ten of the first female academics in educational administration programs in Canada to describe their experiences within the academy and within their discipline. We learned that each woman's trajectory was unique, though some patterns could be discerned. Most of our participants entered these programs with backgrounds in non-traditional disciplinary areas such as music, curricula, adult education, and not-for-profit business. The majority of participants did not enter the academy directly out of school-based administration. These diverse pathways provided them with perspectives on educational administration and leadership that was not the norm, and led them to redefine and transform the masculinist, technocratic, and functionalist discourse of mainstream educational administration (Blackmore 2010; Wilkinson and Eacott 2013). As one woman suggested, "We've, in a way, written ourselves into being." Another woman noted that "It's like breaking down boundaries or crossing boundaries. It's like forcing the new vision into what is called educational administration." For these women, the text *Educational Administration: Theory, Research and Practice*, written by Hoy and Miskel (2012) – a predominant educational administration textbook at the time – was "a metaphor for mediocrity": "We all read Hoy and

Miskel, which was ... incorrect, it was simplistic, it was mind-numbing ... It had no critical content whatsoever, and that was the dominant lens through which most people ... were looking at educational admin. So quite a few of us [women] entered the field hoping to bring life to this because we were leaders of the school ... What is leadership? Let's redefine it."

One participant mentioned that many of the first women in educational administration programs entered at a time when universities were influenced by the women's movement and "there was a bit of a fashion for [feminism] at that point and I was a young-ish woman, you know. So, I was part of this, I was riding this wave, you know?" The influence of feminist theory and the recognition that the embodied experiences of female leaders were not represented in educational administration programs (Brady and Hammett 1999) provided these women with purpose as insiders–outsiders (Hill-Collins 1998). Wilkinson and Eacott (2013) cite Bourdieu (1977) when they suggest that insider–outsider positioning can develop into a "theory of crisis" in which "the habitus falls out of alignment with the field in which it operates, creating a situation in which belief in the game (illusio) is temporarily suspended and the orthodoxy of practice, or doxic assumptions, is raised to the level of discourse, where they can be contested" (200). The struggle for finding legitimacy in educational administration as a consequence of this contestation of the discourse became premised on a "misalignment by choice ... the desire to maintain intellectual autonomy and the choice to not conform" (200).

Though none of these women could be considered conformists, not all of them claimed to be feminists, even though their scholarship focused on equity issues. One woman suggested that she had not started her work in the academy with a feminist consciousness, even though she recognized herself as being unconventional. Others, however, claimed feminism from the moment they entered graduate studies. As one woman noted, "I wasn't quiet about being a feminist. I was very confrontational ... But we quickly got to be 'known,' which was a good and bad thing." Although faculty appointments were relatively plentiful at the time of their entry into educational administration programs, self-proclaimed feminists had difficulties finding positions: "I ended up being the only applicant, and one of my feminist colleagues was on the search committee and told me the guys on the committee tried to close the search down because they didn't want me, they didn't want a feminist ... within the department. And then to their credit, the women who were in the department ... actually came to my defence and said they did want a feminist."

Stories like these suggest that feminists were deliberately barred from positions in educational administration because of the threat they represented to an established, highly normative, patriarchal discipline (Hart 2006). Though these women had been successful graduate students with recognized individual abilities, their movement into academic positions was often contentious, and was supported by the political organization of male and female allies already in the academy.

TRYING OUR WINGS

After spending two years as a faculty member at the University of Texas–Pan American, I was offered a position at the University of Manitoba specializing in educational administration in 2003. That year, the Canadian Society for the Study of Education (CSSE) was held in Winnipeg. My journey with feminism began once I indicated that I would help co-chair the Canadian Association for the Study of Women in Education (CASWE) Institute. I worked with a colleague on a program that celebrated CASWE's tenth anniversary with the theme of "Sexism in the Academy: 10 Years Later." The Institute focused on the legal challenge to the inequitable, sex-based distribution of Canada Research Chairs. I was initially taken aback when I was "reminded" that I needed to think about my tenure and promotion while I was organizing an event with this theme. That same year, I became president-elect of CASWE. I was "rewarded" in my scholarly ambitions with a leadership position focused directly on feminist issues, while at the same time being cautioned about potential repercussions on tenure and promotion. My situation paralleled Asher's (2010) assertion that "Women academics, being implicated in the very structures and processes they are attempting to transform, encounter catch-22s or contradictions as they participate in leadership work" (64).

The potential repercussions of their academic activities on tenure and promotion is not a risk that women should consider lightly. One participant in our study spent time as a faculty representative supporting untenured women who found themselves in precarious positions: "I saw the vicious position between a tenured position and an untenured position, and I walked that walk with about three women and I know I was able to help out. One case we didn't win ... there seemed to be things coming up all the time with untenured women and it was not pleasant that way." The paradoxes between the promotion of equity in scholarship/practice and the potential repercussions of institutional practice when that scholarship threatens the embedded privileges of the system are very real, and not all of them lead to successful resolutions.

My research pursuits coalesce around issues of gender equity, career patterns in administration, and rural education. I quite intentionally found safe spaces of acceptance for my work because gendered topics were not part of the "regular" program in educational administration circles. Gender issue papers went to the CASWE and the social justice special interest group at the American Educational Research Association (AERA); rural education papers went to the Canadian Association for the Study of Educational Administration (CASEA), the National Congress on Rural Education, or the rural education special interest group of AERA; and leadership papers went to CASEA, the University Council for Educational Administration (UCEA) or Division A (Leadership) in AERA. I do not believe my experience is unique. One of the participants in our study, for example, described her similar experience: "We were going to conferences together, [another female scholar] and I, and we were meeting up with many of you. And we didn't exist as far as many of those people ... By that time, all of us were writing in our own other fields and we were publishing in our own other fields, but we weren't in existence in Ed Admin ... I got more play when I went to Europe as someone doing something interesting. I got more play at AERA as someone cutting edge."

At the level of praxis, I was fortunate to work in a province where the provincial leadership groups, the provincial government, and faculty members had close working relationships. Some might say I contributed more to Manitoba's education system in the areas of rural education and administration/leadership than I did on gender issues. Or at least that is what one might assume if success is presumed to be that which is more publicly recognized. As many of the participants in our study attested, however, while gender work is "quiet work," it is work that has the potential to revolutionize individuals. This work can lead to what Oliver (2004) calls a psychic revolt that "can take place in the everyday lives of ordinary people who resist domination" (35), thereby becoming a liminal space of resistance. I may have had more invited addresses, school division presentations, and requested research papers based on my rural and administrative work, but I have engaged in hundreds more conversations with female (and to a lesser extent male) students, school and system leaders, and academics who have found something in my gender work that resonates with their personal experience. Sadly, these individuals tend to initiate conversations in covert settings: in the dark corners of a school building where no one else can see or hear us; in the washrooms after a presentation where they feel compelled to share with me a quick story; over drinks at a conference; or in an email that pours out the pain of betrayal. Where am I making the most difference? Is it in the systems change that some of my work can offer for large numbers of faceless individuals, or is it in the personal transformation of an individual who will teach and lead differently as a consequence of their deeper understanding of power and privilege?

Our academic institutions have increasingly made it their business to decide which aspects of our work are more important. Collegial governance of the academy is being usurped by the corporatization of higher education. Performativity has infiltrated into every aspect of academic life (Ball 2003; Blackmore 2004; Wilson and Holligan 2013), shaping the mindsets of those responsible for the "measurable success" of the institution's ability to increase the GDP. One of our participants discussed this growing trend using the example of impact measurement: "At our university, we are arguing about what are the impact measures and how do you quantify and how at tenure review, where there's supposed to be evidence of impact, what do you use ... So surely if your work changed the work of 1000 classroom teachers who then changed the work of 10,000 or more students, isn't that more impact than having citation in the *McGill Journal of Education*? ... When [students] sat me down and said, 'We never told you this, but you changed our lives.' That, I put in my heart. That is worth everything to me. That, to me, is my impact." Asher (2010) writes that "the leadership work of academic women – and especially women of colour – is often devalued in the corporatized, masculinist culture of the academy, in which economic rationality and the ability to make hard decisions are associated with maleness" (2010, 63). It is partly for this reason that some of the women in our study deliberately chose not to become administrators, even though they were presented with opportunities to lead: "Especially as we moved into a corporate university, I had nothing but disgust for that whole model. So, my choice, very consciously, was to *do* the educational administration theory. Be the kind of leader I was talking about ... I had such distaste for those other things that I would have had to do. And I could see that those would have to be done in an administrative position. You can change some things, but you are walking a line ... that kind of line that muzzles a person." Her words echo those of Blackmore (2004) who suggested that performativity "produces increased compliance not creativity, increased use of silencing through authority rather than persuasion and critical dialogue, increased dependence on leaders rather than professional activism, and a lack of trust" (454).

Although the participants of our study critiqued the growing emphasis on performativity, many of the women in our study took on administrative roles in the hopes of opening up avenues for change. They spoke honestly about the realities of their efforts and ability to effect long-term institutional change. One participant noted: "I've become much less naïve about my own ability to change the world, and I'm much more likely to think that if you're in a position of leadership, what that's good for is trying to mitigate harm during the period when you're in leadership and that's it. I don't think it's appropriate to look for durability as some sort of an indicator of whether I did a good job or I didn't do a good job. It's too harsh an environment to really expect that … It's much bigger than you and me." In her view, administrators can effect change for a certain amount of time, for certain initiatives, while they remain in leadership positions.

Even with all the gains women have made in the academy, our participants noted that status, power, and ideology remain shaped primarily by hypermasculine ideals. More males are hired overall into senior positions and as Canada Research Chairs, and with higher salaries than women. In one woman's view, "the domination by men and by masculine values and points of view is still very much a part of Ed Admin, of the department, of [Faculty], of the University." In the face of this awareness, women recognized that it was important for them to find niches of support with like-minded colleagues so that they could create opportunities to influence the construction of knowledge itself.

FINDING THE ECLIPSE

Although faculty members tend to be independent, very few of us hope to be isolated as scholars, teachers, colleagues, and human beings. Yet we typically work in institutions where there are limited numbers of scholars who work in our niche areas, even though we are connected to large disciplines such as educational administration. In my case, the few scholars in Canada who work on issues of rural education and/or gender issues in leadership were not employed at the University of Manitoba. Although I engaged in many good conversations with colleagues who work in other areas of administration and leadership, I had to find colleagues passionate about rural education and gender elsewhere.

Practical realities such as these can be compounded for feminists who are trying to resist local hegemonic practice and to advocate for social transformation. They can quickly find themselves in "interstitial locations" on the margins of the academy. Although these spaces can appear isolative, Fitzgerald (2010) suggests that it is in these spaces-in-between where individuals can move beyond dichotomous understandings of self and other in a way that "offers the disruption and displacement of hegemonic theories" (103). Asher (2010) cites Lowe (1996) who recommends that individuals "build alliances with other groups on the margins and engage in internal critical dialogues among their communities to interrogate the multiplicities, hybridities, and contradictions encountered within and without the academy" (72).

In my case, I found myself building allied relationships with (primarily female) Indigenous colleagues and/or administrators whose efforts to disrupt the impacts of colonialism on Indigenous peoples, women, and learners were a constant challenge. My most meaningful professional and personal relationship to date was found in my friendship with Dr Sherry Peden. Sherry's critical Indigenous worldview constantly challenges my own assumptions about knowledge, feminism, the academy, and myself. In the space in between our two worldviews, we have found an affirmation of our vision for a more equitable future, and an allied desire to effect transformative change in the area of Indigenous educational leadership.

As a means of building initial alliances with others, some of the women in our study found support with female colleagues in other departments who overtly politicized the need to hire female scholars in educational administration programs. Many women used their writing as a third space (Bhabha 1994) that provided them opportunities to connect to others and find release for personal anxieties. As more of these women became administrators with influence, they used their positional locations "to hire people who did not represent the status quo. We did bring social justice into Ed Admin, by not only our own work but by the people that we hired." These women deliberately facilitated the entry of diverse perspectives into educational administration programs in order to avoid homosociability (Blackmore 2010), to bridge interdisciplinary boundaries, and to create interstitial locations for coalition building.

All of our participants spoke about the value of finding like-minded scholars in international or national scholarly associations who helped to create liminal spaces of support: "Life within the department could be very difficult. And that could be because I was outspoken ... and it was very difficult. What I think kept me going, not just the support of individuals, but also, was the existence of CSSE and ... the people within CASEA and CASWE, with whom I had things in common. And I mean really that made all the difference in those early days." As outsiders within educational administration (Hill-Collins 1998; Wilkinson and Eacott 2013), these women supported each other in a variety of ways, such as ensuring they attended each other's sessions and forwarding each other for association awards. This mutual support was not conducted for the purpose of prestige, but was undertaken to ensure that female Canadian scholars and their contributions to knowledge could not be dismissed: "We can all be dismissed by some people. But together it's a little harder to dismiss us. The more of us that win the awards and recognitions, the harder it is to dismiss. The more writing that we do, it's harder to dismiss. It isn't that we want to be the centre of attention, it's that the agendas that are being put forward are also being dismissed. When we can't be dismissed so easily, neither can the agenda be dismissed." CASWE was the association mentioned most fondly. This association was designed for the express purpose of bringing women together from multiple disciplines to discuss feminist issues that were not being taken up in other associations, and to create networks for feminists across Canada. CASWE became a powerful vehicle for transformative possibilities, and a sanctuary for women who needed a venue for sharing their experiences.

Many of our participants developed their relationships with each other as a consequence of feeling alienated from CASEA. Blackmore and Sachs (2000) noted that female academics often struggle with a sense of ambivalence toward their place in the academy when they are positioned on the margins. Our participants told many stories of being ostracized from the mainstream discourse of educational administration in Canada and the "club" that was CASEA. These experiences are detailed more fully in the next section. Although this group of women was highly critical of CASEA, they all maintained some kind of connection to the association. One woman spoke of the role that CASEA members had played in helping her develop scholarship and career networks across Canada. Another suggested that her presence at CASEA was "a way of giving. I always took students. It was a way of nurturing. And it was connecting us ... It was to take students, mentor them, introduce them, kind of give back to that field." A third woman spoke of the importance of CASEA in keeping her connected to Canadian scholarly friends: "I go to CASEA because I love the people ... Every year it's like meeting my friends and learning what's going on in their lives, scholarly lives. And what's going on in Canada in the field."

As this section indicates, women in educational administration programs have been placed within, but have also created and claimed, liminal spaces in which they were able to create alliances and challenge hegemony. They demonstrated through their writing and leadership "substantive and normative alternatives to how we theorize and practice leadership" (Blackmore 2013, 139). However, their work in these spaces was infused with personal risk for themselves and for their careers.

FLIRTING WITH DANGER

With time, tenure, and experience, I have more luxury to "safely trouble" my place and space in life, and I recognize the privilege, paradox, and responsibility this incurs. I have averted the groping of powerful men and remained silent, because I knew that speaking out could negatively affect my career. I have supported and blocked women in their bids to obtain leadership positions. I have deliberately positioned myself within competitive structures in the academy even though I critique those structures in my scholarship. I jumped at the opportunity to work as a junior faculty member on a book with internationally renowned scholars/friends, but I now live with the personal and professional recriminations that accrue because one of those scholars/friends pled guilty to crimes against women and children. How do I come to terms with all of these tensions as someone who claims the label of feminist?

I am not the proverbial "angry feminist," although I believe that people have the right to rage at abuses of power. If I were an angry feminist, I would be eaten alive with anger at myself. I am neither victim nor heroine, but on occasion have been both. Like all human beings, I am oppressor and oppressed, and a product of my natural personality and (sometimes unnatural) socialization. I am acted upon, but I also act, and I have the agency to transform myself, and maybe the world, in liminal moments. We are all performers in our own social worlds, and as Lander (2001) notes, "Just as the theatrical rehearsal and performance of everyday work life can reproduce and naturalize gendered identities, this theatricality can also perform the resistance that goes into crafting masculine-feminine selves within the cultural and historical matrices of power" (64). Each of us is a writhing mass of contradictions living lives of paradox.

In her discussion of what it means to engage in social critique, Culbertson (2013) suggests that individuals must be willing to question themselves as well as others: "Though we are never free of presuppositions, we must nevertheless step back from the frameworks that provide the character of self-evidence to our desires, beliefs, and pursuits. And this involves at times, not just a willingness to question who one is oneself, but who others are – to question our deepest normative commitments, where our decisions and desires are not just our own" (462). The participants in our research project regularly questioned themselves and the dominant hegemony reigning in the practices and ideologies of educational administration. They also learned quickly that they assumed much risk as a consequence. As one woman admitted, "We can't use the word risk unless there was the chance of failure. Otherwise it's not risk. And I think we're in a risk position often."

Women who questioned the discourse of educational administration faced bitter personal recrimination: "I can't imagine, you know, what it cost to be an outspoken woman. To raise any kind of feminist concern and to be patronized and dismissed and belittled and, you know, even have people angry with [me] ... It was bad, it was not good in my day." One woman was told by a male colleague that an outspoken graduate student would "never get a job in academia because she was too passionate." Both of these examples suggest that attempts were made to ensure that female academics in educational administration were "individuals who are contained" (Martin 2000, cited in Hart 2006): "Women are not outsiders, evidenced by their increasing presence. Yet, their voices, and particularly feminist voices, are silenced to such a degree that the patriarchal culture is replicated rather than transformed. Thus, traditional disciplinary scholarly outlets remain consistent over time with regard to the inclusion of feminist voices and theoretical influences" (Hart 2006, 50).

This attempt to contain was exemplified in our research discussions about a paper that was given at CASEA in the 1990s. The male presenter, a well-known scholar from a large university, expressed concern in his paper that a feminist scholar had been hired for a faculty position for which one of his students, whose professional background and scholarship were more acceptable among traditional scholars in educational administration, had applied and been interviewed. The paper caused quite a stir among the membership: One of the study participants who attended the presentation noted, "It was about the kinds of people who were getting hired and were talking about things that had nothing to do with educational administration. It was wrong. [The paper presenter claimed that, by hiring such a person,] 'We weren't serving the profession [in hiring a feminist scholar over one with a bureaucratic background]'. [After the paper was presented, the participant left the room] [a]nd there was a huge big congregation out in the hall ... I came down this hallway and there was this big group of women just frustrated and outraged."[1] Given the very small world of departments of educational administration in Canada, the CASEA membership who attended the presentation and/or participated in the subsequent discussion, were able to easily identify the unnamed female and male scholar alluded to in the paper. As the study participants discussed this anecdote, they expressed a determination that, despite resistance, their contributions be accepted and valued rather than dismissed. They noted that female scholars began to "write themselves into existence" despite the difficulties experienced by "women from across Canada [...] trying to live in the same kind of chilly climate in various Ed Admin departments across the country, [who] were trying to change the discipline." As these women became prolific and their work was recognized internationally, the discourse of educational administration began to reflect a more diverse perspective. Some of the personal risk to female academics lessened because resisters "couldn't ignore the fact that my scholarship was published and recognized. And so, it was a way of writing myself into being, even as an Ed Admin colleague."

Some of the risks that female leaders faced are part of the inherent nature of feminism that advocates for relationality, or of the socialization of women to be caretakers, or both. Blackmore (2004) found in her work with school and academic leaders that a tension exists between care for others and care for self. Many of the leaders in our study spoke of the pressure they faced because of the need to be available: "For a long time, I succumbed to that pressure as a woman that you want to be emotionally available, physically there, you ought to be using your skills ... But all of that makes me very, very tired ... I've had a realization that I have to take care of me, nobody else is going to be taking care of me ... By the end of the day, when I'm supposed to go to the Senate meeting and be there for them, I'm totally exhausted because I've been carrying all day their troubles on my shoulders ... and I haven't been taking care of me."

Another theme that caused concern in the focus group discussion was the "quietness" with which women in the group discussed their engagement in risky work: "Despite our moxie and our grit, we, too, know that what's really expected of us in some ways is silence. I love how someone said, it's quiet work. That many of us not only have done a lot of quiet work but we have an expectation on us to continue to do quiet work. And to be quiet about it." One participant discussed how acquiescing to silencing affected her personal wellness "because you may not realize how much anger you are suppressing ... I don't think I've sold out but I have that internal churning of my stomach. Ought I have let out my righteous anger?"

Participants talked about their growing weariness, the stresses of this work, and "the tiredness of dealing with this, with the problems ... the lengths of time we spend in this particular kind of battle." The exhaustion and differential experiences did not end when they became senior faculty: "Nobody shouted at the senior guys about what all they had to do." Women alluded to the physical and spiritual exhaustion that could take hold when they saw resurging resistance to feminist efforts in educational administration. It was particularly hard when the resistance was initiated by women whose gains in leadership could be at least partially attributed to the earlier women's work. It was often difficult for them to reconcile that later generation women did not value the purpose of feminism in the same way, if at all: "They had these full-blown careers going on and they had families and they sometimes had supportive husbands. So there was a real shift but it was certainly not a real feminist consciousness and they certainly wouldn't want to have anything to do with being associated with that. Yet, of course, they had taken on a lot of this stuff and they had the opportunities that we had worked for women to have. And so that was pleasing and puzzling at the same time."

As a second example, one woman mentioned being the adviser of a graduate student who had claimed herself a feminist, but who ignored her adviser's advice and instead took the advice of a male colleague that wound up putting her into a compromising, career limiting situation. Though the student stated that she "didn't know why she had done it," our participant suggested, "Of course, we all know why she did it. You don't shed a lifetime of living in a paternalistic world right away ... But, it's very painful when that happens."

A third woman described a situation in which she knew that a younger female colleague was going to be compromised by a female department head in ways that would damage future career opportunities. The young woman had no idea that it was entirely possible that the female department head could act paternalistically toward other women. Our participant was caught between the boundaries of her administrative role, her own feminist principles, and her knowledge that if she did speak out, she was potentially putting the younger female in jeopardy: "I can't just go into the committee and say, 'Hey, everybody, she's being shafted' ... when I have the Dean's hat on and I'm chairing the committee ... I guess I can but I would hurt her more ... The risks that I have the hardest time [with] are when I'm risking somebody else. The personal risk that I'm taking, that I'm going to pay the price of, I can handle that. This is a risk on her behalf that I would have to take. And if it doesn't go well, she will bear the brunt."

In response to this comment, a participant observed that the balancing act female leaders play between their administrative role and their own individuality is "an important aspect to being a leader in less than warm and fuzzy places. It's very much about how I balance being myself, holding my values, thinking about how best to do that short-term and long-term. How to speak through another persona." It is not easy for a feminist to remain true to her ideals when she assumes a prescribed role in an institution premised on corporate agendas and hypermasculine ideals. Barad (2007) describes the tension that arises between the relevance and the ethics of responsibility for each action performed, and each decision made that will affect future possibilities: "The boundaries we articulate and the exclusions that we thereby perform are simultaneously ones about relevance and about ethics; since many different possibilities for (intra-)acting exist at every moment ... these changing possibilities entail an ethical obligation to intra-act responsibly in the world's becoming" (Barad 2007, 178, cited in Bell 2012, 117). For female academics, Asher (2010) suggests that "grappling rigorously with the nuances and complexities I encounter is difficult and demanding because it pushes me to arrive at integrity between theory, lived experience, practice (be it leadership or teaching), and scholarly writing" (64). Yet, that is exactly what is required of women who believe that academic institutions need a voice for equity and change.

Although they worked toward this change, one woman suggested that female leaders have to come to terms with their limited ability to individually control and predict the outcomes of their actions. A second woman acknowledged that she had learned the hard way not to take things too personally, particularly when heated emotions were involved. A third woman admitted that hurt can bottle up when resistance feels like a personal betrayal: "I don't know that the generation of women that I'm working with right now, I don't know that they are aware of this invisible underbelly. I don't know if they're aware of some of the consequences of their actions when they buy in, when they sell out. What that does to the women who were not selling out, the ones who are speaking out. And how it just completely takes your breath away and it hurts."

As Blackmore (2013) suggests, "Recognizing the emotional management work of leadership is not merely being sensitive to others' feelings or exploiting passion, but requires recognition of one's own emotions and how they are displayed and perceived, as well as being aware of the emotional economy of the organization so critical to a sense of well-being and trust upon which leadership is premised" (147). The participants in our study discussed the emotional labour of their work, and that they had learned to control how they (re)presented those emotions to others. The danger is that sensitivity to these concerns can feed into a Foucauldian sense of governmentality as women learn to self-regulate emotions and manage their presentation of self (Tyler and Cohen 2010) under the "gaze" of the institution. Emotional work is also exhausting, particularly when people begin to question their efficacy. Sachs and Blackmore (1998) examine a growing collective or individual sense of disenchantment or disengagement that can develop as individuals start to question their ability to effect change. In their research, they noted "a wider shift in the emotional or psychic economy toward greater introspection and negativity, rather than a sense that education is a force for social justice" (455).

Although these women acknowledged moments when they questioned their individual efficacy, they were adamant in their belief that the risky work of feminist leadership was indeed an important force for social change. Each woman suggested that their collective efforts have transformed the knowledge base and institutional practices of educational administration over time, and have been worth the trials and tribulations each person may have individually faced.

SINGED WITH PURPOSE

The women of our study were singed with a purpose to promote equity of one sort or another from the beginning of their careers. One woman suggested that the feminist movement brought women together in a collective purpose to challenge the knowledge base of educational administration: "The feminist movement was starting to really jar a lot of disciplines ... We knew there were people in the United States, we knew there were people in Australia, we knew there were people in New Zealand, so we began to get those of us who were doing this kind of work together, thinking we really could make an impact, we really could challenge the discipline of Ed Admin."

This collective purpose became a personal obligation for participants that placed additional expectations on their work as female scholars: "I became a bit of a lightning rod for women and gender and feminist stuff around here ... There were women who expected me to step up and defend them in whatever situation or speak up about a situation. And I did some of that, certainly. I mean, that is an obligation ... This was another of these kinds of layered expectations or, doubling the expectations on someone." These women also enacted their power unabashedly to make institutions more equitable for women and others (Shields 2005). Their "moxie" reared its head regularly in conversations when they talked about working for equity: "Somebody has to be on people's backs to make this place more accommodating and it's not just in the classroom, it's not just in the bathrooms, it's not just walking in the building. It's way more than that, and that's a whole area that I could probably work on until I die and it will never, never be addressed properly." They also came to see their identities as scholars and private individuals coalescing into their overarching human purpose: "I don't see my life as compartmentalized. I see it as everything as being interactive and interconnected. I don't think of it as, this is work, this is writing, this is scholarship, or this is private ... It's just that it's all integrated and ... it sort of takes over. But it's more than that. It's that it's an interconnected whole." One woman mentioned that her life and work "has been all about emerging, groundedness, rootedness, but also about multiplicity." This coincides with what she believes to be her purpose as a social historian and feminist: "I'm trying to help people see some things that are hard to see. And often you can't show them something totally visible as you are doing that work with them because it isn't fully formed yet. And so, what you are doing is challenging them to have things like faith, hope, optimism, all of which are very hard to formulate and to prove. But they are, what I've tried to do [in] my work, they are insights, they are impactful moments. They are the ah-hahs that push us forward." These women learned to believe in themselves as leaders via their lived experiences, and they capitalized on those experiences as learning opportunities that could help them improve their future efforts. They demonstrated grit and moxie, and they persevered with purpose regardless of the struggle.

CONCLUSION

What do these women's experiences teach us about life in liminal spaces for feminist leaders in educational administration? They teach us that feminist leadership is a complex balance between one's own principles and institutional expectations. They teach us that caring for others and advancing equity agendas have the potential to deeply affect personal wellness. They teach us that isolation is common and self-doubt regarding one's efficacy to promote change continues to follow even those who have achieved international renown: "I know how to do this stuff with my eyes closed and one hand tied behind my back. There are still ways in which I feel like I still need to prove myself ... gender dynamics are alive and well ... It's a bit lonesome ... How much of it is just endemic to the larger academic world, and how much of it seems to be about where you started out, which is to say, this has been a male field." The experiences of these women teach us that gaining ground for equity is a never-ending battle that morphs into new territories with new means of resistance. With that constant struggle can come physical and spiritual exhaustion, particularly when that resistance stems from other women who have benefited from feminist efforts.

Life in a liminal space carries with it risk, but it also creates opportunities for alliance building and for challenging hegemony. The women of our study recognized their own embeddedness in the discourses and practices of educational administration, yet they continually worked to open up liminal spaces where alternate discourses and practices were possible. Their sense of purpose became that of a calling. As one woman noted, "It was very tough for me to come to sense that really ... I had no alternative. The work had, by then, chosen me, and so there certainly was no going back once I got in." They gained their strength in finding like-minded colleagues and creating and engaging in scholarly associations that supported their work. As they explained, they wrote themselves into being and, in doing so, transformed the nature of scholarship in educational administration, creating space for others to consider leadership from a variety of diverse perspectives. Their actions as leaders transformed what departments of educational administration looked like, studied, and did.

Their experiences reinforce the ideas presented by St Pierre (2000) who proclaims that, "though they are regulated and inscribed by discourse and cultural practice, subjects can resist those normalizing inscriptions and their material effects by moving from a discourse where only certain statements can be made to another where different statements are possible" (503). These women mentioned the unmentionable in the discourses and practices of educational administration, and they refused to be silenced. They flew into the flames and emerged scarred, but strengthened with purpose. As one woman noted, "I do know that I will get out the other side, and I will have some bruises and bumps, and I will learn. And I will be better able to handle the next time."

These women have taught us that "the feminist gaze needs to refocus on the wider gender restructuring of the social, political and economic in ways that they produce patterns of inequality that position women leaders and teachers in particular ways that limit or enable their leadership practices in specific contexts" (Mabokela 2007; Blackmore 2013, 149). In addition to their public efforts, the "quiet work" of these women has probably done more to advance feminist principles than they will ever know. Resistance to hegemony and social transformation has been fostered in the liminal moments of conversations they have had with other female scholars, with graduate students, with new colleagues, and in their continual role modelling for equity and change. It is time for the rest of us to acknowledge and thank them for their efforts. And it is time for us to put Kevlar suits on the wings we have achieved because of their efforts, strap on fire extinguishers, and fly toward the flames.

NOTE

1 In order to clarify the meaning and context, more detail has been added to the quote to assist the reader. The meaning remains the same.

REFERENCES

Asher, N. 2010. "How Does the Postcolonial, Feminist Academic Lead? A Perspective from the US South." *International Journal of Leadership in Education: Theory and Practice* 13 (1): 63–76. doi:10.1080/13603120903242915.

Ball, S. 2003. "The Teacher's Soul and the Terrors of Performativity." *Journal of Education Policy* 18 (2): 215–28. doi:10.1080/0268093022000043065.

Barad, K. 2007. *Meeting the Universe Halfway: Quantum Physics and the Entanglement of Matter and Meaning*. Durham: Duke University Press. doi:10.1215/9780822388128.

Bell, V. 2012. "Declining Performativity: Butler, Whitehead and Ecologies of Concern." *Theory, Culture & Society* 29 (2): 107–23. doi:10.1177/0263276412438413.

Bhabha, H. 1994. *The Location of Culture*. London: Routledge.

Blackmore, J. 2004. "Leading as Emotional Management Work in High Risk Times: The Counterintuitive Impulses of Performativity and Passion." *School Leadership & Management* 24 (4): 439–59. doi:10.1080/13632430410001316534.

– 2006. "Deconstructing Diversity Discourses in the Field of Educational Management and Leadership." *Educational Management Administration & Leadership* 34 (2): 181–99. doi:10.1177/1741143206062492.

– 2010. "'The Other Within': Race/Gender Disruptions to the Professional Learning of White Educational Leaders." *International Journal of Leadership in Education* 13 (1): 45–61. doi:10.1080/13603120903242931.

– 2013. "A Feminist Critical Perspective on Educational Leadership." *International Journal of Leadership Education: Theory and Practice* 16 (2): 139–54. doi:10.1080/13603124.2012.754057.

Blackmore, J., and J. Sachs. 2000. "Paradoxes of Leadership and Management in Higher Education in Times of Change: Some Australian Reflections." *International Journal of Leadership in Education* 3 (1): 1–16. doi:10.1080/136031200292830.

Bourdieu, P. 1977. *Outline of a Theory of Practice*. Trans. R. Nice. Cambridge, UK: Cambridge University Press. [Originally published as *Esquisse d'une theorie de la pratique, précédé de trios études d'ethnologie kabyle* (Switzerland: Libraire Droz S.A., 1972).] doi:10.1017/CBO9780511812507.

Brady, J.E., and R.E. Hammett. 1999. "Reconceptualizing Leadership from a Feminist Postmodern Perspective." *Review of Education, Pedagogy & Cultural Studies* 21 (1, July): 41–61. doi:10.1080/1071441990210104.

Butler, J. 2005. *Giving an Account of Oneself*. New York: Fordham University Press. doi:10.5422/fso/9780823225033.001.0001.

Coulter, R. 1996. "Gender Equity and Schooling: Linking Research and Policy." *Canadian Journal of Education* 21 (4): 433–52. doi:10.2307/1494895.

– 2007. "Gender Equality Policy in Canadian Schooling." In *Gender and Education: An Encyclopedia* 2, ed. B. Bank, 747–54. New York: Greenwood.

Culbertson, C. 2013. "The Ethics of Relationality: Judith Butler and Social Critique." *Continental Philosophy Review* 46 (3): 449–63. doi:10.1007/s11007-013-9271-z.

Fitzgerald, T. 2010. "Spaces In-Between: Indigenous Women Leaders Speak Back to Dominant Discourses and Practices in Educational Leadership." *International Journal of Leadership in Education: Theory and Practice* 13 (1): 93–105. doi:10.1080/13603120903242923.

Foucault, M. 1977. *Discipline and Punish*. Harmondsworth: Penguin.

– 1995. *Discipline and Punish: The Birth of the Prison*. Trans. A. Sheridan. New York, NY: Random House. Original work published 1975.

Giroday, G. 2013. "Leggings Off-Limits in St. B. High School: Form-Fitting Tights Don't Make the Grade." *Winnipeg Free Press*, 31 January, A2. http://www.winnipegfreepress.com/local/leggings-off-limits-in-st-b-high-school-189157771.html.

Hart, J. 2006. "Women and Feminism in Higher Education Scholarship: An Analysis of Three Core Journals." *Journal of Higher Education* 77 (1): 40–61. doi:10.1080/00221546.2006.11778918.

Hill-Collins, P. 1998. *Fighting Words: Black Women and the Search for Justice*. Minneapolis: University of Minnesota Press.

Hoy, W.K., and C.G. Miskel. 2012. *Educational Administration: Theory, Research and Practice*. 9th ed. Boston: McGraw-Hill.

Hudson, K.D. 2012. "Bordering Community: Reclaiming Ambiguity as a Transgressive Landscape of Knowledge." *Journal of Women and Social Work* 27 (2): 167–79. doi:10.1177/0886109912443957.

Lander, D.A. 2001. "Re-Casting Shakespeare: Gendered Performances and Performativity of Leadership." *Studies in Cultures, Organizations and Societies* 7 (1): 55–79. doi:10.1080/10245280108523552.

Mabokela, R. 2007. *Soaring beyond Boundaries: Women Breaking Educational Barriers in Traditional Societies*. Rotterdam: Sense.

Martin, J.R. 2000. *Coming of Age in Academe: Rekindling Women's Hopes and Reforming the Academy*. New York: Routledge.

Mills, C.W. 2000. *The Power Elite*. New York, NY: Oxford University Press. Original work published 1956.

Oliver, K. 2004. *The Colonization of Psychic Space: A Psychoanalytic Social Theory of Oppression*. Minneapolis, MN: University of Minnesota.

Sachs, J., and J. Blackmore. 1998. "You Never Show You Can't Cope: Women in School Leadership Roles Managing Their Emotions." *Gender and Education* 10 (3): 265–79. doi:10.1080/09540259820899.

Shields, C. 2005. "Hopscotch, Jump-Rope, or Boxing: Understanding Power in Educational Leadership." *International Studies in Educational Administration* 33 (2): 76–85.

Sinner, A. 2012. "Transitioning to Teacher: Uncertainty as a Game of Dramatic Hats." *Teachers and Teaching* 18 (5): 601–13. doi:10.1080/13540602.2012.709734.

St Pierre, E.A. 2000. "Poststructural Feminism in Education: An Overview." *International Journal of Qualitative Studies in Education: QSE* 13 (5): 477–515. doi:10.1080/09518390050156422.

Tyler, M., and L. Cohen. 2010. "Spaces That Matter: Gender Performativity and Organizational Space." *Organization Studies* 31 (2): 175–98. doi:10.1177/0170840609357381.

Wallace, J., D. Wallin, M. Viczko and H. Anderson. 2014. "The First Female Academics in Programs of Educational Administration in Canada: Riding Waves of Opportunity." *McGill Journal of Education* 49 (2): 437–58. doi:10.7202/1029428ar.

Weber, M. 1978. *Economy and Society: An Outline of Interpretive Sociology*. Ed. G. Roth and C. Wittich. Los Angeles: University of California Press. Original work published 1956.

Wilkinson, J., and S. Eacott. 2013. "'Outsiders Within'? Deconstructing the Educational Administration Scholar." *International Journal of Leadership in Education: Theory and Practice* 16 (2): 191–204. doi:10.1080/13603124.2012.750762.

Wilson, M., and C. Holligan. 2013. "Performativity, Work-Related Emotions and Collective Research Identities in UK University Education Departments: An Exploratory Study." *Cambridge Journal of Education* 43 (2): 223–41. doi:10.1080/0305764X.2013.774321.

6

Performing Boundaries

Feminism Entanglements in Educational Administration

MELODY VICZKO

And really, what I think is coming out here is the way we have incorporated the idea of educational administration, but not as we received it. We've made it something else that we've taken on ... So we've, in a way, written ourselves into being.

Participant

It is difficult to make the case that feminism has been taken up in a substantial way in the field of educational administration. While there has been an increase of female faculty in the Canadian departments of educational administration and a dent made in the large body of scholarship in the field focused on female leaders and administrators, the ways in which the field itself has changed through the engagement of feminist scholarship are difficult to assess. For example, while the increasing enrolment of female students and faculty members is creating a greater demand for the inclusion of the diversity of women's experiences, there is uncertainty about how this has influenced our knowledge in the field. In 1994, Young argued that, while the opening of educational administration as a focus of study in Canadian universities was an important historical moment, urgency for understanding gender issues was not acknowledged as important in the field (Young 1994). Although the weaving of issues of equity, social justice, and difference into educational administration is possible through interactions with feminism (Shakeshaft et al. 2007), reviews of scholarship in educational administration suggest that little research draws upon feminist theory (Blackmore 1996) and that female leaders themselves are ambivalent toward feminism (Blackmore and Sachs 2007). More recently, Blackmore (2013), almost twenty years after Young's argument, suggested that so much focus has been given to the numbers of women in educational leadership that the depoliticizing and decontextualizing of leadership has rendered feminist research domesticated. Such conditions may lead to a proclamation of the failure of feminism to make a tangible difference in the research and scholarship in educational administration. If feminism remains hidden, how can we legitimate its power in shaping the practices and knowledges of educational administration? It is this question, I suggest, that disturbs our claims of what we know about the influences of feminism in contemporary educational fields.

My purpose in this chapter is to consider the *entanglements* of feminism in education. Tor Hernes (2008) discusses the appeal of the word *tangled* to understand complexity: the word "conveys an imagery illustrative of how processes may be both distinguishable and indistinguishable ... It is descriptive of how a shape is temporarily formed while at the same time it is unformed" (xv). The word tangled connotes that the boundaries that define a shape will shift as something is always on the move toward becoming something else (Hernes 2008).

How can we know the entanglements of feminism in education? I draw here on Actor-Network Theory (ANT) (Latour 2005; Law 1999, 2009a; Mol 1999) to consider what feminism is, as an entity of knowledges, in the lives of female scholars in the field of educational administration. I do so by considering how female scholars have drawn feminism into their practice as scholars and how this entanglement has shaped the field itself. I draw on ANT to consider how feminism has been performed in the academic lives of female scholars, questioning the ways in which realities are enacted in practice (Law and Lien 2013). Consequently, it is essential to understand feminism itself as it is entangled into how women practised their teaching, research, and scholarship in the knowledge production of educational administration.

My goal is not to define what feminism *means*, but rather, to engage a political discussion of defining what feminism *does* through the interactions of female scholars and the field of educational administration. Specifically, two questions are addressed in this chapter. First, in what ways have women's entanglements with feminism contributed to their academic contributions in educational administration? Second, in what ways have these contributions helped to perform the field of educational administration itself?

The chapter begins with a brief introduction of the ways in which ANT addresses concepts of performativity, enactment, and reality. I follow with my personal entry point into this topic. I use data collected through interviews and focus group sessions from a research project studying the experiences of the first female scholars in educational administration in Canada[1] to examine how two of these women spoke about their academic productions throughout their careers.

Drawing on ANT, I rely on two concepts: the performative nature of academic practices and the notion of boundary object, concepts that I elaborate upon in the next sections. In my analysis, I explore how entanglement with feminism not only shaped the academic lives of these women, but this interaction also came to enact a different and more meaningful field of educational administration for them as they began to shift the boundaries of what became knowledge in the field. In this way, feminism became a boundary object (Star 2010) that mediated the relations between the female scholars and the performed boundaries of knowledge in the field.

I suggest that a part of the problem in tracing feminism's influence may be related to the way in which we take up feminism in educational research in the first place, as a categorizing unit in its own right. I propose that by considering what feminisms do in the lives of female scholars, we can better theorize and imagine its agency in education.

PERFORMING REALITIES

As a sensibility toward research (Mol 2010), ANT analyses focus on the interactions between people and things as networks, or assemblages, that produce practices and knowledge. Consequently, what we deem as stable entities, such as knowledge and fields of research, are seen to be an effect of connections and activity (Fenwick and Edwards 2010). The focus in ANT research takes us away from actors as individuals toward "a more complex and less defined phenomenon that is the interaction" (Cordella and Shaikh 2006, 9). Here, researchers trace the assemblage of heterogeneous actors (Latour 2005) – the interactions between human and non-human actors in everyday practices. Interactions are key in ANT in order to trace the assembly, and reassembly, of actions, actors, and interests that produce what is deemed to be authoritative and powerful. ANT researchers question those things that appear as stable entities. Understanding how assemblages hold particular knowledges as static, authoritative, and impermeable is the work of ANT (Fenwick and Edwards 2010).

Donna Haraway (2008) theorized a process of "becoming with" in the interactions between the human and non-human, in that both beings are co-constituted through these interactions. The socio-material nature of reality requires that, to understand our world, we must understand these entanglements. Performativity in ANT is central to understanding the relational nature of reality. As Law (2009b) stated, "Practices, then, are assemblages of relations. Those assemblages do realities. Realities, including the incidental collateral realities, are inseparable from the patterning juxtapositions of practices" (2). By extension, realities can be collateral and multiple. In the context of this research, entities, such as fields of research and bodies of knowledge, are assumed to be assembled and performed into being, rather than simply received and transferred by scholars working in the field.

BOUNDARY OBJECTS

Indeed, in ANT, the notion of field is problematic if we assume it to be a bounded entity that exists outside of the practices from which it emerges. That is, a field is something that has to be performed. Consequently, educational administration and feminism can be conceptualized as fields but only so far as they are performed as such. Through processes of separation, what Latour (1993) termed "purification," bounded contexts are enacted (Edwards, Ivanic, and Mannion 2009). Purification refers to the way in which a field comes to be assembled, to appear as something fixed and stabilized, in the "denial of the play of multiplicity and difference and the valuing of specific practices over others" (488). In using ANT, researchers hope to show how fields that appear to have stable boundaries are made to seem so through complex processes of assembling and reassembling these boundaries, as knowledges, ideas, actors, and interests are enrolled into the assemblages.

In ANT, the notion of boundary denotes both a separation and a connection between fields. That is, boundaries work to contain a set of knowledges in defining one field, but, in doing so, they are connected to help define other fields, too. Consequently, the term boundary object is a helpful term to understand how two spaces that are bounded as separate may still in fact work together. As Edwards, Ivanic, and Mannion (2009) explained, "Boundary objects do not sit between the borders of different contexts, at the edge, but express a relationship between domains brought together" (493) through acts of purification, exclusion and inclusion, and boundary setting. Boundary objects, they suggested, are defined as such by the connections that they seek to make.

Boundary objects are "a sort of arrangement that allow different groups to work together without consensus" (Star 2010, 602). Boundary objects are common objects that form the boundaries; they are the "stuff of action" (603). The notion of object here denotes material and process, a thing that people act "toward and with" (603). In this sense, argues Star, things that are not so physical, such as a theory, may be powerful boundary objects. Boundary objects reside between social worlds and are used by local groups not in interdisciplinary fashion but in ways that are meaningful and useful to the action in local domains. Importantly, Star noted that boundary objects bring groups together, not through consensus, but rather in a back and forth way that acts to shape the object itself. The actions of local groups engaged with a boundary object are not simultaneous, but they do act collectively in how the object comes to be defined or, in ANT terms, enacted and realized.

MY OWN ENTANGLEMENT

Educational accounts themselves produce particular realities (Law and Lien 2013). Indeed, researchers are a part of the messiness that is performed in research. My contribution in this chapter is a particular assemblage that requires my own reflexivity (Fenwick and Edwards 2010; Gorur 2011). Therefore, I begin with my personal entry point into this research. The data for this chapter were collected for a larger research project in which I was engaged that examined the experiences of the first female scholars in educational administration departments in Canadian universities. The data collection took place through individual interviews with each of the women, and through a dual set of two-day focus group sessions. In this chapter, I narrow the focus to look specifically at the ways in which two of the women participants talked about their engagement with feminist scholarship, particularly related to how their scholarship enabled their own agency in performing the field of educational administration.

As a doctoral student in an educational administration and leadership department, I was a research assistant on a research project, as outlined above. I pursued graduate work because I wanted to explore some of the practical experiences I had gained through several years of teaching and administration. My first courses in the graduate program involved interacting with the Canadian literature considered core to the field of educational administration. The work of male scholars dominated the coursework, and feminism was only ever briefly touched upon (if ever) through the work of female scholars who were writing on topics related to educational administration. Often, these works were positioned within one week's readings near the end of the course, and, almost inevitably, along with the other "special topics" such as race, social justice, and equity. In the practice of these courses, feminism was certainly not enrolled into the centrality of what was deemed to be important knowledge for educational administration.

Like others who felt tension with the technorational assumptions underpinning much of the educational administration scholarship (Blackmore 1996), I, too, toiled to reconcile the way in which feminism was bounded as outside the centre of core knowledge in educational administration, and how the experiences of women were represented as "special issues" in the field. I was intrigued by the notion of working on a research project that examined the work and experiences of female scholars in educational administration, including their time as graduate students, and I sought it with a hope of coming to understand my own discomfort with some of the scholarship and practices I encountered twenty or so years after these women began their professional careers in the academy. I was surprised to see how their experiences resonated with my own, and I listened with curiosity to how they managed to navigate through their own tensions as the first female scholars in a highly masculinized field. Consequently, the assemblage presented in this paper also represents my journey in coming to know myself as a new scholar in this field and how my own entanglement with feminism sits in relation to the educational administration that is performed through my own work.

INTRODUCING THE ACTORS: A BACKGROUND INTO THE WOMEN AND THEIR SCHOLARSHIP

The discipline of educational administration has been in Canadian faculties of education since the early 1950s, when the first department was opened at the University of Alberta. Since its inception, male scholars, both at the professorial and graduate level, have dominated the discipline. The first women entered graduate programs in the 1970s and the first few women began taking up faculty positions in the 1980s. The two participants featured in this chapter are among the first women scholars working in the area of educational administration in Canadian universities. Both are white, middle-class women, who acknowledged their own privilege that enabled them to be among the first women educated as scholars in educational administration. Their experiences are used to understand the situated knowledges (Haraway 1998) they enacted in the field of educational administration, even as they acknowledged that their experiences do not constitute a generalizable "women's experience" of/in educational administration.

One participant began her career in educational administration after time spent teaching in both K–12 school systems and adult education settings, as well as in administrative work at the university level. She began her career as a professor in educational administration shortly after completing graduate school. She taught and researched in both K–12 and post-secondary education topics related to educational administration. She talked about doing a study early in her graduate program that was "somewhere in those boundaries of adult and higher ed[ucation]." For this participant, coming to educational administration "had nothing to do with being a school administrator." She explained that she had several administrator roles and experiences, though not in the K–12 school system, which made her an anomaly at the time in her department: "So this brought me in through an unconventional route, which, you see, was what set my thinking around notions of what are conventional routes in careers and what are not so conventional and women's, you know, lives and experiences that way. So, that's how I ended up [in an educational administration field]." The second participant came to the field of educational administration when she was well-advanced in her career in adult and community education. She pursued graduate work in educational administration because of a passion for learning about organizations. Through her work chairing a provincial educational council, she "became more and more interested in leadership and more and more interested in the other perspective – the administrator's perspective." She described her plans for academia: "I knew I had fifteen years [potentially ahead of me as a professor] and I thought of this as an exciting run for it." She was a faculty member in more than one Canadian university, with an appointment at one of the universities in teaching and researching in educational administration and leadership.

Both of these women's scholarship was imbued with a concern for examining the political aspects of educational administration. Their work shared an interest in searching out how women have negotiated the political boundaries of working, teaching, and leading in educational organizations. Both women used historical methods in their research as they sought to illustrate the ways in which female teachers and educational leaders have managed their way through the school system, balancing their personal life commitments and their passion for educating in the K–12 school system and adult education settings.

Each woman contributed toward theorizing what the field of educational administration is and ought to be. For both of these women scholars, there was a need to take up and challenge the technorational dominance in the field of educational administration, in educational organizations, and in community settings. They drew on social theory, including feminism, to critically examine the field of educational administration they encountered as female scholars. One participant's work addressed philosophical questions in educational administration, questioning the historical direction of the field. She urged that feminist research and scholarship could make a more significant impact on the practice of educational administration with sincere and concentrated effort. She focused on the ways in which women were situated in educational organizations and how feminism and gender has been taken up in the field. Her work involved deep study of individual women's experiences, providing a depth of knowledge about what it means to be a female educator. She invoked life story research of women's experiences as they transitioned between roles and leadership positions in the education arena. Her writing was always steeped in a sense of the broader social, economic, and political forces that influenced the careers of women educators. She recognized the agency of individual women based on their particular contexts and structural barriers and supports for women.

The other participant was deeply engaged in philosophical discussions and critical theory. Her research aimed primarily at changing educational contexts to recognize and acknowledge issues of social justice, such as democratic and participatory practices, equality of access, and equity in programming. She focused her work on theorizing situational, creative educational leadership, and demonstrated, through historical research, the leadership of a female educator. Drawing upon philosophy, she wrote about leadership as being embedded in issues of social justice. While the influence of a particularly defined feminism is not substantial in her writing, the extent to which she wrote about leadership from a woman's perspective is indicative of her belief that there are other ways of performing leadership.

ENROLLING FEMINISM

Both women reflected that they did not enter their graduate programs with a desire to pursue feminism. However, their personal experiences among the few women in the program influenced how they thought about their position relative to their colleagues and professors. One of the participants elaborated about coming to an awareness around her position among her colleagues: "I was Mary Magdalene. I think this is very important. I was the only woman and there were twelve guys in my course and before that time I didn't consider myself to be a competitive person. But, after a few episodes of the guys coming in and saying, 'Have you applied for the job at the Department of Education?' looking at all their male counterparts, never asking me, I started to think there was something wrong with this scene."

Later, she described how she was advised to avoid doing a thesis and devote her studies to a course-based route. This exclusion from the academic rigour of completing a thesis troubled her as it signified a taken-for-granted assumption – one she did not share – that she would not be up for pursuing further graduate and academic work. She chose not to follow this advice and did not regret it: "I said, well why do a Masters if you don't learn how to do research? Oh, to them [her male colleagues] the Masters was the end, that was the end point, so I did that, I did the thesis and learned more doing a thesis than anything else."

Additionally, these women referred to other graduate student colleagues and friends from whom they sought mentorship. One participant confided that she did not come into the program with an interest in women in educational administration. She developed an interest in this work through later encounters with feminist and philosophy scholars. However, she reflected on how her own work experiences in adult education had influenced her world view at the time of entering the program: "I would say now that most of the people in charge [in the education sector where I came from] were men, but I wasn't particularly conscious of it at that time. And I did come from a long line of independent women, so there was an element, you know, I was never very all that conventional, never all that conformist about a lot of things. But I certainly hadn't articulated any kind of feminist awareness or consciousness at that stage at all."

However, as she began her doctoral program, she began to take notice of the way the educational administration field was set up in the department: "I looked around, I was the only woman in the room [among the male graduate student colleagues]. And there were eighteen men ... Anyway, that was a real shock to me. And that was what jolted me immediately ... to think about women. And women's role in the area of administration. And I started reading and working in that area immediately."

She elaborated on other influences in her life outside of her department, including people who were close to her that were graduate students and friends who were scholars in feminist philosophy and sociology. These people were great supports to her as she began to interrogate the role of women in society and as she developed her own consciousness around her position as a female scholar in the field. She talked about being the "public feminist entering the classroom" in her early career in the academy, and later she introduced a course on women in education that focused on women in administration in the first instance. This feminist grounding remained with her throughout her career: "There was always a feminist underpinning to what I [did] ... I do think a certain underpinning in valuing voice and expecting rigour, you know. And, trying to be quite creative about involving people in and raising gender as an issue. It was always there in my classes, you know, and it wasn't in lots of others."

While neither of these women sought to become feminist scholars, their early experiences led them to question the conditions in which they found themselves. For these women, the ways in which they thought of educational administration began to shift as they were challenged, beginning in their graduate student experiences and continuing into their careers as scholars. Feminism became an entity of knowledges about what it means to be a female scholar in a male-dominated department, about the ways in which women's voices were both represented and valued in the field of educational administration, and the position of women as scholars. Their subjectivities as female students evolved as they came to express themselves as a competitive female student or the "public feminist" in educational administration. The stability of the boundaries of educational administration were called into question for these women as they came to terms with "women's role in educational administration," as one participant put it.

PERFORMING EDUCATIONAL ADMINISTRATION

Both women had to negotiate how their work fit into educational administration and other educational fields. One participant talked about her doctoral work as it "crossed boundaries" by appealing to those in both the K–12 and post-secondary sectors. For her, there was an unconventionality to her studies with which she was comfortable. She admitted, "I did both the regular route and, as options or whatever, I did the other courses [related to post-secondary contexts]. And my study, of course, straddled the two in a way that I felt suited me, let me put it that way." Her doctoral work also reflected this unconventional approach as doing "feminist work" brings one to an "undefined" place in the field:

> Because many women's careers have actually, because they tend to be more interrupted, women have moved around to where there was work. Teaching work, or related work of one kind or another. So, of course it turned out, indeed, [half of the participants] in my doctoral study had crossed those boundaries themselves, had done work in both sectors. K–12 and post-secondary or adult ed. So, I kind of liked that about my study but it meant I was very undefined in terms of the specialization. And I've seen this so often with the younger, the women, since, who have done feminist work and have particularly taken a focus on women and their activities. It leaves you kind of undefined in the conventional [educational administration field].

Additionally, the participants reflected a concern they had about the way their work was bound as either inside or outside the field. One of the participants spoke about the ways in which her interactions with feminism in her research bounded her work as knowledge outside of educational administration. She talked about how she felt she had to fight against an assumption of essentialism, that her work generalized women's experiences while also being relevant only to female administrators. She recalled a time at a conference at which she was delivering a presentation on a study of female administrators in schools with other junior female colleagues when a senior male colleague from her department commented about "the women's session being over there," simultaneously addressing her work as diminutive and "other." There was great interest in the work, she said, as "the room was absolutely packed" yet as she related this episode, she remembered that it was difficult to overcome the way her work had been bound in an essentialist assumption that limited the scope of its relevance and acceptance:

> I became, because of some work I did with graduate students, I was treated as an essentialist with women and leadership, you know, for a while. But I wasn't. It was a mis-reading, actually, of that work. Because it was also a lot easier for other feminists who wanted to reject liberal or essentialist work to just, you know, pick on some stuff. And I resent that kind of thing. I think there was criticism that was unfair. If people had read closely what we were talking about, [be]cause I had never said anything more than there have always been men who have led in these kind of ways but there seem to be women who have been taking up these kinds of leading. You know, related to ethic of care and connectedness and that sort of thing.

One participant spoke about encountering the sense that a lot of women working in educational administration chose to work in this field of study and research because they wanted to "shake up the administrative side of education." She reflected that the research and scholarship she was encountering as dominant knowledge was "simplistic, it was mind-numbing, although I didn't know that when I covered it as a Master's student." She elaborated on how she sought a criticality in her approach to the work:

Later I realized that [the majority of research in the field] had no critical content whatsoever, and that was the dominant lens through which most people, of the male variety, were looking at educational [administration]. So quite a few of us [women] entered the field hoping to bring life to this because we are the leaders of the school and the whole section of leadership. What is leadership? Let's redefine it. Is it the guy in the pinstripe suit? No, I don't think so. It's the person who's influencing other human beings. Who can it be? Can it be one person one day, it's [the suit] or the teacher. So, I found that just a very exciting challenge and that's why I wanted to do it.

For this participant, one of her biggest accomplishments was the way she changed how her students and those who came across her work might think about the nature of the field of educational administration itself. She reflected that this was something she had to work on as she progressed throughout her career: "I would say that was probably the most innovative thing I did and it was a growth experience for me. I didn't know how to do it so I stumbled along for a few years and developed it." For this participant, introducing the notion of a different kind of leader made educational administration become more meaningful for her, and, she theorized, others whom she encountered.

In one of the focus groups, the question of whether the women's scholarship was bound by educational administration was raised by one of the study's participants. Most of the women rejected the field of educational administration as the boundary of their work. Rather, they avowed an expanse to their work, in that their scholarship drew from areas beyond the traditional, structural-functionalist assumptions based in educational administration, and contributed to a broader audience. In fact, one of the participants featured in this chapter reflected that by engaging with these different knowledges, female scholars were encountering educational administration as they created it: "And really, what I think is coming out here is the way we have incorporated the idea of educational administration but not as we received it. We've made it something else, that we've taken on ... So we've, in a way, written ourselves into being."

In a similar way, in her personal interview, the other participant stated that writing was a way for her to develop her self as a scholar in the field. She commented, "I almost wrote my way through what I had to say there but not quite. You know, there's always some stuff left." However, it was not only themselves as scholars that they reflected on as "becoming." Rather, the enrolling of these different knowledges performed a "crossing of boundaries" that resulted in the emergence of "an educational administration" that was more meaningful for them. As one participant elaborated: "You know, each of us, I think, brought a new ... again, it's like breaking down boundaries or crossing boundaries. It's like forcing the new vision into what is called educational administration, though we call it different things."

The notion of "boundary crossing" from the participants suggests a stability that is deemed somehow natural within the field of educational administration. However, as Latour (2005) suggests, there is benefit in tracing how stability appears as fixed, and how the purification processes at play mask the multiplicity of actors who continually shape the knowledges and practices that construct the field. The process of becoming is not only for the field as an entity of knowledge and practice, but also for the scholars themselves, as their own "becoming with" (Haraway 1990) is performed.

PERFORMING, BOUNDING, BECOMING

The purpose here is not to make claims about a causal relationship of feminism in these women's lives, but rather to look at the ways in which feminism has been enrolled into educational administration through interactions with these women scholars. The assemblages woven here in this analysis are partial (Fenwick and Edwards 2010), but offer some insight into how we understand the relation of feminism to educational administration. I focus on two aspects that emerged in the conversations with these women. First, I consider the ways in which there was a process of "becoming with" as the field of educational administration was performed in new ways with these women's scholarship and teaching, and, consequently, how the women themselves came to be performed as scholars. Second, I discuss the nature of feminism as a boundary object that connected the women to the political activity of the field.

"BECOMING WITH":
PERFORMING KNOWLEDGES, SCHOLARS, AND THE FIELD

Knowledges take material forms, but they are produced through the bits and pieces of actors that are juxtaposed together (Law 1992). This ordering comes to organize and shape realities, including particular actors while excluding others. The processes of inclusion and exclusion work to stabilize certain knowledges, to hold some realities as possible, while making others seem illegitimate and impossible (Law 2009b). The experiences of these scholars as the first women in the field brought them face to face with tensions in the ways in which educational administration was performed as a field of knowledges and practices, in their professional careers, in their doctoral programs, and in the pursuit of their research. For these women, there were uncomfortable tensions and power relations developed in the knowledges they encountered as mainstream in the field of educational administration. They referred to these knowledges as uncritical, structural-functionalist, geared at maintaining the status quo. They sought to reject the ways in which educational administration was represented and instead aimed, in one participant's words, to "redefine" it. In ANT terms, they sought to create the field differently through their research, scholarship, and teaching, and, through such practices, they were involved in reassembling a different reality of what constituted knowledge and what it meant to be an educational administration scholar.

For one participant, writing about leadership from the perspective of a woman, and detailing how this leadership was practised and enacted in community related to the work of a female leader, positioned women centrally into the concept of leadership. By doing so, her work aimed to construct leadership as participatory and democratic, which was a radical shift from the structural-functionalist assumptions of leadership that were posited as real in the academic literature she encountered throughout her career. In writing about a creative, democratic leadership, she enacted a different leadership into the realm of possibility. Her work created the possibilities for a leader to be female and focused on democratic ideals, rather than functionalist conventions of status quo maintenance found in educational organizations. Her work reordered the knowledge that was deemed relevant and pertinent to the field.

For the other participant, writing about women's careers in educational administration not only refocused women's experiences in the field as important and worth knowing but also brought about a site of contention, as the relevance of scholarship labelled as "the women's session" was called into question. Indeed, both of these women's scholarship performed a reordering of the field that in some ways began with their early encounters with feminism as the first female academics when they questioned for themselves who they were as women and as scholars. This questioning continued throughout their careers as they sought to develop scholarship and teaching that they saw as necessary in the field, even though it was excluded as an "other" by their colleagues. In this way, they performed themselves as scholars that involved a "becoming with" feminism.

For these women, the field of educational administration became something different through their becoming as scholars. As one participant stated, these women did not set out to respond to the field but actively shaped it through their scholarly contributions. Through their scholarship, educational administration as a field was involved in its own "becoming with" these women, not separate from them. As they became scholars, the field also became something new to which they contributed their own knowledge. These women showed that educational leadership could be assembled differently, as different actors are entangled in researching, reading, writing, and teaching. Educational administration came to be meaningful for these women in its democratic, creative materiality in one instance and in its gendered materiality in the other.

PERFORMING BOUNDARIES

Boundary crossing was a metaphor used by both of these women to describe the performance of their scholarship. These women talked about their work as though it were not bound by the field of educational administration. Indeed, both of the women's scholarship draws from theoretical concepts outside of the field of educational administration. For them, there is significance in how they took educational administration into new spaces. However, the notion of a bounded field for research and teaching does not hold when we consider fields as performed through assemblages of knowledges and practices. ANT analyses show us that there is work to be done in performing and stabilizing the boundaries of an academic field. This work is never finalized as it is always performed through the practices of scholars and other "things."

In what ways did the female scholars' interactions with feminism influence the knowledge contributions to the field? To answer this, I suggest we look at the ways in which their work enacted boundaries, rather than crossed boundaries as though they were static entities existing outside of practices of the field. In some ways, feminism acted as a boundary object among these female scholars in their process of becoming, as their own scholarship and teaching constituted knowledges in the field of educational administration as well as their own subjectivities as scholars.

Perhaps we can better understand the influence of feminism in educational administration if we consider feminism as a boundary object that connected the women to the politics of defining the field of educational administration. If we accept the notion of "becoming with," then these women's engagement with their scholarship, as it emerged in response to the problems they saw in how the field was being constituted, was part of their process of becoming scholars, as well. Their interactions with feminism called into question who they were as students and as scholars and helped them to identify their own circumstances and the gaps in the field.

Defining what comes to be performed is an act of politics (Mol 1999). These women were not satisfied to continue in the knowledge production of the contributions that were dominant. Their interests were sparked because of their positioning in the field, as they conceived of other, important knowledges that were left out. Consequently, they became enrolled into the political aspects of the field itself. While these women suggested they crossed the boundary, from the perspective of performativity offered here, they did not cross to pre-existing entities, but rather were involved in the "becoming with" of what it meant to be a scholar in the field of educational administration. Indeed, these women wrote themselves into being, but they also wrote into being the field and the knowledges that constructed it.

While one may theorize that feminism remains on the fringes of educational fields, these women's reflections suggest that feminism was entangled in their experiences as the first female scholars in the field, and that this entanglement contributed to the "becoming with" that happened as these women engaged in their scholarship and teaching practices. From their stories, feminism as a boundary object is not located "outside of the field," but rather is enrolled in the performance of the relations between educational administration and other knowledges. In their lives, as a boundary object, feminism cannot be seen as "outside," or as powerless to effect change in how educational administration is performed. Rather, by studying its enrolment, we see how powerful it can become for the women who seek to shape the knowledge practices in the field.

CONCLUSION

Admittedly, the assemblages presented here through the experiences of two women are a small insight into the entanglements of feminism in education. However, given the ontological politics (Mol 1999) at play in how feminism is enrolled to perform different realities in the field of educational administration, I propose that by studying the entangled relations of feminism, we may come to better understand its influence.

Consequently, there is hope that we may continue to ensure that feminism's existence in the field is not only noted but invoked to perform education in a way that is meaningful to female scholars practising in the field. From the insights provided by two female scholars, we may see that its place is not neat and tidy. Rather, as Hernes (2008) reminded us, the imagery of entanglement is descriptive of things "always on the move toward becoming something else" (xv). Such imagery is powerful as we come to see the influence of feminism in performing many boundaries. That is, feminism itself is not disconnected in its own becoming. The power of feminism is not in conceiving of it as a separate entity on its own, but in what comes to be performed as it is enrolled into the practices of researching and teaching in academic life.

NOTE

1 This was a SSHRC-funded research project conducted by Dawn Wallin and Janice Wallace, to whom I am grateful, for their support as a graduate research assistant working on the project.

REFERENCES

Blackmore, J. 1996. "'Breaking the Silence': Feminist Contributions to Educational Administration and Policy." In *International Handbook of Educational Leadership and Administration*, ed. K. Leithwood, J. D. Chapman, P. Corson, P. Hallinger, and A. Hart, 997–1042. London: Kluwer Academic Publishers. doi:10.1007/978-94-009-1573-2_29.

– 2013. "A Feminist Critical Perspective on Educational Leadership." *International Journal of Leadership in Education* 16 (2): 139–54. doi:10.1080/13603124.2012.754057.

Blackmore, J., and J. Sachs. 2007. *Performing and Reforming Leaders: Gender, Educational Restructuring and Organizational Change*. Albany, NY: SUNY Press.

Cordella, A., and M. Shaikh. 2006. "From Epistemology to Ontology: Challenging the Constructed 'Truth' of ANT." London: London School of Economics and Political Science. https://www.researchgate.net/profile/Antonio_Cordella/publication/301295219_From_Epistemology_to_Ontology_Challenging_the_Constructed_Truth_of_ANT/links/57109b2908aefb6cadaaad9b.pdf.

Edwards, R., R. Ivanic, and G. Mannion. 2009. "The Scrumpled Geography of Literacies for Learning." *Discourse (Abingdon)* 30 (4): 483–99. doi:10.1080/01596300903237248.

Fenwick, T., and R. Edwards. 2010. *Actor-Network Theory in Education*. London: Routledge.

Gorur, R. 2011. "Policy as Assemblage." *European Educational Research Journal* 10 (4): 611–22. doi:10.2304/eerj.2011.10.4.611.

Haraway, D. 1988. "Situated Knowledges: The Science Question in Feminism and the Privilege of Partial Perspective." *Feminist Studies* 14 (3): 575–99. doi:10.2307/3178066.

– 1990. "A Manifesto for Cyborgs: Science, Technology, and Socialist Feminism in the 1980s." In *Feminism/Postmodernism*, ed. L.J. Nicholson, 190–233. New York: Routledge.

– 2008. *When Species Meet*. Minneapolis: University of Minnesota Press.

Hernes, T. 2008. *Understanding Organization as Process: Theory for a Tangled World*. London, UK: Routledge.

Latour, B. 1993. *We Have Never Been Modern*. London: Harvester Wheatsheaf.

– 2005. *Reassembling the Social*. Oxford: Oxford University Press.

Law, J. 1992. "Notes on the Theory of the Actor-Network: Ordering, Strategy and Heterogeneity." *Systems Practice* 5 (4): 379–93. doi:10.1007/BF01059830.

– 1999. "After ANT: Complexity, Naming and Topology." In *Actor Network Theory and After*, ed. J. Law and J. Hassard, 1–14. Oxford: Blackwell.

– 2009a. "Actor Network Theory and Material Semiotics." In *The New Blackwell Companion to Social Theory*, 3rd ed., ed. B.S. Turner, 141–58. Chichester, UK: Blackwell. doi:10.1002/9781444304992.ch7.

– 2009b. "Collateral Realities." In *The Politics of Knowledge*, ed. F.D. Rubio and P. Baert, 156–78. London: Routledge.

Law, J., and M. Lien. 2013. "Slippery: Field Notes on Empirical Ontology." *Social Studies of Science* 43 (3): 363–78. doi:10.1177/0306312712456947.

Mol, A. 1999. "Ontological Politics. A Word and Some Questions." In *Actor Network Theory and After*, ed. J. Law and J. Hassard, 74–89. Oxford: Blackwell. doi:10.1111/j.1467-954X.1999.tb03483.x.

– 2010. "Actor-Network Theory: Sensitive Terms and Enduring Tensions." *Kölner Zeitschrift für Soziologie und Sozialpsychologie* 50 (1): 253–69.

Shakeshaft, C., G. Brown, B.J. Irby, M. Grogan, and J. Ballenger. 2007. "Increasing Gender Equity in Educational Leadership." In *Handbook for Achieving Gender Equity through Education*, 2nd ed., ed. S. Klein, 103–29. Mahwah, NJ: Laurence Erlbaum Associates.

Star, S.L. 2010. "This Is Not a Boundary Object: Reflections of the Origin of a Concept." *Science, Technology & Human Values* 35 (5): 601–17. doi:10.1177/0162243910377624.

Young, B. 1994. "An Other Perspective on the Knowledge Base in Canadian Educational Administration." *Canadian Journal of Education* 19 (4): 351–67. doi:10.2307/1495336.

PART THREE

Disrupting Discourses: Speaking Back to Feminism

JANICE WALLACE

Tanya Fitzgerald (2003) has written about the "discourses of privilege" that have surfaced in feminist scholarship in Western educational contexts, particularly related to leadership theory, that produce "a particular kind of consensus ... about the issues which are thought to be important to organize around" (432). She argues that Western feminist theorizing has focused on profiles, patterns, and practice that narrow efforts around particular issues, such as representation, career aspirations, access to opportunities, barriers, retention, leadership style, or pedagogy that were considered in parts 1 and 2. In her view, the focus on these issues often obfuscates the differential experiences of those whose intersectionalities position them as Other within feminist educational discourses. Specifically, the complexity of issues concerning the intersections of race, class, sexuality, ability, religion, geographical origin, language, and so on, with gender, are not attended to adequately, if at all (see Loreto 2016).

In particular, "feminism's white default" (Loreto 2016) in mainstream feminism has become a flashpoint for painful debates and elicited the concept of an intersectional feminism that speaks back to the dominant position of white, cisgender, middle-class, largely urban, able-bodied, educated feminists. Out of those discussions has come the recognition that feminism in its various forms, but particularly liberal feminism, has not been inclusive, to the degree that it needed to be, of the experiences, desires, and hopes of women who are Other. Drawing largely from the work of Black antiracist feminists, Carastathis (2014) notes:

> It has become commonplace within feminist theory to claim that women's lives are constructed by multiple, intersecting systems of oppression. This insight – that oppression is not a singular process or a binary political relation, but is better understood as constituted by multiple, converging, or interwoven systems – originates in anti-racist feminist critiques of the claim that women's oppression could be captured through an analysis of gender alone. Intersectionality is offered as a theoretical and political remedy to what is perhaps the most pressing problem facing contemporary feminism – the long and painful legacy of its exclusions. (304, citing Davis 2008, 70)

The term intersectionality was coined by Kimberlé Crenshaw (1989), a Black feminist legal scholar, in her analysis of a case in which "the Federal courts dismissed the complaint" of African American women who felt that they had been denied access to better jobs. The court ruled that the complaint fit neither race discrimination (because Black men were not barred from better jobs) nor sex discrimination (because white women were not barred from better jobs) (Gordon 2016, 341). This tortuous logic revealed the limits of so-called identity politics and "the dominance of a particular orientation that disaggregates social problems into discrete challenges facing specific groups" (Gordon 2016, 341). Instead, intersectionality offered a way to consider oppression across categories in ways that revealed rather than concealed multiple layers of exclusion.

Intersectionality is certainly not an unproblematic term and may have lost some of its efficacy given its take-up in widely disparate locations in both academe and the vernacular of the popular press and social media (Gordon 2016, 354). Crenshaw (cited in Berger and Guidroz 2009, 65) is quoted as saying, "Sometimes I can't even recognize it in the literature anymore." Carastathis (2014) argues, however, that intersectionality can be seen as "a paradigm for contemporary feminist theory and research" (307). Such a position offers three distinct benefits that enable us to, first, consider "the phenomenological claim that intersectionality captures how oppressions are experienced simultaneously. The second is the ontological claim that intersectionality can theorize the convergence, co-constitution, imbrication, or interwovenness of systems of oppression" (307). Third, "it accounts for or captures experiential and structural complexity" (307). On the other hand, as Ludvig (2006) notes, "The endlessness of differences seems to be a weak point in intersectional theory (247)." Razack (2005) proposes the term interlocking rather than intersecting to denote the ways in which systems of oppression are connected and work together but, theoretically, it remains closely aligned with intersectional feminism.

As this brief history reveals, intersectional feminism has been critiqued, like other feminist theories. However, it has also been highly generative, particularly in concert with critical and post-structural analysis, in talking back to feminism and calling it to an inclusive and strategic resistance to patriarchal capitalism. Each chapter in part 3 offers an opportunity to reconsider the possibilities for feminism more broadly in diverse social institutions such as educational organizations. This is particularly important as educational organizations are reshaped within neo-liberalism's reductionist reforms that have pushed back so vehemently on the gains that were made under second-wave reforms. The chapters in this section detail some of the concerns that surface within these tensions in educational settings, while also providing avenues for feminist scholarship and practice that is more inclusive. Not all of the authors explicitly adopt an intersectional feminist approach, but all speak back to feminism in a way that pushes the work of feminist analysis and activism forward in theorizing difference.

Drawing on her activism, work, and scholarship in anti-oppression adult education, Evelyn Hamdon considers the possibilities of feminist intersectionality as a means of informing feminist research. In her chapter, "Lessons in Dismantling the Master's House: An Adult Educator's Reflections on Intersectional Feminism," Hamdon recognizes that retheorizing epistemic and ontological relations that subjugate women has been the general focus of feminist theory. However, feminist intersectionality points to both "the micropolitics of context, subjectivity, and struggle, as well as to the macropolitics of global economic and political systems and processes" (Mohanty 2003, 223). An expansion of feminist theorizing, Hamdon suggests, is vital to broaden and deepen both methodological and conceptual possibilities for feminism in adult education. These extensions of feminist thinking take into account the complex locations of women, but also examine the ways that both women and men, and those who do not identify within the traditional binary considerations of gender, are oppressed by patriarchal capitalism.

Marlene McKay's chapter, "Indigenizing My Roots in Feminism," presents an enlightening post-structural feminist critique of Canada's colonial history and its impact on Indigenous women. As she considers the interlocking structural and personal layers of her experience as an Indigenous woman, she suggests that feminism has been rejected and avoided in Indigenous educational theory and practice because of the patriarchal and misogynistic ideas inherent in Christian traditions and in traditionalist practices that have proliferated through colonial relations in Indigenous communities. In McKay's view, an essentialized view of Indigenous women's experiences and knowledges have limited their opportunities for voice and participation in educational discourse. McKay concludes by advocating for the inclusion of Indigenous feminist perspectives in curricula and educational practice so that the diversity of Indigenous women's experiences is affirmed, and their positionality in educational discourse can move from margin to centre.

Thashika Pillay, in "Visible Minority Teachers in Canada: Decolonizing the Knowledges of Euro-American Hegemony through Feminist Epistemologies and Ontologies," uses a post-structural feminist autoethnobiographical approach to explore the meaning of intersectionality in her own experience as a student, teacher, and scholar from the Global South who relocated as a young girl to the Global North. Drawing on her experience as a young student in Alberta, a beginning teacher in Canada's far north, and a doctoral candidate and academic, she notes that the majority of teachers are white, middle-class women, while visible minority women continue to be excluded and disadvantaged in the education workplace, as is the knowledge that they would bring to their classrooms. Instead, Pillay argues for the recognition of multiple knowledges and world views and the dehegemonization of Euro-American ways of seeing the world. Doing so, she claims, will open up opportunities for minority women educators, provide a more representative learning environment for minority students, and make available a broader range of knowledges for all students to bring to their learning about the world in which they will live, work, love, and participate as citizens.

Each of these papers is speaking back to feminism in education, questioning its assumptions and creating a space for an Other voice using theoretical perspectives that decentre dualisms of white/black, male/female, mind/body, colonizer/colonized. As Brah and Phoenix (2004) argue, the voices of women who were not the normative subject of feminism have always spoken back, but they have not always been heard and their lives, desires, experiences have not been represented within feminism. But those voices, "part lament, but defiant, articulating razor-sharp politics but with the sensibility of a poet ... performs the analytic moves of a 'decolonised mind,' to use Wa Thiongo's (1986) critical insight. It refuses all closures. We are all in dire need of a decolonised open minds today" (77). In speaking back, the authors in part 3 are working through their own everyday practices and subjectivity from their position within a complex "postmodern imperialism that stalks the world" (Brah and Phoenix 2004, 83) and, in doing so, ask questions of those of us who identify with and live in the "West" on essential issues of social justice in a globalized world.

REFERENCES

Berger, M., and K. Guidroz, eds. 2009. *The Intersectional Approach: Transforming the Academy through Race, Class, and Gender*. Chapel Hill: The University of North Carolina Press.

Brah, A., and A. Phoenix. 2004. "Ain't I a Woman? Revisiting Intersectionality." *Journal of International Women's Studies* 5 (3): 75–86.

Carastathis, A. 2014. "The Concept of Intersectionality in Feminist Theory." *Philosophy Compass* 9 (5): 304–14. doi:10.1111/phc3.12129.

Crenshaw, K. 1989. "Demarginalizing the Intersection of Race and Sex: A Black Feminist Critique of Antidiscrimination Doctrine, Feminist Theory and Antiracist Politics." *University of Chicago Legal Forum* 1 (8): 139–67.

Fitzgerald, T. 2003. "Interrogating Orthodox Voices: Gender, Ethnicity and Educational Leadership." *School Leadership & Management* 23 (4): 431–44. doi:10.1080/1363243032000150962.

Gordon, L. 2016. "'Intersectionality,' Socialist Feminism and Contemporary Activism: Musings by a Second-Wave Socialist Feminist." *Gender & History* 28 (2): 340–57. doi:10.1111/1468-0424.12211.

Loreto, N. 2016. "Feminism's White Default." *Briar Patch* 45 (3): 4–6.

Ludvig, A. 2006. "Differences between Women? Intersecting Voices in a Female Narrative." *European Journal of Women's Studies* 13 (3): 245–58. doi:10.1177/1350506806065755.

Mohanty, C. 2003. *Feminism without Borders: Decolonizing Theory, Practicing Solidarity*. Durham, London: Duke University Press. doi:10.1215/9780822384649.

Razack, S. 2005. "How Is White Supremacy Embodied? Sexualized Racial Violence at Abu Ghraib." *Canadian Journal of Women and the Law* 17 (2): 341–63.

Wa Thiongo, N. 1986. *Decolonizing the Mind: The Politics of Language in African Literatures*. London: Currey.

7

Lessons on Dismantling the Master's House

An Adult Educator's Reflections on Intersectional Feminism

EVELYN HAMDON

REFLECTIONS

In the late 1970s, when I was learning feminist thinking and organizing, I bought the story that we were all the same in the struggle to emancipate ourselves from patriarchy. It never occurred to me that I, who had the luxury of sitting in a consciousness-raising group in my friend's hip Toronto brownstone, was in fact complicit in erasing or ignoring Other women's differing experiences of patriarchy. It took me a long time, even as a woman racialized as non-white, to figure out that there were other issues at play in the lives of women – issues of life and death – the very same issues that precluded their voices from shaping the struggle for equity and justice. In short, there was a lot of "speaking for Others" at the beginning of the movement.

Eventually my own lived experiences of being silenced and marginalized woke me up to the centres and margins being reproduced within the sisterhood. In the early eighties, and accelerating into the nineties, contemporary politics sparked a resurgent Orientalism (Said 1978), and the discourse of the already oppressed Arab/Muslim woman[1] began to surface. Surprisingly, even the most understanding and knowledgeable of the feminist sisters expressed a troubling essentialism through their articulations that I was an anomaly (and "not really an Arab/Muslim at all"), and that all Arab/Muslim women (at least the "real ones") were totally ignorant of their subjugation to an oriental patriarchy (the implication here was that it was a particularly virulent form of patriarchy). What I was encountering was gendered racism (although that concept had not surfaced at that time), which sparked my retreat from feminist politics and organizing and my turn to anti-racism education and organizing.

My encounters with the anti-racism community were, however, no less problematic; I encountered a lack of awareness about the ways in which gender-based discrimination was working within anti-racism contexts. In other words, I exchanged racism within the feminist movement, for sexism within the anti-racism movement. "Why," I wondered, "were folks who were so engaged in dismantling systems and structures of discrimination, unable to see the ways in which they were reproducing centres and margins and identity-based hierarchies?" It was this question that eventually led me to return to the academy and to pursue graduate studies with a focus on identity and difference as they are taken up within activist contexts. And it was upon reading the work of Sherene Razack, bell hooks, Chandra Mohanty, Audre Lorde, Gloria Anzaldúa, and Himani Banerjee that an analytic frame of reference for these experiences began to emerge.

Although I have always included a gendered analysis in my teaching and activism, increasingly I am extending my analysis to become more intersectional. This chapter marks my return to feminist theorizing, to consider the possibility of a feminist orientation that embeds within it a fundamental concern about the hierarchical arrangements of identities – that is, a feminist-inspired, intersectional, and anti-oppressive practice. To myself, and potential readers of this chapter, I pose the question: "Can we as feminists hold as central to our politics and our project the dismantling of patriarchy and make intelligent links to the ways in which patriarchy is itself complicit and implicated in other oppressive structures?" I offer the following as a meditation on this question.

POSSIBILITIES

Feminist anti-essentialist theorizing (Stone 2004; Young 2004), subaltern feminisms (Anzaldúa 1987, 2000; hooks 1981, 1996, 2000; Minh Ha 1989; Yegenoglu 1998, 2003; Spivak 2010; Mohanty 2003; Bannerji 1993, 1995, 2000; Razack 1998, 2004, 2005), queer feminisms (Butler 1999), and other feminisms from the so-called margins have repeatedly called attention to the absence of marginalized subjects within dominant feminist discourses. The capacity of feminist education scholars to address socio-political complexities is important to avoid further fragmentation within activist and academic circles and a dilution of the liberatory possibilities that an intersectional feminism affords.

In this chapter, I explore the prospects for feminist intersectionality to address complex forms of gendered oppression that exceed the capacity of analytic frameworks based on identity politics and second-wave feminism. This analytic approach is useful in refocusing scholarly and practical attention on the ubiquity of patriarchy and its implication in other systems and structures of oppression such as racism, colonialism, homophobia, and ableism. A feminist intersectionality has the capacity to address, for example, gendered forms of racism, heteronormativity within feminist activism, and so forth. It would take into account the complex locations of women, but it would also take up the ways in which those whose gendered identity is fluid are also subject to marginalization within systems of patriarchy.

To open up a conversation on this broad topic, I will touch upon the presences and absences in our historical recounting of feminist thinking and action, then map out one understanding of intersectionality as a possible way back from the fragmentation of identity politics. Next, I will reflect upon a possible intersectional feminism that recentres the effects of globalized patriarchy on all subjects feminized through and by a phallocentric logic. I will conclude with questions for feminist-identified adult educators engaged in anti-oppressive education.

THE SILENCED AND THE ABSENT

Gendered racism has been one contributing factor in the fragmentation of the feminist movement, and one with which I am most familiar. A contemporary and pervasive example of this is the gendered Islamophobic binary: the always emancipated Western women and the always oppressed Muslim and/or Arab women. This type of gender-based binary can also extend to Other people, including women who challenge gender binaries – who refuse the subject-position offering of male/female.

One factor that contributes to the formation of such binary thinking is the exclusion of feminisms that flourish within other national, cultural, religious, social, or geographic locations. These are rarely included in nor referenced by the Western feminist canon, which contributes to the impression or perception that the most robust and legitimate forms of feminism have their origins in Western academies and movements. Thus, the term Muslim feminist seems oxymoronic to many Western feminists (Razack 2004; Abu-Lughod 2001; Yegenoglu 1998, 2003).

In *Telling Feminist Stories* (2005), feminist philosopher Clare Hemmings invites (or perhaps, more accurately, challenges) feminists to rethink the storying of feminism that, she says, has taken on a form that suggests a linear progression marked by a series of ruptures. I would add to Hemmings's reflections that they have been predicated on one particular notion of progress – that is, a Euro-Western enlightenment idea of progress – that has served to erase the stories of other struggles with and against patriarchy.

Hemmings's critique enables new starting points, such as recognizing that the struggle against patriarchy has had multiple, often untraceable, points of origin, and that the many developments in feminist thought, unplottable on the Western feminist trajectory, have been and are imperative to an intersectional, transbordered feminism. Indeed, opening up the story of feminist theorizing and activism to include the (uncensored) work of Other feminists would begin to address and redress what Breanne Fah (2003) has referred to as the "pathologization of non-Western women" (3); I would also include women who do not situate themselves within white, heteronormative, and ableist notions of femininity.

While a thorough discussion of non-Western, queer, and ableist critiques of feminisms is beyond the scope of this chapter, challenges to patriarchy are not limited to feminisms as articulated and performed by white Western women (Mohanty 2003; Yegenoglu 1998, 2003). One of the rifts that requires healing, potentially through an intersectional approach and a renewed attention to global patriarchy, is the old first/third world binary and its variations. While it is true that women living with the effects of imperialism and colonialism have to struggle against differing microcontextual issues, these issues can be traced to macro-level socio-political processes that embed and are embedded in the patriarchy/capitalist/colonial matrix (Fraser 2013; Razack 2005; Weeden 1999).

Of course, these critiques of the biased storying of feminism are not new. In *Feminist Theory: From Margin to Centre*, hooks (2000) challenged her contemporaries by pointing out that "while it is evident that many women suffer from sexist tyranny, there is little indication that this forges a common bond among all women" (4). Audre Lorde observed that "The failure of the academic feminists to recognize difference as a crucial strength is a failure to reach beyond the first patriarchal lesson. Divide and conquer, in our world, must become define and empower" (2003, 27). Indeed, the failure of second-wave or liberal feminism to employ an analysis of the complexities of gender-based oppression has sparked a great deal of so-called subaltern feminism, resulting in a rich field of postcolonial feminist scholarship, Latina and Black feminist scholarship, and queer theory. This theorizing, scholarship, and subsequent activism have been of critical importance to sustaining the relevance of feminism. To offer a small sampling of scholars/activists, I refer the reader to Audre Lorde, Gloria Anzaldúa, Chandra Mohanty, Sherene Razack, Trinh T. Minh Ha, Himani Bannerji, Judith Butler, and Kim Hall, whose loving, if sharp, critiques of liberal feminism have been integral to the intellectual and literal survival of racialized, queer, differently abled, and poor women/scholars. The work from this list reflects a complex theorizing from their subject positions as Marxists, feminists, women of colour, queer women, and Others. I am suggesting adult anti-oppression educators turn to these works, especially those of us who identify as feminists and with feminism. Within these conceptual spaces, these absences may be repaired and these splits healed.

REORIENTING THE STORY: TOWARD AN INTERSECTIONAL FEMINISM

So the question arises, how do we heal these rifts and build a feminist movement that addresses the identity categories and hierarchies? For ideas, I turn again to poet and scholar Audre Lorde who, in her germinal lecture entitled "The Master's Tools Will Never Dismantle the Master's House" (2003), reminds the scholar/activist that there is an ongoing need to address the structure of patriarchy in conjunction with analyses of other structures. That is, feminism's continued relevance and success will have something to do with feminists' and feminisms' capacities to ensure that any analysis of patriarchy occurs in conjunction with an interrogation of the way patriarchy and neo-liberal capitalism work together at this historical moment to affect the lives of human beings not only here in the West but elsewhere, and not only women- but men-identified subjects as well (see, for example, Fraser 2010). Further, and perhaps even more importantly, such an analysis will be critical to the development of new ontological and epistemic starting points that release binary constructions such as Western woman/Other woman, straight women/gay women, able-bodied women/women with disabilities, or men/women, and make space for Other ways of knowing.

Of vital importance to this new understanding will be to interrogate the ordering of patriarchies. A strange discourse has emerged in the West, that is sometimes internalized by women-identified subjects in the East, whereby Western patriarchy is viewed as being less virulent, less oppressive, more amenable and open to dismantling, while patriarchy elsewhere is considered to be more intractable, more vicious and resistant to change from within, thus requiring the intervention (another form of colonization) from outside, by Western women. This kind of reasoning has resulted in what has come to be known as gendered racism and has given rise to a kind of feminist maternalism. This maternalism is often expressed by and through Western or European feminists travelling outside of their locations (social or geographical) to rescue Other women or to bring Western feminism to Other women. This feminized colonialism has been the subject of a great deal of what has been called third-wave feminism or Third World feminism, and while this writing back or speaking back to Western, liberal feminism has been vitally important for feminist thinking as a whole, it is only a partial response to the fragmentation of feminism.

A deeper and more critical taking up of the politics of difference within feminist struggles against patriarchy ought to be the object and subject of our feminist analyses. That is, the road out of patriarchy is not through a modified version of it, which only enables some women, or women-identified subjects, to participate at the margins, but rather human liberation demands the complete dismantling of the structure of patriarchy. Intersectional feminism requires feminists to engage with difference in a radically new way – to recognize the creative potential of difference without romanticizing or minimizing its effects on peoples whose differences have been constructed as deviant or subordinate (Lorde 2003). A contemporary relevant feminism requires a complex and simultaneous understanding of the ways in which various systems come together in particular ways on the bodies of women.

My own entry point into intersectionality has been through postcolonial and anticolonial feminist theory for the purpose of addressing gendered racism. One significant contribution from this body of scholarship has been "to racialize mainstream feminist theory and to insert feminist concerns into conceptualisations of colonialism and postcolonialism" (Lewis and Mills 2003, 3). The particularities of women's social locations due to racialized, classed, or national location has been neglected or only partially addressed. And as Mohanty succinctly states, "Beyond sisterhoods, there are still racism, colonialism, and imperialism" (2003, 36). These foci are variously taken up and reflected in the work of other postcolonial feminists such as Mohanty, Razack, Bannerji, hooks, Anzaldúa, Morega, Trinh, Yegenoglu, Abu-Lughod, Zine, Eisenstein, and others whose scholarship and writing highlights not only the differing effects of patriarchy on the lives of women but also takes up the problematic discourses within Western feminism, including some radical feminists (see Alison Stone's critique of McKinnon and Dworkin). Mohanty (2003) and others have written extensively about the tendency for liberal feminism in particular to reproduce colonial and imperial relations within the movement as well as abroad. Thus, one significant contribution of postcolonial feminist analyses has been to decentre dominant feminist discourse, which has also had the effect of recentring the problem of global patriarchy. In *Casting Out: The Eviction of Muslim from Western Law and Politics* (2008), Razack carefully traces the complex relationships between gendered, colonial/imperial, and racist discourses that serve to privilege Western women and to buttress multiple systems, including patriarchy and racism:

> Just as men claim the universal for themselves through confining women outside of it as non-rational subjects, so the Western woman requires the culturally different body to make her own claim of universality. Unveiling the Muslim woman, rendering her body visible, and hence knowable and available for possession, renders the Western woman as the colonial, observing possessing subject. Thus old colonial technologies enjoy renewed vigour. (86)

These anticolonial (and anti-capitalist) feminists remind scholars (and activists) that colonialism and patriarchy are interpenetrated – that is, they work together to (re)produce patriarchal systems that are experienced by Other women, in material ways that exacerbate their already existing subordination as racialized, classed, sexualized, and other de-privileged subject positions. In addition to these important postcolonial and anticolonial critiques, post-structural theories of gender (e.g., Judith Butler and Alison Stone) have opened up space for feminist theorizing that questions the category of woman as a biological or social construct, which also serves to redirect attention to the epistemic and socio-political systems that continue to operate through and on bodies. As Hemmings observes, feminists can work toward "stressing the links rather than the discontinuities between different theoretical frameworks, as a way of challenging the linear 'displacement' of one approach by another. Firstly, schools of thought conventionally pitted against one another, for example sexual difference and gender theories, might productively be read for their rather different approaches to the common problem of power in the production of sexual and gendered meaning" (2009, 131).

These compelling and cogent arguments put to rest any claims that an intersectional approach diverts attention from issues pertaining to women, by pointing out that such claims have problematically and erroneously conflated identity politics (which was counterproductive for the building of broad-scale movements) with a rigorous intersectional approach. Rather than hobbling the movement politically, an intersectional feminism addresses head-on the symbolic and material violence reproduced on and through bodies that are viewed to deviate from the norm. As Kim Hall (2011) has observed, "Within feminist disability studies, exploring conceptual and lived connections between gender and disability helps to make visible the historical and ongoing interrelationship between all forms of oppression" (4). Her observation echoes the intersectional call to not only interrogate at a conceptual level – the intersecting and interlocking nature of oppressions that rely on the surveilling and patrolling of identity norms and boundaries – but also to develop a radical coalitional activism that holds this conceptualization as the foundation of a political project.

Within this space/these spaces, the possibility exists for an intersectional feminist theorizing and practice, a possibility that (re)turns attention to the presence and effects of patriarchy on all subjects. In the following section, I turn to the history of feminism within the field of adult education in Canada and then map out and begin to demonstrate the value of an intersectional approach to adult anti-oppression education within that broad field.

FEMINISM IN CANADIAN ADULT EDUCATION

The field of adult education, within the Canadian context, has had a varied, complex, and contested history. As Miles (1998) stated, "Adult education has always been an enterprise too broad and diverse to be contained within any professionally defined field. It is deeply rooted in all the projects of our lives and communities and in all our social, economic, political, and cultural institutions" (250). Within this broad, diffuse, and diverse field, an interesting tension has always existed between the instrumental and the critical or emancipatory aspects of adult education. Vocational training, post-secondary education, and workplace education and training stand beside the more emancipatory projects[2] associated with adult education (Collins 1998). The latter are reflected in such notable examples as the Antigonish Movement and Frontier College (Selman 1998), both of which focused on supporting working-class members of Canadian society to become politically informed and active citizens. During the early years of adult education in Canada, there was, arguably, less tension between the instrumental and social aspects of the field. However, the rise of globalization (the new movement of people and capital across borders) and the emergence of neo-liberal capitalist economics have contributed to changes in the discipline, including sharper divisions between instrumental and non-instrumental foci in adult education.

Throughout this history, the education of women has had a place within the broad field of adult education, and issues considered to be of specific and particular concern to women learners are documented in Canadian adult education anthologies (Stalker 1998; Miles 1998; Butterwick 2013; English 2013; Taber 2013). While some of the more formal aspects of adult education for women have focused on instrumental learning as a way of emancipating women by preparing them for higher education or the workplace (Stalker 1998), there has also been a concordant stream of adult education that was perhaps more overtly political within which I would locate anti-oppression education. A feminist intersectionality has much to offer this field at the level of both theory and practice. In the following section, I suggest some possibilities for a feminist intersectionality within anti-oppression education.

FEMINIST INTERSECTIONALITY AND ADULT EDUCATION

The underpinnings of an anti-oppressive practice, guided by feminist intersectionality, will require a complex simultaneity that is not, I argue, impossible. The continued decolonizing of feminist theory through the use of an intersectional approach might mean the articulation of a set of organizing principles that does not take as its starting point the inevitability of the phallic symbolic order (systems of patriarchy) that we have inherited. I refer to Mignolo (2011), who offers this perspective: "Modernity and postmodernity are options, not ontological moments of universal history, and so are subaltern, alternative, or peripheral modernities" (279). While Mignolo is referring to modernity per se, I extrapolate from this observation the possibility that the ubiquity of patriarchy does not mean that it is a natural or inevitable state of affairs. We can trace its origins and map its genealogy, recognizing that, while we have inherited it, it does not have to be our legacy. Thus, the first requirement of an educational curriculum and pedagogy would be to include a clear elucidation of the noninevitable nature of patriarchy, and to interrogate the effects on all human beings of this political system. With this principle in mind, educators would endeavour to support learners to develop an understanding of the material conditions of people living under patriarchy: that is, human beings living within a system that organizes subjects hierarchically on the basis of their identities. Curricula founded upon this requirement would enable an analysis of social systems and political structures that have evolved around and embed a patriarchal ethos.

Second, feminist intersectionality has the potential to correct certain shortcomings of anti-oppression curricula currently favoured by many engaged in emancipatory forms of adult education. According to Kumashiro (2000, 2001, 2002, 2004, and 2006), anti-oppression education has been inadequately theorized to account for complex and fluid identities and for interlocking systems of oppression. Kumashiro emphasizes the need for complex, adaptive, mobile forms of theorizing to create curriculum and pedagogy that is effectively disruptive. One of the advantages of an anti-oppressive education, informed by intersectional feminism, is that it draws from a number of theoretical and disciplinary traditions including critical race theory, queer theorizing, postcolonial feminist theories, and cultural studies. In doing so, it is able to articulate a non-essentialist view of identity, while addressing relations of power and social location that are mediated by identities that have been shaped by patriarchy. An educational practice that locates itself as being anti-oppressive is intended to draw attention to Otherness as an effect. It rejects and interrogates normativity while highlighting the way that difference is marshalled to organize social relations in hierarchical arrangements. Feminist intersectionality contains the potential to disrupt essentialist thinking and link the oppressive nature of essentialism with the project of patriarchy.

One of the drawbacks of earlier iterations of anti-oppression education, including curricula and pedagogy that draw primarily upon feminist theory, is its partiality (Kumashiro 2002). The challenge of any feminist adult education practice is to avoid defaulting to the partial addressing of systems and relations of oppression (e.g., sexism) at the expense of other forms of oppression. The pedagogical aim is to develop a theory and practice that guards against or works against what Kumashiro calls "repetition" (2002). Drawing upon Judith Butler, Kumashiro describes oppression as "characterized by the repetition in society of regulatory identities, knowledge, and practices. In particular what is oppressive is having to experience, again and again, the privileging of only certain ways of identifying, thinking, or relating to others" (68). An educational practice that draws upon the intersectional is concerned with the development of pedagogies that enable "learning against repetition" (Kumashiro 2002, 70).

Finally, an intersectional feminism has one other important contribution to make to an anti-oppressive adult education practice: the promise of more careful and skillful attention to learner resistance. In their respective work on anti-racism education, Schick (2000), Aveling (2006), and Arber (2000) all caution educators to recognize, plan for, and respect learners' needs to protect a deeply held sense of themselves. Articulations of hostility, rationalization, and defensiveness often mask the subject's struggle to preserve the imaginary and to stave off any encounter with their symbolic ordering of the world. The students' investment in the symbolic is significant. Kumashiro (who is drawing upon the work of Britzman) reminds the educator that learners will need to learn how to "interrupt their resistance to disruptive, disaffirming knowledge" (2002, 70), and, I would add, to develop methods of working with that resistance, and to find fertile possibilities for exploring the nature and origins of such resistance.

If the purpose of feminism has been to both interrogate systems and discourses of oppression and also dismantle them, then an education to build a mass movement in that direction will necessarily require that we draw upon theories of difference that enable students, learners, and indeed educators to become conscious of the ways in which both normative and regulatory identity-based regimes have been used to divide human beings. A feminist intersectionality offers one way out of the cul-de-sac that was and is identity politics. It enables us, as Chandra Mohanty once famously said, to turn our attention away from identity politics and to focus on the politics of identity. Future-oriented adult education will take heed of Mohanty's advice and continue to rethink, reconfigure, and reimagine the theoretical and practical terrain.

INTO THE FUTURE

I began this chapter with a reflection on my own history within both feminist movements and anti-racism movements, observing that identity essentialisms operating within feminist activism and scholarship have sometimes resulted in incomplete analyses of how power operates. I then focused my critique on some of the more predominant forms of feminist theorizing, pointing out, as many others have already done, that the absences and silencing of certain lived experiences helped to give rise to a proliferation of feminisms to address microcontextual (Mohanty 2003) sites of gender-based oppression.

The binary ordering of subjects, including but not limited to woman-identified subjects, has regulated social and political life in such a way that even liberatory projects like feminism become caught up in reproducing these dividing practices. I have been reflecting on and imagining a deep analysis of systems of thought and social structures that have been the legacy, at least in significant part, of patriarchy. I am suggesting that feminism – an intersectional feminism – may contain within it the possibility for such an analysis, which has the potential to heal these splits. It is important to clarify that I am by no means proposing either a totalizing feminist ethos or a return to the universality of modernity to address this fragmentation, but rather I view an intersectional approach as one way of deepening our analysis to reveal the profoundly interconnected nature of our seemingly disparate liberatory struggles. In a strange way, this intersectionality marks a return to the original socio-political project of feminism reminding us that its intent was, and continues to be, to disrupt patriarchy, to challenge the logic of it, and to imagine, theorize, and enact other ways of knowing and being.

An intersectional feminism points to the symbolic phallocentric privileging of masculinism, initially within the family structure through the father, and then extended to other forms of authority, which becomes conflated with the masculine or the phallic. Thus heteronormativity, whiteness, and standardized notions of ability, which have become markers for phallic authority, *are* feminist concerns. Simply put, the dismantling of phallocentrism or patriarchy will necessitate and include the dismantling of other binary orderings of subjects. This is the intersectional point of such future work. And a future-oriented adult education practice that subscribes to a feminist intersectional approach would take as its starting point the consideration of how these logics are at work in curriculum, pedagogy, and systems of adult education practices.

I write and reflect on these issues because the fragmentation of the movement and the growing divide between and among feminisms poses a threat to the greater struggle for equity and against inequity (gendered or otherwise) produced and reproduced through patriarchal systems. An intersectional feminism has the potential to bridge these divides and to contribute to Mohanty's (2003) vision of a feminism that embodies "egalitarian and non-colonizing cross-cultural scholarship" (502) and practice.

There have been significant epistemic and ontological changes within feminist scholarship over the past thirty-five years. What was once the purview of middle-class, straight, white women, has been transformed by – at the insistence and thoughtful persistence of – Other voices and perspectives. Issues that were considered ancillary to the movement and not salient to "the struggle" have made their way into feminist discourses and activism. We can no longer ignore the ways in which skin matters, who we love matters, what our bodies look like matters. We can no longer ignore the complexities and effects of privilege and the ubiquitous workings of normativity within scholarly, educational, and activist domains. As Cho, Crenshaw, and McCall (2013) remind us, intersectionality (including feminist intersectionality) is an analytic approach that enables us to see and act on the world differently:

> What makes an analysis intersectional – whatever terms it deploys, whatever its iteration, whatever its field or discipline – is its adoption of an intersectional way of thinking about the problem of sameness and difference and its relation to power. This framing – conceiving of categories not as distinct but as always permeated by other categories, fluid and changing, always in the process of creating and being created by dynamics of power – emphasizes what intersectionality does rather than what intersectionality is. (795)

Intersectionality is most certainly not the master's tool, and it may indeed help us in our (educational) attempts to dismantle the master's house.

NOTES

1 I use the term Arab/Muslim woman or women (with the backslash) to denote the way in which these two identifiers or subject positions are often confused and conflated.
2 I locate both social reformism and transformative or emancipatory education within the latter, although there are important distinctions.

REFERENCES

Abu-Lughod, L. 2001. "'Orientalism' and Middle East Feminist Studies." *Feminist Studies* 27 (1): 101–13. doi:10.2307/3178451.

Anzaldúa, G. 1987. *Borderlands/La Frontera: The New Mestiza*. San Francisco: Aunt Lute Books.

– 2000. "(Un)natural Bridges, (Un)Safe Spaces." In *This Bridge We Call Home: Radical Visions for Transformation*, ed. I.G. and G.A. Keating, 1–5. New York: Routledge.

Arber, R. 2000. "Defining Positioning within Politics of Difference: Negotiating Spaces 'in Between.'" *Race, Ethnicity and Education* 3 (1): 45–63. doi:10.1080/713693012.

Aveling, N. 2006. "'Hacking at Our Very Roots': Rearticulating White Racial Identity within the Context of Teacher Education." *Race, Ethnicity and Education* 9 (3): 261–74. doi:10.1080/13613320600807576.

Bannerji, H. 1993. "Returning the Gaze: An Introduction." In *Returning the*

Gaze: Essays of Racism, Feminism, and Politics, ed. H. Bannerji, ix–xxiv. Toronto: Sister Vision Press.
- 1995. *Thinking Through: Essays on Feminism, Marxism, and Anti-Racism.* Toronto: Women's Press.
- 2000. *The Dark Side of the Nation: Essays on Multiculturalism, Nationalism, and Gender.* Toronto: Canadian Scholars' Press.

Butler, J. 1999. *Gender Trouble: Feminism and the Subversion of Identity.* New York: Routledge.

Butterwick, S. 2013. "Class and Poverty Matters: The Role of Adult Education in Reproduction and Resistance." In *Building on Critical Conditions: Adult Education and Learning in Canada*, ed. T. Nesbit, S.M. Brigham, N. Taber, and T. Gibb, 129–38. Toronto: Thompson Educational.

Cho, S., K.W. Crenshaw, and L. McCall. 2013. "Toward a Field of Intersectionality Studies: Theory, Applications, and Praxis." In *Signs: Journal of Women in Culture and Society* 38 (4): 785–810. doi:10.1086/669608.

Collins, P.H. 1998. "Lifelong Education as Emancipatory Pedagogy." In *Learning for Life: Canadian Readings in Adult Education*, ed. S.M. Scott, B. Spencer, and A.M. Thomas, 107–13. Toronto: Thompson Educational.

English, L. 2013. "Gender and Literacy in Historical Perspective: A Newfoundland Case Study." In *Building on Critical Conditions: Adult Education and Learning in Canada*, ed. T. Nesbit, S. M. Brigham, N. Taber, and T. Gibb, 62–71. Toronto: Thompson Educational.

Fah, B. 2003. "Analytic Dualisms, Stunted Sexualities, and the 'Horrified Gaze': Western (Feminist) Dialogues about Female Genital Mutilation." *Michigan Feminist Studies* 17:47–70.

Fraser, N. 2010. ""Who Counts? Dilemmas of Justice in a Postwestphalian World." *Antipode: A Radical Journal of Geography* 41 (1): 281–97.
- 2013. *Fortunes of Feminism: From State-Managed Capitalism to Neoliberal Crisis and Beyond.* Brooklyn: Verso Books.

Hall, K. 2011. *Feminist Disability Studies.* Bloomington: Indiana University Press.

Hemmings, C. 2005. "Telling Feminist Stories." *Feminist Theory* 6 (2): 115–39. doi:10.1177/1464700105053690.

hooks, b. 1981. *Ain't I a Woman? Black Women and Feminism.* Boston: South End Press.
- 1996. *Reel to Real: Race, Sex and Class at the Movies.* New York: Routledge.
- 2000. *Feminist Theory: From Margin to Centre.* Cambridge: South End Press.

Kumashiro, K. 2000. "Toward a Theory of Anti-Oppressive Education." *Review of Educational Research* 70 (1): 25–53. doi:10.3102/00346543070001025.

- 2001. "'Posts' Perspectives on Anti-Oppressive Education in Social Studies, English, Mathematics, and Science Classrooms." *Educational Researcher* 30 (3): 3–12. doi:10.3102/0013189X030003003.
- 2002. "Against Repetition: Addressing Resistance to Anti-Oppressive Change in Learning, Teaching, Supervising and Researching." *Harvard Educational Review* 72 (1): 67–92. doi:10.17763/haer.72.1.c1161752617k46v6.
- 2004. "Uncertain Beginnings: Learning to Teach Paradoxically." *Theory into Practice* 43 (2): 111–15. doi:10.1207/s15430421tip4302_3.
- 2006. "Toward an Anti-Oppressive Theory of Asian Americans and Pacific Islanders." *Race, Ethnicity and Education* 9 (1): 129–35. doi:10.1080/13613320500490879.

Lewis, R.L. 2003. "Introduction." In *Feminist Postcolonial Theory: A Reader*, ed. R.L. Mills, 1–28. New York: Routledge.

Lorde, A. 2003. "The Master's Tools Will Never Dismantle the Master's House." In *Feminist Postcolonial Theory: A Reader*, ed. R.L. Mills, 25–8. New York: Routledge.

Mignolo, W. 2011. "Geopolitics of Sensing and Knowing: On (De)Coloniality, Border Thinking and Epistemic Disobedience." *Postcolonial Studies* 14 (3): 273–83.

Miles, A. 1998. "Learning from the Women's Movement in the Neo-Liberal Period." In *Learning for Life: Canadian Readings in Adult Education*, ed. S. Scott, 300–12. Toronto: Thompson Educational.

Minh Ha, T. 1989. *Woman, Native, Other: Writing Postcoloniality and Feminism*. Bloomington: Indiana University Press.

Mohanty, C.T. 2003. *Feminism without Borders: Decolonizing Theory, Practicing Solidarity*. Durham, NC: Duke University Press. doi:10.1215/9780822384649.

Razack, S. 1998. *Looking White People in the Eye: Gender, Race, and Culture in Courtrooms and Classrooms*. Toronto: University of Toronto Press.

- 2004. "Imperilled Muslim Women, Dangerous Muslim Men, and Civilised Europeans: Legal and Social Responses to Forced Marriages." *Feminist Legal Studies* 12 (2): 129–74. doi:10.1023/B:FEST.0000043305 .66172.92.
- 2005. "Geopolitics, Culture Clash and Gender after September 11." *Social Justice (San Francisco, Calif.)* 32 (4): 11–31.
- 2008. *Casting Out: The Eviction of Muslim from Western Law and Politics*. Toronto: University of Toronto Press.

Said, E. 1978. *Orientalism*. New York: Vintage.

Schick, C. 2000. "'By Virtue of Being White': Resistance in Anti-Racist Pedagogy." *Race, Ethnicity and Education* 3 (1): 83–101. doi:10.1080/713693016.

Selman, G. 1998. "The Imaginative Training for Citizenship." In *Learning for Life: Canadian Readings in Adult Education*, ed. S.M. Scott, B. Spencer, and A.M. Thomas, 24–34. Toronto: Thompson Educational.

Spivak, G. 2010. "Can the Subaltern Speak?" In *Can the Subaltern Speak? Reflections on the History of an Idea*, ed. R.C. Morris and G. Spivak, 21–80. New York: Columbia University Press.

Stalker, J. 1998. "Women in the History of Adult Education: Misogynist Responses to Our Participation." In *Learning for Life: Canadian Readings in Adult Education*, ed. S.M. Scott, B. Spencer, and A.M. Thomas, 238–49. Toronto: Thompson Educational.

Stone, A. 2004. "Essentialism and Anti-Essentialism in Feminist Philosophy." *Journal of Moral Philosophy* 1 (2): 135–53. doi:10.1177/1740468104001002o2.

Taber, N. 2013. "Learning War through Gender: Masculinities, Femininities, and Militarism." In *Building on Critical Conditions: Adult Education and Learning in Canada*, ed. T. Nesbit, S.M. Brigham, N. Taber, and T. Gibb, 139–48. Toronto: Thompson Educational.

Weeden, C. 1999. *Feminism, Theory, and the Politics of Difference*. Oxford: Blackwell Publishers.

Yegenoglu, M. 1998. *Colonial Fantasies: Towards a Feminist Reading of Orientalism*. Cambridge: Cambridge University Press. doi:10.1017/CBO9780511583445.

– 2003. "Veiled Fantasies: Cultural and Sexual Difference in the Discourse of Orientalism." In *Post-Colonial Feminist Studies: A Reader*, ed. R.L. Lewis and S.M. Mills, 542–66. New York: Routledge.

Young, I.M. 1994. "Gender as Seriality: Thinking about Women as a Social Collective." Signs: Journal of Women in Culture and Society 19 (3): 713–38. doi:10.1086/494918.

8

Indigenizing My Roots in Feminism

MARLENE MCKAY

The community called her Awcheecheet, and she was my maternal Cree French grandmother who helped raise me while my mother worked. Awcheecheet is a Cree word meaning the person with the hands. I believe she was given this name because she was known to be a hard worker. My granny taught me many things about being responsible and the importance of contributing. When we were younger, she would often get us out of bed by saying, in a thick Cree accent, "You can't sleep all day. You have work to do." She did not speak much English, but she was able to articulate these words to get the grandchildren up for school or chores. These are words I have internalized that now function as an alarm to get me up to go to work. I am grateful I had Awcheecheet in my life as she taught me the significance of hard work and that, even though we were poor, our integrity was worth something.

I was raised in a Cree community in Cumberland House, Saskatchewan, populated by both Métis and First Nations people. In my generation, everyone spoke Cree; even those non-Indigenous students whose parents worked in the community learned to speak Cree. I learned English when I became a student at the local public elementary school that, at the time, was taught by nuns. I also had to leave my community to attend grade 12, though the local school now offers a full K–12 program. For many families, fishing, hunting, and trapping were the primary means for supporting the family, and they continue to be a source of sustenance. In our Cree community, we learned the importance of kinship, speaking Cree, and being able to live off the land.

Like many other communities in Northern Saskatchewan, forms of Christianity are dominant systems. Many Aboriginal people have become devout practitioners. When I was a child, there were two major Christian denominations in the community: Catholic and Anglican. Now, there are approximately four different churches that operate, and often there is competition about who has direct access to God. Unlike many of the Central and Southern Saskatchewan Aboriginal communities, there is little talk or practice of traditional Aboriginal ceremonies, such as sweat-lodge ceremonies or powwows. If observing spirituality exists, it is largely linked to the Christian church.

My mother was a single parent who had some support from my maternal grandparents. She carried the sole responsibility for providing for and parenting her children. My mother does not have any post-secondary education, but she worked at various long-term jobs until she retired. She has a strong work ethic and she modelled the ethic that no matter how hard things might seem, one must keep going. My mother is also a devout Catholic, and we endured most of the rituals involved in that denomination. As much as the church is a form of strength for her, it has also contributed to her having shame and guilt for bearing illegitimate children.

In this chapter, I draw on my lived experience and I engage Aboriginal people in a feminist conversation. Discourses that acknowledge male dominance and female subjugation in Aboriginal communities are relatively recent. Although our colonial history continues to be monumentally felt in education, administration, band policies and elections, a gendered analysis is often not welcomed in Aboriginal contexts. Hence, I approach my discussion on feminism in education from an Aboriginal perspective within a broad context. Given my Indigenous roots and its impact on my understandings of life, I elaborate on what theory has to offer for understanding subjectivity, what societal rules are imposed upon Aboriginal women, what international Indigenous women are saying about Indigenous feminism, what Aboriginal feminism is, and feminism in education from an Indigenous perspective. I draw on recently conducted research on experiences of Aboriginal women.

WHAT DOES THEORY OFFER FOR UNDERSTANDING SUBJECTIVITY?

The theories that inform this analysis come from feminist poststructuralism (Davies 2000; St Pierre 2000; Weedon 1997) and Michel Foucault's (1990) notion of relations of power. Of particular relevance are the ways in which discourse, power, and knowledge operate to silence or affirm subjects. The positioning of Aboriginal people will be examined through these theoretical lenses.

According to St Pierre (2000), feminist poststructuralism has no fixed meaning because there are a number of discourses in play at any given time. People who advocate a feminist post-structural position have ceased attempting to understand. This position is a troubling stance for many who insist that there is a unified reality and truth in which all people are included and are knowable if only the right methods are followed. For example, a unified reality would suggest that being manly and womanly are easily recognizable. However, the discourses made available to women vary because women's issues are not all the same: women's social and political positions and subjectivities vary across class, race, sexuality, and political stance. Given that women are diversely located, feminist poststructuralism recognizes a multiplicity of locations. Weedon (1997) explains that in feminist poststructuralism, gender is understood to be socially produced, and that different forms of gendered discourses are made available to women. Weedon suggests that we look at social processes and institutions to understand how power relations work to produce and reproduce familiar gendered discourses and to identify strategies for change. We must be cognizant that discourses and social processes are fundamental to understanding our positioning as women. This chapter examines the discourses and social processes particular to my local context.

Weedon (1997) suggests that "in poststructuralist feminism, we can choose between different accounts of reality on the basis of their social implications" (28). When men and women are defined by specific characteristics, ideas emerge that contribute to a belief that identities are stable and unified as male or female. This further entrenches women into particular roles, such as women as nurturers and caretakers. St Pierre (2000) finds that women have historically been considered to be natural, sensual, and emotional, while men have been perceived to act within the realm of culture, thought, and reason. Feminist poststructuralism opens up opportunities for women to reposition and to act on these accounts of social and political constructions that have social implications for them. Agency is possible through attention to social and political constructions that are useful in developing a critical understanding of the colonial legacy on gender relations in Aboriginal communities.

At the individual level, feminist poststructuralism offers an explanation of how our experiences are produced, why those productions can be problematic, and how they can change (Weedon 1997). This theory offers a mode of knowledge production in which theories of language, subjectivity, social processes and practices, and institutions are entangled in relations of power. Through an analysis of historically produced discourses, feminist poststructuralism is able to explain how power has worked on behalf of specific interests, a result of which has opened opportunities for resistance. When we see how discourse works in power relations, we learn that the subject is not a unified stable self, but rather one whose subjectivity is contingent upon the discourses that are made socially available at any given time and place. This chapter focuses on gender and the production of colonial social relations of Aboriginal people.

Foucault (1990) explicates a theory of relations of power that is applicable to this analysis. Foucault notes that power is omnipresent, "not because it [power] has the privilege of consolidating everything under its invincible unity, but because it [power] is produced from one moment to the next, at every point, or rather in every relation from one point. Power is everywhere; not because it embraces everything, but because it comes from everywhere" (93). Power operates with aims and objectives; it is productive. Power functions as actions upon actions, but it does not involve persuasion or coercion (Prado 2000). Rather, this power modifies the actions of others through surveillance and discourses. Prado agrees that "power is a total structure of actions brought to bear upon possible actions in the sense that power enables or enhances some actions and inhibits or precludes others" (68).

When we understand that power circulates among and through individuals, we understand the relations of power. Power relations operate in a complex system and our socialization reproduces the same subjects through binaries such as man/woman, good/bad. Prado (2000) holds that "to act in defiance is to act within power, not against it. To escape power, one would have to be utterly alone and free of all the enculturation that makes us social beings" (73). In addition, there is a persuasive element to power where particular discursive practices are enforced. Therefore, enmeshed as we are within social and institutional relations, resistance inevitably circulates within those relations of power (Foucault 1990; Prado 2000). Individuals cannot escape power because, as Prado notes, power "is the intricate web of constraining interrelationships that exists the moment there is more than one agent" (73). Foucault's theory of relations of power helps to contextualize how individuals are socialized through a system of powerful forces.

The discourses that come from both Eurocentric and Aboriginal traditions affect Aboriginal people's understandings and experiences of colonialism. One of these discourses is that of authenticity. Although we cannot claim a pure Aboriginal culture because of colonizing interruptions, we are nonetheless left to live within a colossal colonial mess of contradictory ethical discourses. For example, I have introduced myself as a Cree-speaking Indigenous woman. I have also identified as being schooled in Western institutions and being raised in the Christian value system. As a consequence, there are contradictions and choices I must make in order to claim agency. Davies (2000) contends that "persons as speakers acquire beliefs about themselves that do not necessarily form a unified coherent whole. They shift from one to another way of thinking about themselves as the discourse shifts as their positions within varying storylines are taken up" (102). With regard to the discourses that are made available, I concur with Davies that we must speak ourselves into existence because we must position ourselves in the discourses that are made available in order to enact agency.

SOCIETAL RULES IMPOSED ON ABORIGINAL WOMEN: CHRISTIANITY, TRADITIONAL CULTURE, AND PATRIARCHY

In my doctoral research, I examined the ways that single-parent Aboriginal women of Northern Saskatchewan experience marginalization. One theme that emerged was the imposition of discursive rules onto Aboriginal women. Some of these discursive rules come from Christianity and the effects of colonialism on Aboriginal traditional cultural practices. These rules operate to oppress, manage, denigrate, and silence Aboriginal women. To be clear, I am neither advocating a rejection of Christianity nor am I promoting a dismissal of Aboriginal cultural traditions. However, what I am asserting is that rules operate to celebrate some identities and silence others. These discursive rules are imposed by specific subjectivities with a particular learned patriarchal perspective that operates to monitor Aboriginal women's performance of their subjectivity.

Brown and Parker (1989) critique women's positioning in Christianity and they propose that women are anesthetized into abuse in the context of male privileging and male domination in the Christian Church. The abuse is often a part of women's enculturation: women are expected to stay in abusive marriages, to stay silent when raped, use their/our energy to support other lives, and even to punish themselves if successful (Brown and Parker 1989). The authors contend that, for those who are deeply invested in the Christian tradition, self-sacrifice and obedience are the measures of a faithful and moral identity. Brown and Parker also propose that "Our full personhood as well as our rights have been denied us. We have been labelled the sinful ones, the other; and even when we are let in, so to speak, we are constantly reminded of our inferior status through language, theological concepts of original sin, and perpetual virginity – all of which relate to sex, for which, of course, women are responsible" (3). Based on my family and community upbringing and the information provided by the single-parent Aboriginal women from my research, this is the social and moral context of many Aboriginal women's lives: to be self-sacrificial, obedient, and to aspire to a biblical virgin ideal.

Ruether (1989) examines women's reproductive rights in Christianity. She contends that "It is not primitive ignorance but patriarchal ideology that decrees that women should not use contraceptives or seek abortion and should accept whatever pregnancies 'God' and males impose on them" (38). It is oppressive to use God as the rationale for keeping unplanned or unwanted pregnancies, which ultimately leads to silencing and marginalizing women. For Aboriginal women living in Aboriginal communities, particularly in remote areas, the scrutiny, or the breaking of the rules, is often marked with judgment, while the guilt and shame is paralyzing.

Additionally, women's purity before marriage is often closely monitored (Ruether 1989). Ruether finds that "women's chastity before and in marriage has been rigidly regulated, in contrast to the sexual freedom allowed males, in order to assure the paternity of the child" (38). There is a preoccupation with legitimacy. Ruether observes that a woman's "sexuality was defined in canon law and moral theology as the 'debt of her body' which she owes her husband in the marriage contract" (39). Within this understanding, then, women become property. There are many Aboriginal women who want to be in relationships and end up investing much emotion, time, and energy into keeping a stable or long-term, albeit dysfunctional, relationship. Many of these relationships result in children being born and, when the men leave, it is the women who become the parent and financial provider, while the men are often absolved of any responsibility and move on to other relationships. The Aboriginal woman becomes the image of sin, leading to a presumed state of degeneracy and immorality. Further to this, I argue that even if Aboriginal women were to follow all the rules in Christianity, her personhood is additionally marked by her racialization as uncivilized (Kuokkanen 2007). Discursive rules that affect Aboriginal women come from the norms of Christianity that position them in particular ways through relations of power that emerge from socialization.

Another way in which rules are imposed to regulate Aboriginal women is around activities surrounding traditional Aboriginal cultures. Martin-Hill (2003) warns us that there is often pressure for Indigenous structures to produce authentic cultural knowledge keepers and spiritual leaders. She warns that "we must be mindful of the gender issues that it raises" (112). Martin-Hill explains that she has been involved in the healing movement for Aboriginal people and that many people are profoundly affected by these efforts. She shares that at one healing event, she was charged with ensuring that elders were properly accommodated. One of the male elders at this event informed her he would be staying at her house during the conference. When she replied she did not have any room, his reply was "Well, I was planning on sleeping with you" (114). At the elder's words, she found herself dumbfounded, and even offered to pay for his hotel room. In response, this elder publicly commented at the conference about her inability to work with elders and her lack of organization skills. Martin-Hill refused the respected elder's sexual advance, thereby breaking the cultural rule that an elder's instructions cannot be questioned or refused, especially in places of healing and learning.

Another rule in traditional Aboriginal cultural events involves the drum. Deerchild (2003) writes, "The drum has been translated into a rule – women cannot sit in the first row behind the big drum, nor are they allowed to play the drum" (100). The place for women surrounding the drum is either sitting or standing in the second row and behind the male singers. When she questioned the reason for this, often the response was, "That's the way it's always been done" (100). Many Aboriginal women, however, question this rule and wonder if this rule is tradition or colonial patriarchal sexism?

Blaney (2003) offers a useful analysis regarding priorities and rules at the First Nations band offices. She writes about the work that is being done by the Aboriginal Women's Action Network. Blaney believes that many Aboriginal agencies and bands lack an analytical perspective and are often unable to recognize sexism. She finds that racism and sexism operate as a double jeopardy for Aboriginal women, with many First Nations women experiencing discrimination. In reference to one of these women, she writes: "They are not willing to help women. In fact, [despite] all of the paperwork that I supplied, my Indian band pushed my brother's status through and totally ignored mine. In the end I had to get [name of the person] to give a little shove to hurry mine up because we ended up in the dead file" (165). This example is much like my experience in becoming a registered Indian, but I had another obstacle to get through. First, I had to get my father to sign an affidavit attesting that he is indeed my father. He finally agreed with much reluctance and ridicule at first, after the lawyer I hired talked to him. Second, I waited for fifteen years and two applications to become an official band member of my ancestral community roots. Since I was raised in a poor single-parent family, I believed that becoming a registered Indian might entitle me to some educational benefits. Unfortunately, the patriarchal rules imposed through the Indian Act are now being policed and managed by First Nations band offices, often at the financial, social, and political expense of Aboriginal women.

At an educational institution in which I was previously employed, I had an experience that blatantly reveals the subjugation of Aboriginal women. My job was to help coordinate and facilitate an Aboriginal cultural camp for Aboriginal adult learners. My employers told me that I had to wear a dress and abstain from any ceremonies during my moon-time – moon-time refers to when women are menstruating. There were cultural practitioners present who were policing this for the Aboriginal women. The facility where this camp was being offered included a residential component. As I toured the facility with a director, she asked to see where I would be sleeping because "she wanted to make sure I would be sleeping alone." I was insulted and dumbfounded, yet I felt powerless to say anything as I had just been recently employed. At that point in my career, I had completed three degrees, one focusing on Aboriginal feminism. I also had fifteen years of previous experience in an organization where I had developed a respected professional reputation. And yet, I did not want to tell anyone about what this Euro-Canadian woman said to me because I was embarrassed and insulted. I had to wear a dress, I was excluded in some of the activities because I was menstruating, and I understood that I could not be trusted because of an assumed promiscuity. This, to me, is the normalization of Aboriginal women's marginalization, when it occurs in such a matter-of-fact manner, and even more so, when it occurs in a place of learning.

Our sense of ourselves as people is acquired through social processes (Burr 1995). It is in the structure of language that we come to understand how this happens. Of particular importance is that we ask ourselves what people are doing with their speech and what is the desirable outcome (Burr 1995). If language is not a reflection of reality, it is necessary to inquire what is being done with speech because it helps us understand how the relations of power are produced through a variety of discourses. For this analysis, I ask, "What are the purposes of imposing these discursive rules that shape the practices and structures mentioned above?"

Wetherell (2001) writes about discourse as a form of social action, referring to discourse involving work. Discourse constructs a version of social reality. If language allows for multiple versions of social reality, then discourse is viewed as productive. Wetherell observes that "It [discourse] is designed to be persuasive, to win hearts and minds ... What is said is often produced, heard, and read in relation to the things which are not said. Discourse is a designed activity. It involves work" (17). It takes work and effort to impose rules onto Aboriginal women, and this leads to positioning them in particular ways. It is important to be mindful of the work and effort that become observable through attention to social and material practices and processes.

Wetherell (2001) suggests that we consider the origins of meaning. Meaning is born out of complex social historical processes and is relational. Wetherell finds that "discourse continually adds to, instantiates, extends and transforms the cultural storehouse of meaning" (18). Meaning is a joint production; it comes out of particular interactions with engaged participants, and in cultural/social and political contexts. Wetherell (2001) reveals that "in the production of discourse we see people cooperating to generate social events which make shared sense" (18). There is often a rejecting or validating of discourses that are co-produced in social action. Through the discourse of social action and the rules involved, the positioning of Aboriginal women is an active endeavour that subordinates; it is not the result of innate inferiority, which some discourses would have us believe. Rules imposed on Aboriginal women originate from a particular subject position that is deeply socialized in historical, patriarchal, and racialized discourses. When Aboriginal women are constructed as inferior, as they often are, it is performed with purpose because of the dominant historical discourses that have served to normalize this social production. Aboriginal feminism is helpful in naming these oppressive discourses.

WHAT IS ABORIGINAL FEMINISM?

For many Aboriginal people, feminism is the new "F" word that is marked by suspicion and is often minimized or ridiculed. Feminism is often considered to be a European construct that is irrelevant to Aboriginal people, suggesting that male privileging does not exist in Aboriginal communities. It is also dismissed because of the belief that women want to be positioned better than men. Of course, this assumption is faulty because feminism is about becoming cognizant of how privilege becomes unequally available to men in heteropatriarchy and then working toward strategies for change that are equitable for men and women. For Aboriginal people to be part of the feminist discourse, an articulation of some of our concerns is necessary. As a self-identified Aboriginal feminist, I must situate my feminist positioning in the discourses that are offered to me as a woman and as an Aboriginal person. These two identity categories intersect to produce significant differences among all women. I turn now to Green (2007) and St Denis (2007), two Aboriginal scholars who define Aboriginal feminism.

Green (2007) likens Aboriginal feminism to socialist, maternal, radical, liberal, and ecofeminist characteristics. She believes that gender is a serious social-organizing process that operates within patriarchal societies. Green writes, "Feminism is usually viewed as multiple: feminisms analyze the diversity of women's cultural, political and in other ways specific experiences" (21). A feminist perspective surfaces when conditions of male dominance are operating, and responds by seeking ways to respond to oppression. Yet, she also asserts there are women's groups such as REAL (Realistic, Equal, Active for Life) Women who reject or malign feminism. The organization, REAL Women, is a group of conservative women who believe that the family is the most important structure in society – in this context, an ideal family would entail a mother, father, and children. Other communities and cultures believe that they are free from patriarchal oppression, and that their cultural practices affirm women's power and positioning, consequently, they see feminism as irrelevant (Green 2007).

As I mentioned earlier, in contemporary society, Aboriginal women are often given secondary status. Green (2007) claims that "contemporary Aboriginal women are subjected to patriarchal and colonial oppression within settler society and, in some contexts, in Aboriginal communities" (22). Whether through original processes or by incorporating the colonizer's patriarchy, Aboriginal communities have become patriarchal. As a result, Aboriginal women endure both sexism and racism within the dominant society and often within their own communities.

Green (2007) holds that, in patriarchal societies, feminists are denigrated because "they question the common understanding of what it means to be a good woman (and a good man), and they challenge the social, political, economic, and cultural practices that validate, perpetuate and enforce these roles" (22). She shares Rebecca West's analysis, who said that people called her a "feminist whenever I express sentiments that differentiate me from a doormat" (22). For feminists, challenging dominant practices is not easy as they are met with suspicion or even hostility from members of their own communities.

Green (2007) questions how liberation will take place for Indigenous women, given that some Indigenous political cultures have internalized racism and sexism as it operates in colonialism. She suggests that a return to traditional culture is often put forward as a decolonizing and liberatory practice, and that traditional culture is often promoted as being purely Indigenous where women are believed to be honoured in their cultural contexts. Yet, the Royal Canadian Mounted Police (RCMP) produced a report on missing and murdered Aboriginal women in 2014 indicating that "most homicides were committed by men, and most perpetrators knew their victims – whether as an acquaintance or a spouse" (Canada 2014, 3). However, an Indigenous liberation theory premised on an untouched traditional culture "has not been attentive to the gendered way in which colonial oppression and racism function for men and women, or to the inherent and adopted sexisms that some communities manifest" (Green 2007, 23). As a result, Aboriginal feminists are often held at a distance when they link the effects of colonialism to sex and race oppression. Many people in the Aboriginal communities consider Aboriginal feminists as political adversaries and Aboriginal men in positions of leadership are often those who are dismissive of sexist and misogynist discourses that circulate within families and communities. For example, Shirley Green (2007) compares the news coverage of an Aboriginal woman who was shot in the back and killed by her husband in the Yukon with the killing of a pregnant cow moose a few weeks later. In the numerous news stories about the dead cow moose, it was suggested that the person responsible be prosecuted to the fullest extent of the law, while there was no attention paid to the woman who was shot by her husband. Green asserts that, in this example, "it was open season on women in the Yukon" (161).

In order to confront accusations that Aboriginal feminists have assumed white colonial theories, many Aboriginal women assert that a feminist analysis helps to challenge racism and sexism. Green (2007) finds that Aboriginal feminists are able to articulate the ways in which colonialism affects women and children, and how some Aboriginal peoples have internalized colonial practices in their communities. She reveals that in some band politics, women who have the courage to talk about the distribution of resources or violence against women are often judged as feminists, as though it is a measure of sin and that there is a little merit in addressing this violence. Matters do not end at being called a feminist; Aboriginal women's authenticity is questioned when they are identified as feminists. Green (2007) finds that "it is as though some authority has decided that Aboriginal women cannot be culturally authentic, or traditional, or acceptable, if they are feminists" (25). Ultimately, the social and political contexts of Aboriginal women's lives are very complex and cannot be easily summed up. Aboriginal women's positioning is not monolithic – perhaps it is the idea that Aboriginal culture is a monolith that contributes to Aboriginal women's subjugation by working against the possibility of naming and recognizing the effects of colonialism, thus providing room for change.

St Denis (2007) makes an important contribution to theorizing Aboriginal feminism. In an effort to understand why Aboriginal women dismiss the relevance of feminism, she identifies six reasons, but for this analysis, I will focus on two. First, St Denis comments that "some Aboriginal women contest the feminist claim that male's domination is universal" (37). That is, some Aboriginal women, including scholars, believe that patriarchy is not universal and that historical Aboriginal cultural practices held women in high regard. She writes: "This claim further asserts that there are fundamental differences between Aboriginal and Eurocentric cultures in regards to gender relations. Some Aboriginal women claim that Aboriginal cultures do not have a history of unequal gender relations. In fact, it is argued, Aboriginal women occupy or occupied positions of authority, autonomy and high status in their communities" (37). Thinking back to the interviews I conducted for my research, as well as the experience of many women from my community, the rejection by some Aboriginal women scholars of the reality that male domination is normalized within Aboriginal communities does a real disservice to women and infers on them an inferior status. Many Aboriginal women have experienced and observed the ways in which patriarchy informs social and political participation. Also, many Aboriginal women feel frustrated and unable to confront male dominance when it happens because, when they do try, they are judged as going against cultural norms and practices, and, hence, rendered silent. I would argue that patriarchy has seeped through the walls of Aboriginal cultures because it was modelled, enforced, and normalized in colonialism and the residential school era.

Just as Green (2007) affirms that some Aboriginal communities believe in Indigenous solidarity, St Denis (2007) makes a similar observation of these Aboriginal women who reject feminism and regard feminism as in opposition to Aboriginal restoration. St Denis explains: "Some Aboriginal women regard it as unnecessary to appeal for the attainment of the same rights as men; rather, they appeal for the restoration and reclaiming of cultural traditions and self-government that would allow Aboriginal women to be restored to their once and continuing revered position" (39). St Denis believes that the call for traditions offered as a solution to patriarchal violence within Aboriginal communities erases the larger socio-political contexts of Aboriginal women's lives. The point made by St Denis is significant because, if all Aboriginal people are affected by colonialism's patriarchal agenda, how could patriarchal colonialism possibly be equitable for Aboriginal women? As a final note from St Denis, she argues that "most, if not all Aboriginal people, both men and women, who are living in Western societies, are inundated from birth until death with Western patriarchy and Western forms of misogyny" (44).

The call to restore Aboriginal cultural traditions as a solution to violence against Aboriginal women is complicated. While on the one hand, many Aboriginal peoples have been dispossessed from their ancestral roots by residential schools, or even through the sixties scoop,[1] many have gone back to their Aboriginal roots to reclaim an identity that was taken away. For many, developing a positive sense of identity could be affirming. On the other hand, reclaiming Aboriginal cultural traditions could lead to essentializing Aboriginal identities that encourage ideas of gendered insider/outsider status. Both reasons for recalling Aboriginal traditions are important to consider but, as St Denis (2007) points out, can we really say these cultural traditions are without patriarchal colonial influence?

As a Cree-speaking Aboriginal feminist who was raised in Cumberland House, Saskatchewan, I am mindful of the political issues discussed by Green (2007) and St Denis (2007). While I reclaim a positive self-identity as an Aboriginal woman, I am aware of the multiple discourses that produce and constrain Aboriginal peoples, particularly those in their essentialized form. As a woman, I espouse feminism because it offers women a positioning that is fluid and is supportive of political agency. As with many feminists, the issues that I am conscious of are the social, economic, and political positioning of Aboriginal women, including an analysis of how Aboriginal communities position women. While I am a product of my Cree family and community, I also appreciate what I have learned in Western education systems. Particularly, I am grateful for learning about forms of patriarchy, and the ways that women have both historically and currently worked to resist gender oppression. Specifically, feminism is useful for me because it enables me to name male dominance when it is happening, as opposed to romanticizing an Aboriginal culture that is also affected by colonial white patriarchy. For the knowledge I have gained and for my Cree background, I will not apologize, as each has brought me to the place in which I situate myself – as an Indigenous feminist.

WHAT ARE INTERNATIONAL INDIGENOUS WOMEN SAYING?

For many Aboriginal women, examining what is happening to other Indigenous women throughout the world is seen as an abstract academic endeavour because the immediacy of issues in local contexts is so profound. The colonial impact of violence and women's oppression has been normalized and is part of their everyday lives. Many Aboriginal women have no post-secondary education and, as a result, do not access scholarship that speaks to how male dominance and patriarchy is normalized. A number of Indigenous women, including myself, questioned many things, but did not have access to documented history about Aboriginal people, and were silenced. It is through academia that I learned that Aboriginal people are produced through a history that, until recently, was written from the Euro-Canadian perspective, power relations, and discourses. Having a wider perspective on Indigenous matters helped me to understand the impact of patriarchal colonialism.

Indigenous people are constantly under the colonial gaze where their performance of "authenticity" – that is, as constructed through colonial discourses – is desirable. They are recognizable by performing "authenticity" and it is demanded by both white and Indigenous societies because it serves specific interests. Performing "authenticity" is more problematic than helpful because it encourages essentialism, and essentialism negates the diversity that exists among Indigenous peoples.

Rauna Kuokkanen is a Sami woman from Finland who writes about the myth of the strong Sami women (2007). She proposes that, "besides as a marker of distinctiveness, the notion of strong Sami women [also] had to do with a desired ideal of Sami society rather than the everyday reality of Sami women" (73). When Sami women advocate for women's issues, this myth is often conjured up and used against them. Kuokkanen finds that Sami women are often disregarded as they are thought to be better off than Sami men "because they are stronger and because the loss of traditional livelihoods has not impacted them as radically as men" (73). In contrast to this general claim about Sami women by Sami men, she believes that Sami women are affected by patriarchal Christianity, attitudes and perceptions of Sami women, and the domestic and sexual violence that they experience. Kuokkanen proposes that the notion of the "strong Sami woman" is an excuse to perpetuate male dominance and continued marginalization of Sami women.

Mohanty (1997) provides a perspective on Third World women whereby Western standards are used to judge legal, economic, religious, and familial structures. She finds that structures are defined as "underdeveloped" or "developing," and when Third World women are placed within these structures, an image of an "average Third-World woman" emerges. The Third World woman is slotted into a category as the "oppressed Third-World woman" within a context of a Third World difference. Mohanty notes Third World differences include a paternalistic approach for those women who are constituents of the Third World. In an extensive elaboration of her concerns about how Third World women are perceived, she writes,

> Since discussions of the various themes I identified earlier (kinship, education, religion, etc.) are conducted in the context of the relative "underdevelopment" of the Third World (a move that constitutes nothing less than unjustifiably confusing development with the separate path taken by the West in its development, as well as ignoring the directionality of the power relationship between the First and Third Worlds), Third World women as a group or category are automatically and necessarily defined as religious (read: not progressive), family-oriented (read: traditional), legally unsophisticated (read: they are still not conscious of their rights), illiterate (read: ignorant), domestic (read: backward), and sometimes revolutionary (read: their country is in a state of war, they must fight). (272)

Third World women are produced in this way while occupying a space of difference, and Western standards are used to judge the Third World woman. Indigenous and Third World women are often read through Western standards, which lead to positioning them as primitive. Instead, Indigenous women need to be understood through a colonial context that is complex and is also rooted in their community of origin.

Leigh (2009) also reveals the complexity of identity and authenticity with regard to North American Indigenous women. She warns that discussions regarding Indigenous peoples run the risk of homogenizing a heterogeneous group. An issue of Indigenous authenticity emerges when Indigenous peoples are portrayed as all the same, and this includes discussion among Native communities. Leigh proposes that Indigeneity is often defined in terms of the colonial relationship; however, there is a dynamism that forms gendered reformulations of Indigenous resistance to colonialism and, I would add, to patriarchy. There really is no ideal Indigenous type because identity is highly complex; identity is not completely clear and is certainly more than simply being a member of a single group. Authenticity – a constructed homogenous enactment of "normalized" and colonized Indigeneity – is often expected by both the white Western observer and Indigenous community. Performing authenticity is often welcomed by Indigenous peoples because these acts develop and encourage a sense of belonging and, for many Native people who have been dispossessed, this can be seductive. For the Western observer, ideas of authenticity encourage white innocence in which racism is denied.

Chow (2003) also writes about how "the Native," in not staying within their "authentic" frame, causes disruption to the colonizing gaze. On this point, particular groups and identities are read through positive or negative stereotypes. Chow asks "in the politics of identifying 'authentic' Natives, several strands of the word 'identification' are at stake: how do we identify the native? How do we identify with her? How do we construct the native's identity?" (325). The notion of identity is often tied to one's own construction of identity and, white people often do not have to consider their identity and privilege (McIntosh 1990) because it is the norm against which other identities are judged. However, as Chow points out, the "Native" is constructed and he or she remains at the level of image identification. This image identification is a process whereby our identity is used to calculate the degrees to which "he" resembles "us." Measuring the degrees of resemblance is also practised in Aboriginal communities, especially when women are devout Christians or wear dresses in cultural settings that lead to social or cultural rewards the more their images resemble acceptable colonial models of femininity. When stereotypical discourses are performed, Aboriginal people become recognizable and our Aboriginal diversity is often denied or silenced. This is an effect of the colonial gaze.

In Chow's (2003) rather complicated version of the Native and authenticity, she wonders why there is so much fascination with history and the Native, especially in modern times, asking, "What do we gain from our labour on these 'endangered authenticities' that are presumed to be from a different time and different place?" (336). Her question is about the irreversibility of modernity. The original witness of the Native's destruction is no longer here, and with "the untranslatability of the Native's discourse into imperialist discourse, Natives, like commodities, become knowable only through routes that diverge from their original homes" (336). As a result, the "Natives" have become knowable through ideas of authenticity in which a powerful and lasting gaze is used to construct them, and now Indigenous peoples are left to ponder how to perform themselves. Many Indigenous people are profoundly affected by colonialism with all the negative assumptions it imposes. It is not surprising that Indigenous people, and particularly Indigenous women, become lured into dominant and essentialized discourses that serve particular interests – but usually not her interests.

FEMINISM, EDUCATION, AND ABORIGINALITY

Any significant talk about the relevance of feminism as a decolonizing strategy is recent to Aboriginal people. As Aboriginal women, we must speak ourselves into discourses we define in order to disrupt discourses that imprison us and keep us locked into contradictory relations of unequal power. Some of these discourses include how we have been historically dehumanized, and continue to be; why we are left to unpack patriarchal colonial contexts, such as, asking why there are so many missing and murdered Aboriginal women in Canada (Canada 2014); and how we might hold Aboriginal men accountable when they help bring children into this world. As Aboriginal women scholars, we need to position ourselves in education in order to resist these kinds of – and other – oppressions.

When I think about my own elementary and secondary schooling, there is very little that was documented about Aboriginal people's history. In my era, during the 1980s, high school curricula did not include a conversation about Aboriginal peoples. When I left to complete my grade 12 requirements at an urban centre, there were many Aboriginal students also enrolled in that high school. Although we were physically present in schools, our history was absent. In grade 12 social sciences in the 1980s, Aboriginal content was almost never part of the curriculum; rather, we learned about white Canadian history, suggesting that Aboriginal people were absent or had disappeared. Today, teaching Aboriginal content is largely optional and many non-Aboriginal teachers choose not to include it. In both situations, gaps about Aboriginal people's history remain. As a result, there is little known about Aboriginal people's history other than the mis-education received through mainstream media and the observation of those who are homeless or have addictions issues as a result of the effects of colonialism and residential schools.

On the other extreme is the representation of Aboriginal peoples in essentialized ways that serves to deny our diversity. One of the images includes the promotion of a male super-Indian who has survived the effects of colonialism (Francis 1997). These stoic Indians are often etched into the minds of many people, both Aboriginal and non-Aboriginal. The promotion of this stoic Indian is often exalted in educational institutions or other human service agencies that attempt to address Aboriginal education. Aboriginal women become frozen into a monolithic dichotomy where we are portrayed as princesses in cultural events, or as the drudges of society to be shunned. This is often what Aboriginal education is summed up to be. When Aboriginal women are produced as this dichotomy, not only is our diversity denied, but the imagery entrenches Aboriginal women as sexually sinful and lustful or too pure to be real.

As analyzed by St Denis (2007), cultural revitalization is valorized to the exclusion of complicated social relations that continue to marginalize within and outside Aboriginal communities. This happens in educational institutions, and probably in many other organizations where Aboriginal people are being served. Cultural reclamation is often served up as the answer for Aboriginal people's destitute circumstances. There are often rewards coming from Aboriginal and non-Aboriginal society when Aboriginal peoples perform the discourses associated with culture. In this dynamic, there is very little gender analysis recognized, or even entertained as a legitimate area of concern. As I have already argued, cultural reclamation does not address gender oppression; it may do the opposite. The effects of colonialism in education are far-reaching and complicated – we cannot deny this.

Statistics Canada (2009) reports that Aboriginal women are more likely to complete post-secondary education compared with Aboriginal men. Given the numerous ways Aboriginal women are marginalized, it is not surprising that many look to post-secondary education for hope. In my own graduate research, all the women I interviewed were either enrolled in university or had completed degrees; all of these women went to school for a better future. Often, it is post-secondary education that gives us access to Aboriginal people's histories. Some Aboriginal peoples are content with the celebration of Aboriginal cultures, but some feel we must look further to understand how historical and political discourses affect us. Frequently, we must intentionally search to find literature about Aboriginal feminism, as it is marginalized or not accessible. However, Aboriginal feminism can be found in higher learning contexts. For those Aboriginal women interested in feminism, we have largely just entered that conversation. Feminist analysis is a useful tool for Aboriginal people interested in challenging and disrupting gender violence and misogyny in Aboriginal communities. The misogyny runs deep in Aboriginal communities, so much so that it can be taken as a form of Aboriginal culture.

CONCLUSION

In this chapter, I have discussed feminism in education as it relates to Aboriginal women in a broad context. For Aboriginal women, feminism is still a fairly new concept. It is with effort and intention that Aboriginal feminism is found and enacted. Aboriginal feminism is often thought to be an academic endeavour because it is not accessible in Aboriginal communities. Not only is it not accessible, male domination is often thought of as acceptable behaviour. The normalization of male dominance persists through the impact of patriarchal colonization, Christianity, and Aboriginal cultural reclamation projects. Often when we question the impact of Christianity and cultural revitalization we, as Aboriginal women, are asserting our diversity. However, our diversity is often denied, refused, or silenced because the discourses of what it means to be an essentialized Aboriginal woman are long-lasting, profound, and limiting. As well, if Aboriginal content in curricula is marginally available, it is unlikely that Aboriginal feminism will be considered at all.

I am not certain how far Awcheecheet went in formal learning, but she was able to read somewhat. When we would go to town to pick up groceries, she often had one of her grandchildren help with English speaking and translations. Although she had basic reading skills, she knew enough to ask when she needed help. One day when we went to town for groceries, as we crossed the street she looked over at the store down the street, and she uttered "The Meet." When I looked at the sign, it was "The Met." My granny was not afraid to laugh at her limitations, but she had a sense of pride when it came to her work. She had no other choice but to be strong given the numerous ways Aboriginal women are positioned in the margins. My Cree granny worked hard and she would not walk passively away from a challenge. Perhaps she knew that life carried many challenges and she embraced them without hesitation.

NOTE

1 The term *sixties scoop* was coined by Patrick Johnston, author of the 1983 report *Native Children and the Child Welfare System*. It refers to the mass removal of Aboriginal children from their families into the child welfare system, in most cases without the consent of their families or bands. For further information, see Erin Hanson, "Sixties Scoop," Indigenous Foundations, University of British Columbia, http://indigenousfoundations.arts.ubc.ca/home/government-policy/sixties-scoop.html.

REFERENCES

Blaney, F. 2003. "Aboriginal Women's Action Network." In *Strong Women Stories: Native Vision and Community Survival*, ed. K. Anderson and B. Lawrence, 156–70. Toronto: Sumach Press.

Brown, J.C., and R. Parker. 1989. "For God So Loved the World?" In *Christianity, Patriarchy, and Abuse: A Feminist Critique*, ed. J.C. Brown and C.R. Bohn, 1–30. Cleveland, OH: The Pilgrim Press.

Burr, V. 1995. *An Introduction to Social Constructionism*. London: Routledge. doi:10.4324/9780203299968.

Canada. 2009. "Canadian Social Trends: Special findings. Catalogue No. 11–008." Statistics Canada. http://publications.gc.ca/site/archivee-archived.html?url=http://publications.gc.ca/Collection-R/Statcan/11-008-XIE/0020311-008-XIE.pdf.

– 2014. "Missing and Murdered Aboriginal Women: A National Operational Overview." Royal Canadian Mounted Police. www.rcmp-grc.gc.ca/en/missing-and-murdered-aboriginal-women-national-operational-overview.

Chow, R. 2003. "Where Have All the Natives Gone?" In *Feminist Postcolonial Theory*, ed. R. Lewis and S. Mills, 324–49. New York: Routledge.

Davies, B. 2000. *A Body of Writing: 1990–1999*. Walnut Cree, CA: AltaMira Press.

Deerchild, R. 2003. "Tribal Feminism Is a Drum Song." *Strong Women Stories: Native Vision and Community Survival*, ed. K. Anderson and B. Lawrence, 97–105. Toronto: Sumach Press.

Foucault, M. 1990. *History of Sexuality: An Introduction*. New York: Random House.

Francis, D. 1997. *The Imaginary Indian: The Image of the Indian in Canadian Culture*. Vancouver: Arsenal Pulp Press.

Green, J., ed. 2007. *Making Space for Indigenous Feminism*. Winnipeg, MB: Fernwood Publishing. http://indigenousfoundations.arts.ubc.ca/home/government-policy/sixties-scoop.html.

Kuokkanen, R. 2007. "Myths and Realities of Sami Women: A Post-Colonial Feminist Analysis for the Decolonization and Transformation of Sami Society." In *Making Space for Indigenous Feminism*, ed. J. Green, 72–92. Winnipeg, MB: Fernwood Publishing.

Leigh, D. 2009. "Colonialism, Gender and the Family in North America: For a Gendered Analysis of Indigenous Struggles." *Studies in Ethnicity and Nationalism* 9 (1): 70–88. doi:10.1111/j.1754-9469.2009.01029.x.

Martin-Hill, D. 2003. "She No Speaks and Other Colonial Constructs of the 'Traditional Woman.'" In *Strong Women Stories: Native Vision and Community Survival*, ed. K. Anderson and B. Lawrence, 106–20. Toronto: Sumach Press.

McIntosh, P. 1990. "White Privilege: Unpacking the Invisible Knapsack." *Independent School* 49 (2): 31–6.

Mohanty, C.T. 1997. "Under Western Eyes: Feminist Scholarship and Colonial Discourses." In *Dangerous Liaisons: Gender, Nation and Postcolonial Perspectives*, ed. A. McClintock, A. Mufti, and E. Shohat, 255–77. Minneapolis: University of Minnesota Press.

Prado, C.G. 2000. *Starting with Foucault: An Introduction to Genealogy*. 2nd ed. Boulder, CO: Westview Press.

Ruether, R.R. 1989. "The Western Religious Tradition and Violence against Women in the Home." In *Christianity, Patriarchy and Abuse: A Feminist Critique*, ed. J.C. Brown and C.R. Bohn, 31–41. Cleveland, OH: The Pilgrim Press.

St Denis, V. 2007. "Feminism Is for Everybody: Aboriginal Women, Feminism and Diversity." In *Making Space for Indigenous Women*, ed. J. Green, 33–52. Winnipeg, MB: Fernwood Publishing.

St Pierre, E. 2000. "Poststructural Feminism in Education: An Overview." *International Journal of Qualitative Studies in Education: QSE* 14 (5): 477–515. doi:10.1080/09518390050156422.

Weedon, C. 1997. *Feminist Practice and Poststructuralist Theory*. 2nd ed. Malden, MA: Blackwell Publishing.

Wetherell, M. 2001. "Themes in Discourse Research: The Case of Diana." In *Discourse Theory and Practice: A Reader*, ed. M. Wetherell, S. Taylor, and S. Yates, 14–28. London: Sage Publications.

9

Visible Minority Teachers in Canada

Decolonizing the Knowledges of Euro-American Hegemony through Feminist Epistemologies and Ontologies

THASHIKA PILLAY

> I must speak bi-lingual
> Neither one of them mine ...
>
> I must study centuries of history
> None of it mine ...
>
> I read a thousand voices
> None of them speak to me
> Not one of them speak of me
>
> Am I entirely obscure?
>
> I see you Talk 'n Teach
> But I can't hear a word you say
>
> Salmon 2013, 85

My father owned a grocery store in South Africa, and he would buy eggs for the store from a "white" lady. I once went with him to buy the eggs. I remember seeing him speak to the white lady and feeling a sense of fear run through my veins; I wondered, "Why is Dad speaking to that lady? What if he gets in trouble?" Even at the age of six, I understood the politics of the time and place, of the status accorded to non-whites and of the repercussions of a man of colour speaking to a white woman. This was the environment that I grew up in. Therefore, I was not prepared for the learning curve that moving to Canada presented. Unlike many visible minority immigrants, I had grown up in a country where I had always known that I was considered an outsider. That status did not change when I moved to Canada. I did not suddenly encounter racism for the first time; I was a product of racism from the time of my birth. My birth certificate has a record of my ethnicity. In black typeface, my identity was reduced to "Indian," not even "South-African Indian" – simply "Indian." It was of no consequence that I had never been to India or that I spoke English as a first language and Zulu as a second. I was not considered South African.

Upon moving to Canada and, in particular, small-town Alberta, I was thrown into a new world, one in which I was a new kind of minority. The teachers and children at my school were not like me. However, there was one teacher – my grade 2 teacher – who was of South Asian descent and the same heritage as all of my previous teachers. It was the only time during my K–12 education in Canada that I had a teacher who looked like I did, who shared a similar culture, who celebrated the same holidays, and who understood what it meant to be a visible minority living in Canada.

Being a student in Canada meant learning how to be friends with children whose lives were nothing like my own. I was too embarrassed to bring curry for lunch; too embarrassed to speak because of my accent; I had never watched *Sesame Street*, and they had never watched *The Pumpkin Patch*. They had no idea what it was like, on a daily basis, to have to overcome every survival instinct to run in the opposite direction and instead speak to "them," to attend class with "them," all the while pretending that nothing was wrong, that I did not feel to the very core of my being that I was in a place in which not only did I not belong but that I was not wanted. I am not stating that my classmates were not kind to me or did not try to reach out – they did. However, I had a decade of oppression to unlearn and no tools with which to unlearn these oppressions. Furthermore, most of my classmates had never been friends with someone whose life experiences were so unlike their own. We were all navigating new terrain without a compass to point us in the right direction.

What I did have was a grade 2 teacher who, by the simple act of being, calmed many of my fears. Her presence allowed me to feel a sense of security in this new environment in which everything was suddenly different. I sometimes wonder if the school placed me in her class because of our shared ethnic identity. In the months I spent in Mrs B.'s class, I learned how to survive in a new world; I learned how to separate the various components of my self – the school version from the home version – to speak, to act, to think in order to become like everyone else. Had I not had Mrs B. as my teacher, I am not sure how I would have responded to living in this new world. In our conversations together, we could discuss how my family had celebrated Diwali, and I knew that she would understand. However, these cultural exchanges were always private and never extended to the rest of my class. As wonderful a person and teacher as she was, Mrs B. had never been taught to teach beyond the curriculum, to bring in epistemologies and ontologies beyond the mainstream. I learned how to adapt who I was to fit in; my classmates were never expected to do the same.

I start this chapter with this anecdote to highlight that, while visible minority teachers can be role models for visible minority students, this role is often extremely superficial. Once the astonishment and pleasure of having a teacher who shares cultural, ethnic, or racial ties is played out, students need teachers with whom there is shared meaning and shared understanding of the world, and they also need teachers who challenge them to experience multiple ways of being, seeing, and knowing. Furthermore, the act of centring these multiple ways of knowing, seeing, and being changes the school environment, not only for students but also for teachers and administrators.

In this chapter, I explore ways to decolonize the knowledges of Euro-American hegemony through feminist epistemologies and ontologies as well as through relevant literature and an autoethnographical perspective. My intention in this chapter is to illustrate that the presence of visible minority female teachers in Canadian classrooms offers Canadian education systems one way in which to challenge the hegemonic dominance of Euro-American knowledges in school systems when such teachers' diverse epistemological and ontological perspectives are supported and valued. Furthermore, given the large numbers of visible minority students in Canadian schools, it is surprising that so few end up as teachers in the school system. This lack of visible minority teachers is due not only to widespread systemic and structural discrimination, but also as a result of an educational system that values only one type of knowledge – that of a hegemonic dominant class from which most visible minorities are alienated.

SITUATING VISIBLE MINORITY FEMALE TEACHERS IN THE CANADIAN EDUCATION SYSTEM

The teaching profession in Canada has been described as a feminized position in which the majority of teachers are women (Prentice 1977; Weiler 2003). However, while the majority of teachers are women, teaching in Canada remains a profession that largely excludes visible minority women from gaining membership, belying Canada's status as a multicultural nation. A study conducted by Ryan, Pollock, and Antonelli (2009) found in 2001 and 2006 that the proportion of visible minority teachers in the overall workforce was less than the proportion of visible minority citizens in the general Canadian population, and, that the proportion of visible minority teachers in the workforce has decreased relative to the proportion of visible minority citizens in Canada, which has increased (597). The current lack of participation by visible minority women in the education sector will be greatly exacerbated unless current structures and policies that exclude visible minority women from teaching are reevaluated and redesigned.

AN AUTOETHNOGRAPHICAL APPROACH

Using post-structural feminism as my foundation, I consider issues of race, gender, and class in conjunction with the diverse epistemological and ontological beliefs of visible minority women. I hope to offer an alternative view of the role of education in society and illustrate the need for multiple epistemologies and ontologies that benefit all, not only the few. This chapter, then, aims to challenge the dominant, hegemonic feminist conventions within Canadian education – the liberal feminist orthodoxies prevalent in Canadian education – while reiterating the call for change.

In highlighting the need to recognize multiple knowledges and world views and to dehegemonize Euro-American-centric ways of seeing the world, I supplement existing literature on the experiences of visible minority female teachers with an autoethnographic perspective based on my own experiences. According to Ellis (1991), an autoethnographical approach uses vignettes, stories, reflexivity, multiple voices, and introspection to "invoke readers to ... consider evocative, concrete texts to be as important as abstract analyses"

(Ellis, Adams, and Bochner 2010). The use of vignettes, stories, reflexivity, multiple voices, and introspective storytelling allows for overcoming the difference in position between the teller and the listener, between telling the tale and hearing it. Storytelling, which is all about subjectivity, is often uncritically understood as a sentimental, personal, and individual horizon – the domain of the female and Indigenous – as opposed to an objective, universal, societal, limitless horizon – the domain of the male and Eurocentric. Yet, stories are a means of obtaining the knowledge we need to create a just legal structure (Razack 2001, 36–8).

According to Metta (2010), placing visible minority women at the centre of scholarly texts ensures that critical analysis and knowledge-making becomes a highly political act that challenges histories that have long erased women and subjugated their experiences. Razack (2001) asserts that within the context of social change, "storytelling refers to an opposition to established knowledge, to Foucault's suppressed knowledge, to the experience of the world that is not admitted into dominant knowledge paradigms" (36). Furthermore, as noted by Metta (2010), "Placing the personal, the cultural, and the familial narratives at the centre ... challeng[es] the dominant masculinist and patriarchal discourse of knowledge-making within scholarly paradigms ... [and] also foreground[s] the importance of relational knowing and engaged practice and pedagogy in the production and transmission of knowledge across difference" (27). An autoethnographical approach, then, is the exploration of personal and cultural narratives as narratives of resistance to discourses of racism, sexism, and marginalization (Metta 2010).

WHY POST-STRUCTURAL FEMINISM?

This paper also uses a feminist post-structural lens to analyze issues of power and knowledge as illustrated in the experiences of visible minority educators such as myself in Canada and the concurrent discourses of the social and political world they/we inhabit. To define feminism purely in gendered terms assumes that our consciousness of being women has nothing to do with race, class, nation, or sexuality, and is solely a result of gender. The central tenet of post-structural feminism is intersectionality: the concept of "woman" is problematized and complexified by issues of class, culture, ethnicity, sexuality, and other aspects of identity (Butler 1999/2002). Post-structural feminism acknowledges that intersectionality is imperative to understanding diverse experiences and identities of women because, as Mohanty (2003) asserts, ideologies of womanhood are a result of intersections of class, race, and gender, which position "us as women" (55).

Marginalization as a result of gender, class, and/or race has varying effects on women, necessitating a thorough understanding of the intersections at play and a possible rewriting of hegemonic histories (Mohanty 2003). Intersectionality is particularly important within Canada where multiculturalism policies promote a universalizing image of "visible minorities," ignoring class, gender, or ethnic and cultural differences, for example (Hogarth 2011). An understanding of intersectionality can ensure greater understanding of the challenges faced by racialized women. Their experiences within the workplace and educational institutions greatly exacerbate feelings of marginalization and increase dependence on family and community (Hogarth 2011). Furthermore, intersectionality ensures that women are characterized by more than simply their gender. A sole focus on gender reduces the world to a construction of binary divisions – men and women – thereby indicating a world in which men have power and women do not, and where men exploit and women are exploited. Intersectionality allows for local responses: decolonization at all levels (Mohanty 2003).

According to Ambwani and Dyke (2007), visible minority women are the most disadvantaged group in Canada. The intersectionality of race and gender often depicts these women as somewhat deficient and lacking a fully established and defined self-identity. The problems women face are seen as a consequence of their own deficiencies as opposed to being attributed to policies and practices that oppress women based on race, class, culture, and religion. The intersectionality of race, gender, class, and nationality positions visible minority women as outsiders, thereby reinforcing discrimination in the workplace and wider society at large (Crawford 2004).

For post-structural feminists, analysis lies within understandings of difference as depicted through women's struggles with patriarchal structures of domination. Therefore, the struggle for women's emancipation is not simply limited to a liberal feminist notion of equality in which equality continues to be defined by patriarchal constructs. Post-structural feminism posits that there are many feminisms and no single truth. Therefore, the solution to women's emancipation must come from a multitude of perspectives in which issues of knowledge construction and devaluation as a result of power and power relations are understood through intersectionalities.

CURRENT DISCOURSE ON PARTICIPATION OF VISIBLE MINORITY WOMEN IN TEACHING

The majority of literature on the absence of visible minority women in the teaching profession in Canada argues that there are structural and systemic obstacles that promote racism, thereby acting as barriers to block visible minority women from entering the teaching profession. Carty (1991) asserts that the racism in educational institutions is very similar to that in the streets. Bannerji (1993) states that her race and gender ensure a loss of respect and authority in the classroom. Haideh Mogissi (1994) argues that racism has an impact on the respect, recognition, and authority of minority educators. Beynon, Toohey, and Kishor (1998) find that parental influence plays a significant role in the decision of visible minorities to pursue a career in teaching: the majority of Asian parents influence their children away from a career in teaching. According to Samuel and Wane (2005), visible minority women are accorded an outsider status as a result of their gender and race. These explanations of the ways in which race and gender work to oppress visible minority women focus exclusively on women being devalued because of their colour and gender. The assumption is that if the "knowledge" being taught by a visible minority woman was instead taught by a white male, it would be deemed valuable. However, these explanations do not question the type of knowledges being privileged or the hegemony of Euro-American knowledges in the decision-making process that leads visible minorities away from pursuing a career in education.

Men and women of various ethnicities have accepted the hegemonic notion that Euro-American knowledge systems are superior. This is exemplified through an examination of educational policies of many countries of the Global South where policymakers and educators who have undergone psychological colonization privilege Euro-American knowledges (Pillay 2010). Therefore, the privileging of a Euro-American knowledge system is not limited to people of one ethnicity or culture. However, given that the knowledge that is privileged is that of dominant white male elites, several important questions must be asked: Why do educational structures privilege the knowledge of dominant white, male elites? Why has the discourse around the lack of visible minority teachers centred on the aesthetic qualities – for example, skin colour – of women, as opposed to whose knowledges are being privileged? In attempting to answer these questions, I concur with Mohanty (1991) that gender, sexual orientation, race, and class should become verbs, rather than predetermined static categories within which to fit women, because we need to understand how women and women's knowledges are constituted and produced within relations and discourses of power in order to recentre these knowledges that have been Othered and excluded.

THE MULTIPLE EPISTEMOLOGICAL AND ONTOLOGICAL POSITIONS OF VISIBLE MINORITY FEMALE EDUCATORS

My very first teaching job was in a small town in Northern Manitoba. The school was composed entirely of Métis and Cree students. There were two teachers on the staff of twelve who were not originally from the area, and who themselves were also not Cree or Métis: a Caucasian teacher who lived in the area and taught at the school for almost twenty years, and me. Teaching at the school changed my beliefs on education in ways that I still cannot fully explain. I learned from other teachers about how to challenge dominant world views, bringing other perspectives into the curriculum and learning ways in which to ensure that my pedagogy reflected the lived experiences of the students and community. There is one particular instance that comes to mind. My grade 10 English class informed me that they had cut down a Christmas tree every year at the beginning of December since grade 6. As someone who grew up in the city, this notion filled me with images of sliced-up body parts, trips to the hospital, and lawsuits – my law and ethics class, taken during my bachelor of education degree, had clearly had an impact on my psyche. Yet after receiving approval from the principal, we all dressed warmly and went out to cut down our class Christmas tree. I was clearly the student in this endeavour. The entire class took part and was engaged in the activity; every student arrived at school on time the morning that we went out. We then decided to use our English class to write up and perform a play for the Christmas concert. The students brought Christian and Indigenous beliefs into the play, acknowledging multiple epistemologies and ontologies. Furthermore, it was the girls in the class who took the lead in organizing and directing the play as well as in set design while the boys agreed that they would be responsible for writing, lighting, and other more technical aspects; acting duties were shared equally.

As a new teacher, the process of allowing the students to engage with language and knowledge that went beyond the objectives and dominant ideology of the curriculum taught me the importance of ensuring that all knowledges are valued and seen as important. It also taught me that education is a two-way process in which both student and teacher must be engaged in a continual iterative learning process. Learning to dialogue with those with diverse experiences, knowledges, and backgrounds is integral to providing an education that ensures the ability to form "communities through joint democratic action for social transformation" and allows teachers to develop the ability to "dialogue across racial, ethnic, and class boundaries" (Austin 2009, 50), which in turn supports a similar development in students.

Educators need to be aware of the inherent dangers of asking students to tell and, thereby, teach their own stories and histories. Brown (2008) contends that such a pedagogical strategy further subjugates certain knowledges as there is no epistemic base upon which to validate and honour the knowledges being brought forward while students continue "to be perennial strangers in their classrooms" (379). It is, therefore, necessary to ensure that educators have the background, knowledges, and capacity to support and honour the knowledges in the classroom. Thus, the creation of spaces in which diverse epistemologies and ontologies are acknowledged and reclaimed is integral in the process of recentring subjugated knowledges (Wane 2008).

Hegemonic knowledges that are supported by school curricula promote the interests of the powerful, and are not in the best interests of either students or teachers. Alberta's grade nine social studies program, for example, specified that when studying core concepts of citizenship and identity, Indigenous and Francophone perspectives and experiences should *also* be taught (Alberta Education 2007). The word "also" signals that these perspectives are Othered; in other words, they are not part of the mainstream. Even within my own teaching, I focused on teaching the knowledge of the dominant group, which is portrayed as objective, but is actually located within a particular social, economic, and political world view, because that is the knowledge students are expected to have for university. The curriculum not only sets up Indigenous and Francophone perspectives as supplementary to mainstream knowledge, but also excludes the perspectives of women – whether Francophone, Indigenous, or racialized. This results in the teaching of hegemonic knowledges and constitutes a world view that is deeply problematic as it erases all other knowledges and world views.

Elabor-Idemudia (2001) contends that the knowledges promoted by educational institutions are those of the elite, white, male world and are alienating to people of colour – in particular, women. Citizenship and identity, as presented through the grade nine social studies curriculum, are concepts in which women of colour are absent. It is the story of white men and, to a much lesser extent, white women. Visible minorities in Canada are mentioned as a proportion of the population they constitute, while Indigenous perspectives, when taught, are narrowly restricted within the confines of Canadian citizenship, of belonging to a political state. The diverse perspectives of visible minority and Indigenous women on citizenship and identity are absent. Their knowledges are devalued to such an extent that they are invisible. It is what Foucault (1980) refers to as "subjugated knowledges," or those of persons who are "located low down on the hierarchy" (208, cited in Elabor-Idemudia 2001). Furthermore, this invisibility of non-majority women assumes that the white male experience is not only the norm but is also the only experience that really matters (Elabor-Idemudia 2001). The Canadian education system, with its tacit commitment to assimilation as a central objective is, therefore, failing visible minority women, including minority teachers and students (Mukherjee 1993).

The privileging of specific knowledges leads to the devaluation of both the knowledges women hold and the work they engage in, by both the larger society and women themselves. Given the ways in which the world of work is constructed, women, who are an exploited and oppressed group, have negative attitudes toward work in general and the work they do in particular (hooks 2000). Work becomes simply an exchange of labour for monetary value, which directly contrasts with the non-paid work of women as mothers, as nurturers, as essential and valuable members of the family and the home. Of course, not all women are homemakers, mothers, and nurturers or they may need/choose to fulfill a double shift of care at home and full- or part-time employment. In whichever way a women's work life is organized, their work in the home and in the workforce is devalued.[1] The work of women in the external workforce is also devalued and those careers that women tend to gravitate toward, such as teaching, are not as highly regarded as jobs that are typically within the purview of men. hooks (2000) argues that "women devalue the work they do because they are taught to judge its significance solely in terms of exchange value ... Like other exploited groups, women internalize the powerful's definition of themselves and the powerful's estimation of the value of their labour" (hooks 2000, 105). Furthermore, women have been conditioned to believe that it is not possible to fulfill their role at home successfully if they are dedicating too much of their time to work outside of the home (Wrushen and Sherman 2008). The challenge they experience to believe in themselves, in their abilities, talents, and strengths is the direct result of a society that teaches women to devalue their ways of being, seeing, and knowing in favour of a world created by and for elite, white men.

Given the feminization of the teaching profession, this is problematic as women's knowledges, centred on the private world of the home and family responsibilities, are seen as less valuable than men's knowledges that are exercised in the public sphere of commerce and the state. Mathematics and science are considered core subjects whereas home economics is an option, not considered valuable enough to be learned by all. When students learn about the way in which the earth was created, they study the big bang theory, not the multiple understandings of the creation of the universe taught in homes and families. There is, therefore, a disconnect between the knowledges taught in the school and the knowledges taught in the homes of many students.

Growing up in an African Hindu family, I was always aware that my family beliefs were not those of the school system. As a teacher, I taught many students who struggled with similar problems, attempting to negotiate the divide between home and school. After all, I only had to spend time on the family farm to understand the harmful effects of climate change; yet, this local and specific understanding of science was not viewed as objective and universal "scientific" knowledge. I eventually became extremely disenchanted with the narrow view of education promoted by schools and decided that the continual devaluation of my identity and world views meant that teaching was not the career for me. This view is shared by a teacher of Métis background in a study by Marie Gervais (2007) in which the teacher points out how the refusal to acknowledge other ways of being and seeing discount her experiences, knowledge, and very existence. She is then seen as deficient, as incompetent. Finlayson (2011) asserts that for many visible minority women, orientations to work, a sense of family, and a sense of community responsibility are powerful determinants in their decisions to teach; when teachers feel that the knowledges that they are privileging are not those of families and communities, the incentive to teach decreases.

It behooves educational institutions, then, to respond to the growing reality of a world of "lives lived differently, lives constituted around different metaphysics of economics, of law, of science, of healing, of marriage, of joy, of dying, and of co-existence" (Odora Hoppers and Richards 2012, 10). Knowledges cannot be divorced from the lived realities of people's lives. The hegemony of a particular Euro-American, scientific, objective knowledge over all other ways of knowing, ways of seeing, and ways of living has resulted in the exclusion of the vast majority of people from engagement in knowledge construction. The exclusion of vast numbers of people perpetuates a society which will simply regurgitate old ways of knowing, seeing, and living; it will be a world without creativity, without thinking (Odora Hoppers and Richards 2012).[2]

DECOLONIZING EDUCATIONAL PRACTICES: MOVING FORWARD

This chapter highlights the necessity for educational institutions to respond to the systems, structures, and institutions that perpetuate the colonization of education by engaging in acts of resistance that have the ability to transform families, schools, communities, cities, nations. Resistance, however, is "not always identifiable through organized movements" but must be looked for in the "gaps, fissures, and silences of hegemonic narratives" (Mohanty 2003, 83). These acts of resistance, as illustrated through the experiences of scholars such Bannerji (1991, 1993, 1995), Elabor-Idemudia (2001), Mohanty (1991, 1997, 2003) and Wane (2008), also depict the determination and refusal of women – and in particular visible minority female educators – to be victims of patriarchy, classism, capitalism, racism, sexism, imperialism, and colonialism. These acts of resistance encompass all that women are, see, and know, thus transforming and, thereby, continually producing new knowledges. Bannerji (1995) articulates the emergence of this new understanding of the world, of new ways of seeing and being through her account of experiencing racism for the first time after moving to Canada:

> I learned to name the new violence that I encountered in Canada – different from other violences that had structured my life in India, of patriarchy and class, but alongside them. This new violence I learnt was "racism," a product of colonial capitalism rooted in slavery and genocide ... I looked to Black history, to history of Indigenous people of the Americas, and re-read the anti-colonial struggles ... The word Black, then a political metaphor rather than a territorial politics, filled me with a sense of pride and dignity, spelling a shared culture and politics of resistance. Those who dismiss so disdainfully all projects of self-naming and self-empowerment as "identity politics" have not needed to affirm themselves through the creative strength that comes from finding missing parts of one's self in experiences and histories similar to others ... For me this process of discovering the many names of my oppression in all its complexity brought sanity (9).

And through this newfound "sanity," Bannerji is able to illustrate for others the ways in which oppression and domination work to subjugate, the importance of naming the oppressions she faces, and then use new knowledges to help her resist the violences inflicted upon her by capitalism, racism, sexism, and patriarchy. The infliction of those very oppressions also propels transformations in ways of being, seeing, and knowing, and that leads to calls for change.

Educational institutions continue to devalue the knowledges, epistemologies, and ontologies of visible minority women. Hill-Collins (2000) calls for a decentring of those who occupy seats of power and the knowledge that defends their power (43). In this chapter, I begin the process of decentring and decolonizing through the use of personal narratives that illustrate the subjugation and inherent value of knowledges of women's experiences through both gendered and racialized lenses. Viewing women's experience in this way problematizes understandings of women's lives, depicts the experiences of marginalized women, and illustrates the necessity for epistemological and ontological decolonization of knowledge construction and valuation (Metta 2010). This decentring and decolonization begins with the question: What is feminism? All that feminism encompasses must be released into multiple significations where "unanticipated meanings might come to bear ... In a sense, what women signify has been taken for granted for too long, and what has been fixed as the 'referent' of the term has been 'fixed,' normalized, immobilized, paralyzed in positions of subordination" (Butler 1992, 16, cited in St Pierre 2000, 505). I am calling for a decolonization of feminism that comes from a rethinking of the ways in which the world – and schooling – is ordered.

NOTES

1 It must be noted that not all women are natural homemakers, mothers, or nurturers. However, these characteristics are not taught in schools but instead taught in the home by family and community and are, therefore, an important aspect of feminist ontologies.
2 Odora Hoppers and Richards argue that there exists a status quo in which Western knowledges are "hegemonic" tools, promoting an ideological vision of what is in everyone's interests that is largely accepted as common sense. This belief continues to prevail even though it is in direct contradiction of the experiences of the vast majority of peoples. Hoppers and Richard, therefore, contend that this *"unthinking"* promulgates a dominant world view that is in need of a transformation – a world view that requires a new way of thinking.

REFERENCES

Alberta Education. 2007. *Social Studies Program of Studies, Grade 9*. Edmonton: Alberta Education.
https://education.alberta.ca/media/1126804/ss9.pdf.
Ambwani, V., and L. Dyke. 2007. "Employment Inequities and Minority Women: The Role of Wage Devaluation." *International Journal of Diversity in Organisations, Communities and Nations* 7 (5): 143–52. doi:10.18848/1447-9532/CGP/v07i05/39459.
Austin, T. 2009. "Conflicting Discourses in Language Teacher Education: Reclaiming Voice in the Struggle." *Educational Foundations* 23 (3): 41–60.
Bannerji, H. 1991. *Unsettling Relations: The University as a Site of Feminist Struggle*. Toronto: Women's Press.
– 1993. "Re: Turning the Gaze." In *Returning the Gaze: Essays on Racism, Feminism and Politics*, ed. H. Bannerji, 220–36. Toronto: Sister Vision Press.
– 1995. *Thinking Through: Essays on Feminism, Marxism, and Anti-Racism*. Toronto: Women's Press.
Beynon, J., K. Toohey, and N. Kishor. 1998. "Do Visible Minority Students of

Chinese and South Asian Ancestry Want Teaching as a Career? Perceptions of Some Secondary School Students in Vancouver, BC." *Canadian Ethnic Studies* 30 (2): 50–75.

Brown, Y. 2008. "Ghosts in the Canadian Multicultural Machine: A Tale of the Absent Presence of Black People." *Journal of Black Studies* 38 (3): 374–87. doi:10.1177/0021934707306572.

Butler, J. 1999/2002. *Gender Trouble: Feminism and the Subversion of Identity*. New York: Routledge.

Carty, L. 1991. "Black Women in Academia: A Statement from the Periphery." In *Unsettling Relations: The University as a Site of Feminist Struggle*, ed. H. Bannerji, L. Carty, K. Dehli, S. Heald, and K. McKenna, 13–41. Toronto: Women's Press.

Crawford, C. 2004. "African Caribbean Women, Diaspora and Transnationality." *Canadian Woman Studies* 23 (2): 97–103.

Elabor-Idemudia, P. 2001. "Equity Issues in the Academy: An Afro-Canadian Woman's Perspective." *Journal of Negro Education* 70 (3): 192–203. doi:10.2307/3211210.

Ellis, C. 1991. "Sociological Introspection and Emotional Experience." *Symbolic Interaction* 14 (1): 23–50. doi:10.1525/si.1991.14.1.23.

Ellis, C., T.E. Adams, and A.P. Bochner. 2010. "Autoethnography: An Overview." *Forum Qualitative Sozialforschung / Forum:* Qualitative *Social Research* 12 (1). http://www.qualitative-research.net/index.php/fqs/article/view/1589/3095#gcit.

Finlayson, M. 2011. "African-Canadian Educators' Perspectives: Critical Factors for Success." *Canadian Journal of Education* 34 (4): 86–103.

Foucault, M. 1980. *Power/Knowledge: Selected Interviews and Other Writings*. New York: Pantheon.

Gervais, M. 2007. "Challenges Faced by Visible Minority and Aboriginal Teachers in Alberta Schools." Centre for Race and Culture website. www.cfrac.com/images/stories/pdf/challenges_faced_by_visible_minority_ _aboriginal_teachers_in_alberta_schools.pdf.

Hill-Collins, P. 2000. "What's Going On? Black Feminist Thought and the Politics of Postmodernism." In *Working the Ruins: Feminist Poststructural Theory and Methods in Education*, ed. E.A. St Pierre and W.S. Pillow, 41–73. New York: Routledge.

Hogarth, K. 2011. "Contested Belonging: The Experiences of Racialized Immigrant Women in Canada." *International Journal of Diversity in Organisations, Communities and Nations* 10 (5): 63–74. doi:10.18848/1447-9532/CGP/v10i05/38928.

hooks, b. 2000. *Feminist Theory: From Margin to Center*. Cambridge: South End Press.

Metta, M. 2010. *Writing against, alongside and beyond Memory: Lifewriting as Reflexive, Poststructuralist Feminist Research Practice*. Bern: Peter Lang.

Mogissi, H. 1994. "Racism and Sexism in Academic Practice: A Case Study." In *The Dynamics of Race and Gender*, ed. H. Afshar and M. Maynard, 222–34. London: Taylor and Francis.

Mohanty, C.T. 1991. "Under Western Eyes: Feminist Scholarship and Colonial Discourses." In *Third World Women and the Politics of Feminism*, ed. C.T. Mohanty, A. Russo, and L. Torres, 51–80. Bloomington: Indiana University Press.

– 1997. "Women Workers and Capitalist Scripts: Ideologies of Domination, Common Interests and the Politics of Solidarity." In *Feminist Genealogies, Colonial Legacies, Democratic Futures*, ed. M.J. Alexander and C.T. Mohanty, 3–29. New York: Routledge.

– 2003. *Feminism without Borders: Decolonizing Theory, Practicing Solidarity*. Durham: Duke University Press. doi:10.1215/9780822384649.

Mukherjee, B. 1993. *The Holder of the World*. Toronto: Harper Perennial.

Odora Hoppers, C., and H. Richards. 2012. *Rethinking Thinking: Modernity's "Other" and the Transformation of the University*. Pretoria: University of South Africa Press.

Pillay, T. 2010. "Critical Perspectives on NGOs and Educational Policy Development in Ethiopia." *Journal of Alternative Perspectives in the Social Sciences* 2 (1): 323–63.

Prentice, A. 1977. "The Feminization of Teaching." In *The Neglected Majority: Essays in Canadian Women's History*, ed. S. Mann Trofimenkoff and A. Prentice, 49–65. Toronto: McClelland and Stewart.

Razack, S.H. 2001. *Looking White People in the Eye: Gender, Race, and Culture in Courtrooms and Classrooms*. Toronto: University of Toronto Press.

Ryan, J., K. Pollock, and F. Antonelli. 2009. "Teacher Diversity in Canada: Leaky Pipelines, Bottlenecks and Glass Ceilings." *Canadian Journal of Education* 32 (3): 591–617.

Salmon, W. 2013. "Curriculum." In *The Great Black North*, ed. V. Mason-John and K.A. Cameron, 86. Calgary: Frontenac House.

Samuel, E., and N. Wane. 2005. "Unsettling Relations: Racism and Sexism Experienced by Faculty of Color in a Predominantly White Canadian University." *Journal of Negro Education* 74 (1): 76–87.

St Pierre, E.A. 2000. "Poststructural Feminism in Education: An Overview."

International Journal of Qualitative Studies in Education: QSE 13 (5): 477–515. doi:10.1080/09518390050156422.

Wane, N. 2008. "Mapping the Field of Indigenous Knowledges in Anti-Colonial Discourse: A Transformative Journey in Education." *Race, Ethnicity and Education* 11 (2): 183–97. doi:10.1080/13613320600807667.

Weiler, K. 2003. "Feminist Analysis of Gender and Schooling." In *Critical Pedagogy Reader*, ed. A. Darder, M.P. Baltodano, and R.D. Torres, 269–95. Westport: Greenwood Publishing.

Wrushen, B.R., and W.H. Sherman. 2008. "Women Secondary School Principals: Multicultural Voices from the Field." *International Journal of Qualitative Studies in Education: QSE* 21 (5): 457–69. doi:10.1080/09518390802297771.

CODA

Rounding Out the Conversation

JANICE WALLACE

A *coda* is a term used in music to indicate the section that brings a piece of music to an end. It may, for example, be added to the end of the last movement of a long sonata or bring down the house at the end of a rock song, and often both draws on familiar themes in the previous musical piece and adds an element of its own. Here, we are using it to signify a chapter that draws together some of the themes in the chapters that precede it while introducing some new ideas to the conversation.

In Carol Harris's paper, "A Critical Feminist Exploration of Arts-Based Education in Canada: Embodied Teaching, Learning, and Research within an Equity Framework," she draws together many of the themes we have already explored in looking at feminism's influence in educational contexts, but uses aesthetics as a fresh lens for the possibilities of critical feminism. She also draws our attention to issues in rural educational settings – a context that is underexplored in education scholarship – and pedagogical possibilities across age groups.

Harris argues that aesthetics as a theoretical and pedagogical stance breaks open the possibilities of feminism to move beyond mind/body dualisms in order to explore the multiple and interlocking layers of subjectivity. In doing so, she offers philosophical and pedagogical possibilities that challenge dominant epistemologies in learning locations for both adults and young people and focuses on the emergence and influence of a critical feminist aesthetics in the work of teachers, community educators, and academics. She posits that aesthetics working with critical feminism provides a theoretical grounding for an arts-based pedagogy that opens up democratic possibilities in education at all levels: K–12, higher education, and adult education.

Two communicative links are explored in which arts-based pedagogy, at the service of improved equity, can be accelerated: between administration and the work of teaching (i.e., leadership, curriculum, and pedagogy), and between child and adult learning. She concludes with an examination of how she and a colleague enacted these communicative links in the context of an arts-based pedagogical project that was helpful in critical place-based research about food practices in a rural setting: Change Islands, Newfoundland.

Harris's paper provides an illuminating coda as it rounds out the conversation around feminist issues in teaching, administration, and equity in contexts that are too often ignored. However, it is important to note that a coda does not tie up a musical – or scholarly – piece of work with a pretty bow. Instead, it references what has been heard, rounds it out with new possibilities, and then invites continued engagement.

10

A Critical Feminist Exploration of Arts-Based Education in Canada

Embodied Teaching, Learning, and Research within an Equity Framework

CAROL E. HARRIS

Tell me, I'll forget. Show me, I'll remember. Involve me, I'll understand.
Chinese proverb

Arts and education, writ large as teaching, learning, and research in school, university, and community, provide the focus for investigating the impact of feminism on contemporary education in Canada. By combining aspects of critical feminism and the feminist art movement, I argue that women's writing about art forms and body awareness, albeit impeded by political neo-liberal conservatism, has benefited educational equity in Canada. This effect, revealed in the examples below, is clearly visible in adult education research but less so in postsecondary and school contexts.

The problem addressed in this chapter stems from the dichotomy of mind and body, as experienced in our educational institutions and wider society. It emanates from the beginning of recorded philosophic thought but takes distinct shape with the Cartesian separation of male rationality and intelligence from the bodily imperatives of female existence (Lennon 2014). Although the problem is complex, many-sided in definition, ongoing, and impossible to measure, I trace examples of arts-based research and pedagogy that bridge this divide. My purpose is to illuminate connections between feminist approaches to mind/body dualisms and improved socio-cultural equity within educational institutions and their larger communities.

First, I contend that the arts offer a powerful source of privilege for some children and, when absent, a serious deprivation for others. This perspective, gleaned during my early years in Nova Scotia, established my own critical approach to what is meant by curricular "basics." Later it led me to appreciate Bourdieu's interconnections among cultural, economic, social, and political capital (Harris 2008). Next, drawing on feminist theory, I trace the subjugation of women artists and indicate why the arts, and other embodied approaches to learning through the senses, continue to be feminist issues (e.g., Gates 2006a and b; Gustafson 1999; Korsmeyer 2004; Naidus 2007).

I build my case through snapshots of two learning sites. The first involves proceedings from the Canadian Association for the Study of Women in Education (CASWE) featuring a rich variety of papers by feminist students, community educators, and university faculty members of CASWE. Selected writings of feminist adult educators, exploring transformative dimensions of community arts, provide the second data source. Adult educators have actively fostered the arts in teaching, learning, and research for several decades and, as a result, are able to speak experientially to the problem and purpose of this chapter. In the end, I return to the personal, drawing from my own research to illustrate points of connection between critical feminism, the arts, feminist pedagogy, and feminist research.

Although the socially constructed and intertwined subjugations of body, women, art, and feminism will be examined through a fine arts lens, this paper is primarily about arts-based education (ABE). Education in the fine arts – a right that I have long defended for all children (Harris 1996a) – calls for in-depth arts literacy as well as performance, and demands specialist teaching. The arts, calling upon a wide range of sentient acuity (i.e., sight, hearing, voice, touch, movement) and expression (visual representation, music, dance, poetry, drama), however, have played a secondary role in schools. They maintain a precarious hold within the curriculum and classroom, and become the first subjects to be cut or severely underfunded in times of austerity.[1]

Arts-*based* learning, because of its greater accessibility, offers diverse means of understanding and expression within reach of all children and adults (Butterwick and Dawson 2006; Desai and Koch 2012). Although not a substitute for arts education, ABE provides an enlarged palette of possibility for those who question the historical dichotomization of mind and body, the societal *status quo,* and the received wisdom of a highly consumerist economy. For instance, ABE provides venues within the bureaucratic structure of schools (Driscoll 2013) and post-secondary institutions (Gustafson 1998; McGregor 2012) for subjugated knowledge to find expression. As with feminist adult education in general, arts- and craft-based learning with feminist intent "reclaims knowledge, promotes activism, raises consciousness, challenges hegemony, builds community, deals with community loss, and works towards social justice" (Clover and Stalker 2005, 4). I highlight these issues as feminist contributions to education advocating strengthened communication between feminist approaches to arts-based pedagogy and research and ABE as it is played out in schools, post-secondary classrooms, and the larger community.

I have limited my examples to the arts, and chosen, where possible, arts that embody learning. My overview of selected documents demonstrates close parallels between feminism, arts education, and the embodiment of learning. This paper is inspired by the stated objectives of the CASWE.[2] Feminists in all fields share successes and learn from one another about components of education "frequently rendered invisible by existing pedagogy, curriculum, philosophy, policy and school organization." This paper extends the search that, I trust, others will join.

SETTING THE STAGE: A PERSONAL STORY

My own awareness of the arts as a connection between mind and body progressed by periods of questioning and leaps of recognition. My earliest questions, as a rural child of eight attending a two-room school, concerned my own good fortune in being given piano lessons and taking part in an exceptionally fine girls' choir. Because of the energy and skill of our choral director, a woman adult and school educator, we young singers were immersed in life-enhancing music (Harris 1998); moreover, we enjoyed our "breaks" from choral singing as we experienced our rural and cultural heritage by performing folk dances. But these were Saturday, and not school, activities.

I was aware that other children, equally talented and eager to participate in music, were barred from participation because opportunities, although "open to all," required considerable parental input. My realization of this situation awakened early thoughts of social and cultural [in]justice. These thoughts, years later, found resonance theoretically with Maxine Greene, Pierre Bourdieu, and others who spoke critically about the socio-economic roots of cultural capital. As an adult, I chose my theoretical home and based my activism on positions of possibility, such as the following: "To tap into the imagination is to become able to break with what is supposedly fixed and finished, objectively and independently real. It is to see beyond what the imaginer has called normal or 'common-sensible' and to carve out new orders in experience. Doing so, a person may become freed to glimpse what might be, to form notions of what should be and what is not yet" (Greene 1995, 19). I absorbed other practical, youthful lessons during the latter years of government support for adult education in Nova Scotia, a period extending from the early 1950s through the late 1960s. In this time of community-based education (itself an outgrowth of the Antigonish Movement, Nova Scotia's renowned experiment in social democracy) the provincial government, through its Adult Education Division, held a series of folk schools. Here farmers, housewives, and miners and their "teachers"[3] combined learning about cooperatives, credit unions, and community organizing through dance, singing, and drama. As these activities were collectively called "recreation," it took me some time to realize that the arts not only offered breaks from study sessions but also, through the dramatization of alternative socio-economic arrangements, provided a forum for social critique. At twenty, I joined the division for one year as its music adviser, a position that brought me teaching experience with teachers and community members, at several folk schools, and at a summer residential school exclusively for the arts. That year set my educational compass for life, although many years passed before I fully appreciated the connections I was establishing between mind, body, and the arts.

Somehow, I had managed to graduate from university in music and English with little awareness of the embodiment of either, apart from the physical discipline involved in piano and vocal performance, and a few music and movement games with children. At age forty, with twenty years of school and government teaching under my belt, I began to study Kodály music education as practised in Hungary. In this approach – named for the composer and theorist Zoltán Kodály rather than for the superb women educators who conducted research in school classrooms – music was approached holistically through song, dance, reading, writing, and composing before instruments were added. When I visited Budapest's Liszt Academy as a music scholar in 1987, I was required to dance to the music of other students and to play the piano while students moved to my mazurkas, waltzes, sarabands, and adagios. This experience, apart from years on the dance floor, was my first conscious movement to the music of others, and my first time seeing the embodiment of music that I, myself, had performed. The experience taught me much about music and, I believe, even more about myself.

Still I asked myself: What is it that one learns from engagement with the arts? What does the body have to do with learning if, indeed, learning takes place? And, if artistic expression and bodily engagement are beneficial, why have we had so little of either? Working backwards through these questions, I first looked for answers in feminist theory.

FEMINIST FRAMING OF THE ISSUE: WHY SO LITTLE EMBODIMENT OF LEARNING?

Feminism is a politics. It is a politics directed at changing existing power relations between women and men in society. These power relations structure all areas of life: the family, education and welfare, and the worlds of work and politics, culture and leisure. They determine who does what and for whom, what we are, and what we might become.

Weedon 1997, 1

These opening words by Weedon, in her discussion of *Feminist Practice and Poststructuralist Theory*, indicate the complexity and scope surrounding the feminist project and, thence, the circuitous route linking dichotomies and definitions of mind and body, constructions of hierarchy, and consignments of gender and power. Weedon's words also signal the feminist objectives of challenging dualisms, healing divisions, and altering language (Ferguson 1984).

We can trace the mind/body split explicitly from the time of Rene Descartes, noting through the intervening years the privileging of the former over the latter. Descartes attempted, more forcefully than earlier philosophers, to establish fundamental principles for distinguishing truth from falsehood (Bennett 2007). Using the gendered conventions of the time, he pointed to man's rationality (that is, the mind) alone as capable of discerning reality; the senses, although helpful in providing evidence of the Real, were prone to position appearances over truth. From this foundation, it does not require a long stretch of reasoning to assign distinct mind/body attributes according to gender.

Well before Descartes – probably from the beginnings of human evolution – rationality and mind had become the purview of men while women, biologically connected with family and reproduction, were representative of emotions, sensuality, and the body. This is but one set of socially constructed divisions separating and privileging the claimed territory of male competence over areas assigned to women. Others, critiqued forcefully by post-structural theorists, separate and prioritize public and private lives, nature and culture, creativity and imitation (Heilbrun 1993; Martin 1994; Sydie 1994) and the significant dualism paralleling the mind/body split: science and art.

Science, as explained by Descartes in 1637, provides the route whereby reasoned thought leads – one proposition at a time – to what is generally regarded as Truth or Reality. Art, as perceived by Plato (1987) some 300 years BCE and accepted by Descartes, is the carrier of impressions and appearances; it emanates from imagination, fancy, and imitation. Plato honoured and applied the arts in his own work, yet feared their possible corrupting influence on society as a whole. He viewed the physical world, and its portrayal in art, as a decadent copy of eternal and perfect Forms of reality. According to Plato, artists ought to be banned from the perfect state, his idealized Republic.

Yet artistic expression is, and has always been, fundamentally important to all societies. Social anthropologist Dissanayake (2000, 1992) thoroughly documents art as permeating all cultural and human experience, present in the earliest relationships between mother and child, and essential to human existence. In *Homo Aestheticus*, Dissanayake (1992) surmises that art, as omnipresent, must be there for good reasons. One surely is the "necessary" pleasure it gives, for "anything as strongly pleasurable and compelling as the arts ... in some ways contributes to biological survival" (in Dutton 1994, 206). She notes that the role of art, through millennia, has been to "make special" celebrations, ceremonies, play, rituals, and other events of personal and cultural significance. Dissanayake's historical perspective on art as an expression of community life invites an exploration of what adult educators have come to know as "community arts" (Clover and Stalker 2005; Harris 2002).

HIGH ART, MISOGYNY, AND THE TURN TO COMMUNITY ARTS

The arts, whether idealized yet feared as in high art, or purposeful as in community arts and crafts, have, for centuries, under the division of mind and body, placed women in a marginalized position. In the fine arts or classical music field, the perspective has been decidedly misogynistic. Female musicians in the nineteenth century were accepted as performers yet deterred from studying theory and composition under their own names (Gates 2006a). Fanny Mendelssohn Hensel, for instance, composed more than four hundred works, but published only under her brother Felix's name. The list of obstacles to her work, sounding painfully like those facing feminist artists today, included "her relationship with her father and brother, her responsibilities as wife and mother, her often debilitating sense of isolation, and her ambivalence about her creative talent" (Gates 2007, 1).

The story for orchestral conductors, who perhaps most intensely embody their art, is no more encouraging. Given their near exclusion from the study and composition of music, women simply did not try to conduct orchestras. Yet they were constantly blamed for failing to create, compose, or lead. Critic and journalist Harold Schonberg, to give one example from the 1960s, refused to admit the possibility that women possess the requisites to assume orchestral leadership. The conductor, in his view, "is many things: musician, administrator, executive, minister, psychologist, technician, philosopher and dispenser ... Above all he is a leader of men ... a father ... The Teacher who knows all" (in Maddocks 2013, 17). Today, female conductors still face sexual innuendo, as demonstrated in the comment by Vasily Petrenko to fellow conductor Marin Alsop. Petrenko quipped that women distract from important business for "a cute girl on a podium means that musicians think about other things" (Maddocks 2013, 2). The implication of this remark, like Schonberg's, is clear: the podium is no place for a woman.

The history of visual art has followed a similar storyline, which sees women barred from studies, studios, and galleries. Chadwick (2007), illustrating the relentless subjugation of women from the sixteenth to eighteenth centuries, traces the artistic talent of three exceptional Europeans. As with music, the stories are of exclusion (by fathers, brothers, and husbands), false attribution of authorship, and the double aesthetic bind in which women's products are seen either to be too sentimental and feminine, or too bold, boisterous, and masculine. Chadwick (2007) and Korsmeyer (2004) describe women's eventual turn in the twentieth century to radical art, and their vehement rejection of social constructions of the mind/body dualism and of taste and artistic talent. In revolutionary spirit, women began to present the body both as the site of sexual desire, gratification, and childbirth, and, at the same time, as an object enchained, tortured, and exploited. In overturning what was hitherto considered acceptable and worthy in art, many artists – including feminists such as Frida Kahlo, Leonora Carrington, and Alexis Hunter – demanded public attention through their presentations of subjects and objects of "sublimity and disgust" (Korsmeyer 2004, 130–51). Feminist artists today are well on their way to reclaiming the body as significant, reinhabiting their own, and inspiring others to do likewise.

As Weedon (1997) contends, feminism is a politics that concerns the power relations that control, to a large extent, our present and future – unless we contest and override the existing political agenda. Not only do we have a radical backlash today against gender stereotyping within the fine arts, but we see a feminist insistence on redefining art itself. Smith (1991) notes that artists of all descriptions possess and apply literacies that subvert and contradict the existing, limited sociological imagination. Addressing feminists, she maintains that her fellow sociologists "have not known, as poets, painters, and sculptors have known, how to begin from our own experience, how to make ourselves as women the subjects of the sociological act of knowing" (Smith 1991, 69). To disrupt the "brutal history of women's silencing" (22), Smith acknowledges women's exclusion from the "high arts" and points to their conscious involvement in the arts of everyday experience as they turn to "forms, materials, and practices quite different from those that, until recently, have been identified with art" (23). Quilting stands as Smith's example of resistance in women's everyday lives, for a "quilt was not a piece of art, therefore, to be seen in isolation from its history and the social relations of its making ... [but] always a moment in the moving skein of family and tradition, raising suspicion against time and its powers of separation" (23).

A seniors' project in British Columbia, "Crying the Blues," illustrates the educational potential of women's engagement in quilting as a transformative fabric art. Clover (2005) followed the BC "Old Age Pensioners" (OAP) as they protested the province's budgetary cuts to public services brought about by neo-liberal government policies. Fabric squares, designed and executed by each of the seventy-five chapters of OAP, were sent to a central quilting team. Themes, drawing attention to the impact of cuts on "the well-being and vitality of citizens" (630), were symbolized as scissors (for generalized cuts to services), tipped scales (for imbalances in provision), a crossed-out letter H (for reductions in hospital beds, and breaches in sanitary conditions), and so on. Although the completed project was not embraced by government or promoted by televised media, it found resonance in local newspapers and at union and academic conferences. Of great importance, however, was the civic lesson of solidarity gained by the senior women who sharpened their critical perspectives and saw their protest come to life in the co-operative production of an art object.

More than a decade before this example of protest and action by BC seniors, the feminist organization of the Canadian Association for the Study of Women in Education (CASWE) had been formed with the broad mandate to "promote exchanges of information about feminist scholarship and pedagogy" (Epp 1999, 140). We turn now to CASWE's early days and continuing importance.

CASWE: A TRAIL BLAZER

CASWE's first summer institute, held at Brock University in June 1996, signalled a difference in learning both through the papers of its proceedings (Harris and Depledge 1996) and the design of its sessions. Under the direction of faculty member Cecilia Reynolds, graduate students Diana Gustafson and Pam Seaman invited attendees to take part in a most untraditional event, marked by an opening tea service complete with small, intimate round tables, white tablecloths and flowers, and a sunrise, fire-circle ceremony led by women from the nearby Six Nations Reserve. For many of us, the Brock conference illustrated that knowledge could flourish through informality, laughter, and a true mixing of educators from town, reserve, and gown. As broadening the circle of participants was an objective, an invitation was extended locally to members of the general public and, further, to the American Association of University Women. Together, participants realized that academe could be organized differently and better, and that women would continue to do just that.

As the theme that summer was inclusivity, it was not surprising that many presenters were concerned with "voice." Balaisis, for instance, spoke of the importance of intuition in reclaiming women's wisdom, claiming that "voicing the known moves the knowing into being, just as sound penetrates time and words have power to touch" (Harris and Depledge 1996, 133).[4] To illustrate this point, Balaisis explored the reclamation of voice though the medium of drama and the "projected play, making believe, and taking on [a] role" (134). Finding freedom and voice through the assumption of a semi-fictional persona marks an important feature of drama to which I return later.

The next two Institute proceedings addressed issues raised in *Centring on the Margins: The Evaded Curriculum* (Epp 1998) and *Engendering Education* (Sanford, Blair, and Schlender 2000). In 1998, music and visual art were cited as "evaded" subjects, deeply gendered in their encompassing presuppositions (Cooley, Pescesky, and Walker 1998, 255–60; Lamb, Bates, and Frederickson 1998, 295–6). The first authors portray "the art making experience as catalytic in their growth towards a sense of self and agency, both as artists and as members of society" (255). The second team of researchers, studying the perceptions of school music teachers, found gender divisions along expected corridors, with men favouring improvisation, dictation, composition, and performance (that is, music literacy) while women called for more affective evaluation, integration of music with other subjects, and movement within music classrooms. All researchers, however, noted the subjugated place of music within the curriculum, evoking the metaphor of a "sweet but silly girl, appreciated for her beauty and charm but not taken seriously as a meaningful contributor to contemporary education" (296).

Elsewhere, the 1998 proceedings reported many embodiments of learning, mostly centred on the development of identity through narrated story lines and poetry. The Institute of 2000, in addition, conveyed an aura of artistry in its overall programming. Although the proceedings contained only two articles of arts-based research, the Institute itself opened with a documentary film and a display of visual art. One entire session was dedicated to a drama presentation by Mirror Theatre, an educational company featuring plays and workshops about social issues as recounted ("mirrored") by citizen definitions of circumstances.

One paper in this collection illustrated art-as-embodiment through dance. Darmaningsih, a Javanese dancer, shared her own journey from classical or high art to a form more expressive of her individuality and emotion. Beginning in a formalized classical vein and following the traditional movements of her art, at age thirty, Darmaningsih asked herself: "Do dances have the ability to speak about larger issues such as justice, power, human rights, and so on? Do I have the need to speak through my own dance to others?" (Darmaningsih 2000, 62). Her response to these rhetorical questions was a resounding yes, freeing her to act on this new awareness. She relates "after three years of continued hard practice (i.e., moving beyond classically rooted steps and precise movements to self-expression), I was finally able to do my own movements and express my own self without feeling guilt and hurt" (62). Then she was able to dance with "eyes no longer averted, arms raised in the air, running, and jumping as the mood dictated." Through her insistence on embodied learning, Darmaningsih came to honour and express her own desires, emotions, and need for artistry and, at the same time, combine her traditional heritage with elements of her new home, Canada.

Although the direction toward embodiment through art was established in these early CASWE Institutes, the 2002 Institute spoke directly to the issue. In "Ways of Knowing in and through the Body," the objective was to "portray what gets left out of scholarly work [because of] our obsession with certainty and our reliance on words and linear rationality to gather and represent our realities" (Abbey 2002, ix). In her own contribution to the proceedings, organizer Sharon Abbey addressed school curricula, recommending the incorporation of "embodied knowing through the use of sensory awareness, yoga, breathing, meditation, intuition, metaphor, visualization, poetry and visual art" (1).

Other papers in 2002 explored the dichotomization of knowledge (cognitive and/or emotional) in schools, universities, adult learning centres, communities, health-care facilities, and homes. Examples directly dealing with embodied learning included papers on information technologies (Coupal 2002, 75–9); dance choreography (Karsemeyer and Karsemeyer 2002, 146–9); transformative learning through dance (Brown and Penniston 2002, 150–2); dance as environmental education (Neilson 2002, 190–3); musical performance as embodied listening (Bogdan 2002, 32–5); Eastern methods of exploring the intersections of body, mind, and spirit (Guénette 2002, 126–9); the physical exploration of poetry and action in distinguishing between factual knowledge and knowledge as understanding (Cooper and Kooy 2002, 71–4; Peddigrew 2002, 203–5); metaphors for changing physical capabilities (Lindsay 2002, 169–73); and one of special interest to me – the knowledge that can come with embodied singing (Mackie 2002, 177–80).

The next two Institutes, like the previous, followed specific feminist topics. The 2004 proceedings, held in celebration of CASWE's first decade, dealt with sexism in the academy (Wallin, Macpherson, and Liwiski 2004). They were illustrated with photographed sketches depicting Michelangelo's Libyan Sybil and other images of prophets and prophetesses from the Sistine Chapel. The editors remind us, noting Sybil's gaze upon the open book at her feet, that our ongoing struggle with "authoritarian, male-dominated institutions [is not new], and neither are we new to the enterprise of knowledge, wisdom, and learning" (5). The papers, although not specifically about the mind/body dualism, come with reminders of women's ongoing hardships within academe, many of which remain embedded in tenacious, gendered constructions of such issues as student and peer expectations, salaries, acceptable research, and the funding of research chairs.

Seventy-two women responded to the topic of 2006, *Women, Health and Education* (Gustafson and Goodyear 2006). Although most papers touched on the mind/body dualism and/or the embodiment of learning, only a few did so directly through arts-based approaches. One deeply moving paper, "Body Sight/Site: A Performance" (Patterson 2006, 211–15), used photography, poetry, and prose to explore and visually represent experiences of women with disabilities. Another paper, collectively written by seven women, described research "On Girls' Disembodiment: The Complex Tyranny of the 'Ideal Girl.'" This study, using drawings and narratives, explored the gap between constructions of "ideal" and "self" which, not surprisingly, was particularly large for girls in lower socio-economic and for different ethnocultural groups (224–8).

In 2008, the first CASWE doctoral award for outstanding feminist scholarship was presented to Amani Hamdan Alghamdi for her metaphorical interpretation in "Quilted Narratives of Arab Muslim Women's Tapestry: Intersecting Education Experiences and Gender Perceptions" (Alghamdi 2006). Hamdan's metaphor of the quilt – again the image of everyday women's lives – stitches together the educational and personal lives of nine Arab Muslim women now living in Canada. The study juxtaposes insider/outsider views of women, gender, religion, and social expectations.

The Institute proceedings from Concordia (Clover and Smith 2010) opened discussion of the sources, transfer, and mobilization of knowledge even more widely, positioning educational sites in the wider community – in families, streets, voluntary and non-governmental organizations, unions, and business offices – and included female learners across a wide range of cultures and abilities. Several papers, following CASWE's theme of "connected understandings," addressed the embodiment of learning either obliquely or directly. The winner of the 2010 CASWE doctoral award was Indrani Margolin who, in the final paper of the proceedings, provided a brief overview of her research into the freeing capacity of movement, and the possibility through poetry of expressing this freedom. Her paper, "Soaring into Dance," opens with the problematic issue of body image: "Many girls in urban schools live under the surveillance of oppressive gendered dominant discourses that dictate they be thin, white, and submissive. These systems of control are seeped into their school, family, and social contexts so intensely that they internalize these notions and begin to relate to the *bodyself* in a critical, objectifying, and segregating manner" (Margolin 2009, 104). Margolin's approach to this problem was to immerse girls in an after-school program of creative dance, focusing on their inner experience of body as a kinesthetic, sensual, perceptual, emotional, and spiritual site of knowledge. The research with four girls aged sixteen to eighteen constitutes little more than an abstract, yet it entices readers concerned with embodied learning to explore the thesis itself for a detailed exploration of the healing potential inherent in *bodyself* techniques.

The 2010 CASWE proceedings, broadening the organization's spatial definition of education to encompass both child and adult research and learning, introduce my next set of examples. In these, feminist adult educators work from informal as well as formal learning sites to explore the power of drama, popular theatre, documentary film, and other community arts to reunite body and mind in teaching, learning, and research.

FEMINIST ADULT EDUCATORS AND ARTS-BASED TRANSFORMATIVE LEARNING

Feminists in Canadian adult education today challenge traditional perceptions of art's autonomy (i.e., art solely for the sake of art) with particular urgency. Valuing art as a teaching and research tool, these women are decidedly pragmatic; they *use* art forms to present contradictions within society and to explore discriminations of all kinds – gender, sexual, class, racial, and ability, as well as acts that insult the environment. And, like the visual artists described above, they frequently use art's shock value to elicit wonder, awe, reflection, and laughter. Through their edited books, journals, and conference proceedings, feminist adult educators engage with one another. Moreover, they inhabit a culture where men and women are for the most part comfortable with aesthetic expression. Illustrating this acceptance, Butterwick and Dawson (2006) point to the tradition at Canadian adult education (CASAE) conferences of including "an arts-space evening ... where members read poetry, sing songs, play music, and share through different art genres their adult education passions and experience" (284). Although not immune to the "great man" culture (Stalker 1998; Taber and Guthro 2006), men and women adult educators have travelled far along the road to healing gender dualism.

An important aspect of feminism within adult education inheres in the educational meaning of transformative learning. Unlike the meaning of transformation as "organizational change," so often adopted in leadership circles (e.g., The Transformational Learning Institute) [5] for the initiation of better business and management practices, the meaning within adult education focuses on individual enrichment and socio-economic emancipation, taking its lead from Freire (1986). His objective was to bring oppressed citizens to an awareness of the conditions in which they live and, in turn, enable them to overthrow their oppressors and determine their own destinies. This is a critical approach to education, fortified by the arts, aimed toward increased social awareness through study groups, cultural activities, and an exploration of alternative arrangements through discussion, reflection, and action.

Drama and popular theatre, when conceived of as "activist art" (Clover 2010, 236; Naidus 2007, 140–1), have been two of the most effective art forms used in bringing about positive educational change. I define drama in this context as the development of skits or scripted plays, often drawn from the experiences of participants and/or from other original research data, designed to evoke reflection and critique, and delivered for institutional, public, personal, and political edification (e.g., Baskwill 2008; Meyer and Young 2013). Popular theatre, on the other hand, delves into collaborative techniques in which the marginalized of society can better see themselves and imagine alternative social situations. This theatre form, inspired by Freire's *Pedagogy of the Oppressed,* was devised by Boal (2002, 2006) in the context of Brazilian poverty and political oppression. Boal believed that all humans are capable of being actors (they act) and spectators (they observe). In his theatre, therefore, both performers and audiences take part as "Spect-Actors" who assume different poses and perspectives in order to portray present conditions and possible alternatives.

Applications of Boalian theatre in Canada include experiments in Vancouver (Butterwick 2002; Butterwick and Selman 2003; Kennelly 2006) where Headlines Theatre (now called Theatre for Living) uses dramatic techniques to help communities tell and revise their stories. One feminist project in the early 2000s involved women who were working to resolve divergences and difficulties associated within feminist coalitions. The participants described by Butterwick (2002) made use of paired storytelling of a critical incident, "deep" listening, and co-operative planning for dramatic representation. Returning to the larger group, the women then created images and body sculptures (a Boalian technique for expressing an emotion, event, or theme), followed by group discussions of each representation and its possible alteration. Etmanski (2007), in the context of a Canadian post-secondary institution, explored international student experiences through popular theatre. In this work, researcher and participants questioned, together, the gap between the rhetoric of Canadian multiculturalism and the overt and covert racism often experienced by those who arrive with too few language skills, little spending money, and no one to familiarize them with their new culture.

An objective of community activist visual art also concerns the collective participation of men and women in transformative learning. Roy (2012), for instance, observes in her study of documentary films that people come together to watch films with a purpose; they are seeking edification about aspects of the world and the experiences of others. Their learning may simply affirm their own views, or it may offer information and an example of a different reality. Roy contends that "watching television at home was very different from watching films with others in a dark theatre, listening to stories of challenges and success ... even if there were no direct exchanges between viewers" (297). One viewer observed that he had more "responsibility to the present" in the collective context. Embodied learning is evident in this propulsion of the collective toward new energy and solidarity.

Clover and others (Clover, Sanford, and Butterwick 2013), in literature reviews and articles, have contributed greatly to knowledge about the theory, methodologies, and outcomes of feminist art pedagogy and research internationally. In an overview of feminist aesthetic practices, Clover (2010) calls on selected journal articles and conference proceedings to demonstrate research and learning through fabric arts, theatre, poetry, traditional basket weaving, painting, and "motherwork." Clover has given us both an understanding of this aspect of her field and a model from which we may draw in other educational disciplines. Much the same can be said of Clover, Sanford, and Butterwick (2013) where, again, the spotlight falls on feminist goals of inclusivity, risk, and defiance to focus on the advancement of social justice, civic engagement (as participants move from observers to become public actors), the mobilization of knowledge, and art education itself.

These are but a few examples from the broad spectrum of feminist adult educational research and pedagogy. The common thread binding these projects is the perceived need for researchers, teacher/facilitators and participants to challenge the status quo of educational and political power and influence, and to recognize the possibilities inherent in collective action.

UNITING THE TRANSFORMATIVE POTENTIAL OF ABE AND FEMINIST/EMBODIED LEARNING

Feminist teaching and learning, in many ways, are one. The feminist teacher, as defined in this chapter, sees herself as a lifelong learner who benefits constantly from the ideas and experiences of her students (Duckworth 2006; Tisdell 2000). The learner, as well, embarks on an adventure of mutual discovery with his or her teacher, aware that roles may be reversed in different contexts. Feminist research, likewise, depends on the establishment of a mutual learning space for researchers and participants. Feminist researchers do not gather and hold priority over information but, rather, pass it – and thus power (Foucault 1980) – back to participants in a spirit of reciprocity (Lather 1991). Of course, not all feminist teachers and researchers fulfill these objectives, and some may not attempt to do so. Perhaps we can consider the Teacher–Researcher as an Ideal Type – with goals never entirely realized by feminist academic, school, and community workers, but goals, nevertheless, that inspire.

Critical feminist educators emphasize particular issues about their work, such as positionality (Tisdell 2000), voice (Hayes 2000), and transformative learning (Cranton 2006; Manicom 1992; Smith 1991; Weedon 1997). Concerning positionality, teachers are called to recognize and reflect upon their own backgrounds of power and, in turn, do their utmost to learn from the backgrounds (social, economic, and cultural) that each student introduces to the classroom or community setting. What privileges and presuppositions does the teacher or researcher bring to the questions posed? What responses does she seek? And how does she assess the success of her teaching and research? Second, the discovery of voice, in recognition of women's constructed subjugated position in society, has become a recurring theme in feminist education (Gilligan 1982). An objective of feminist teachers, therefore, is to provide a safe space in which students may express themselves and a listening and responsive atmosphere in which their feelings, beliefs, and experiences are taken seriously. Third, the journey from silence to voice involves many instances of transformative learning. The task of critical feminist pedagogy is political; these feminists have an agenda. They recognize that neither they nor their students and research participants come to the classroom and research site tabula rasa. The pedagogical objective is that all students become aware of existing power relations – of class, gender, sexuality, age, prior learning opportunities, physical ability – and their role in either securing and perpetuating these relations, or challenging and changing them.

In considering the possible role of ABE in feminist teaching, learning, and research, we can ask first how, or *if*, the arts contribute to our personal and overriding learning goals. A major goal for many of us involves initiating or fostering, in each child and adult, the kind of excitement that motivates lifelong learning, opens doors to new perspectives, and stimulates creative imagination. To reach each child, we need to call on the widest possible range of expressive devices embedded in the arts, conversation, and numbers. Although not all children come to school with well-developed numeracy and literacy skills – that Holy Grail of educational and labour necessity (Green and Riddell 2001) – each child possesses some verbal, visual, musical, dramatic, or kinesthetic ability to share ideas and impressions about the world. Yet these basic embodiments of knowing are far too often ignored or underacknowledged, with the resultant dulling of sentient perception as the child moves into adulthood (Collingwood 1958, 162–3).

Butterwick and Dawson (2006) counter the present market-driven culture in Canada, contending "the goal [of teaching and learning] should be to prepare people for artistic forms of thinking" (282). Eisner (2002) reminds us of several benefits from an arts-inclusive education. First, he contends that learning through the arts, dependent as it is on sensory messages, promises to transform our consciousness of the sights and sounds, tastes, and smells of our environment. Further, Eisner, like Greene (1995), claims that this refinement of the senses enlarges the imagination and, therefore, provides models through which we can experience the world in new ways. A related learning lies in the realization, prevalent throughout aesthetic experience, that there can be several "answers" to a given problem. Third, there exists such a thing as "rightness of fit" whereby our judgment depends on a physical and emotional response to the issue at hand (Eisner 2002, 201). Finally, and relevant to goals of identity formation, Eisner maintains that education is a process of learning how to become the architect of one's own experience and, therefore, how to create oneself. This final reference to the development of agency and identity applies to every branch of school and adult education.

In the rural schools of Newfoundland and Labrador (NL) where I have conducted research over the past fifteen years, some students have limited language skills in the conventional sense. The arts provide an avenue for their voices that otherwise might be silent, and for visual, musical, and body imaging. In an ongoing study, my research colleague and I build on the recognized literacy of the traditional curriculum (i.e., language arts) to develop artistic literacies among students from grades 4 to 12 (Harris and Barter 2013). We do this while working with the students-as-researchers of past and present-day food practices in their own village. The identification of a significant phrase in a student's research data, for instance, may lead to poetic elaboration as in the example of Sean and Charlie. These high school youth identified the following exclamation as "significant" to the senior citizen with whom they talked: "Look what's happening to the fishery today!" From these words, the lads developed a poem in free verse that they felt encapsulated the meaning of the interview, and their own quest for identity in a community that once was a vibrant fishing centre. Their verse, entitled "Times past, Times to come," begins with "Boneless pink salmon ... Thailand/but where's the fishery?" and ends with "where do I stand?"

In the arts, we seek "the ability to perceive things, not merely to recognize them" (Eisner 2002, 5). These lads have seen their community decline, and now they perceive that the diminished fishery is somehow related to the importation of foods from the far corners of the globe. Their use of "found poetry" (Glesne 2010) allows them to express this new connection.

MENDING FENCES AND BRIDGING DUALISMS

Although bringing body and mind together in harmonious and mutual benefit for individuals and collectives remains the major challenge addressed in this chapter, several other divisions have surfaced from the literature examined here. One concerns the socially constructed rift between fine arts and community arts; another divides adult and child learners.

Regarding the fine arts/community arts dualism, some feminists have rejected the former as hopelessly enshrouded in the theoretical foundations of a modernist and patriarchal era. Others would retain the best of historical worth, regardless of foundational bias, and build upon it a better, more inclusive future (Clover 2010). My own approach favours the combined arts route, taking seriously the history of misogyny and paternalism surrounding the fine arts, and recognizing – but not prioritizing – the distinction between artists and their art works, and individuals and groups who engage in community arts. Practising artists and art historians combine traditional knowledge and skill gleaned from those who have gone before. To produce or speak of "art," however, they create anew and, at times, take risks, as in the case of radical visual artists who shock with embodiments that challenge local mores. Community arts-based processes and products, created *by* the people, tend to speak more directly *to* the people, their needs, and perceived injustices.

Distinctions between fine arts and arts-based pedagogy are important as well. Without their clear definition in educational discourse, we run the risk – especially likely in a period of economic austerity and cuts to education – of substituting one for the other in our classrooms and of confusing the meaning of arts literacy. Both the fine arts and arts-based teaching/learning are needed in a socially just school system, but for different purposes and with different objectives. Eisner (2002) presents a comprehensive rationale for the inclusion of fine arts, but for economic and ideological reasons, few school systems adequately provide these programs. It is in integrated (or community) arts that teachers and students can explore together new ways of representing their experiences and observations. Everyone can participate because specialization is unnecessary. However, to do so, teachers (and researchers) who are novices to ABE must gain sufficient confidence through enriched pre-service and in-service experience.

The other dualism that surfaces exists between adult and child learners. The assumption seems to be that children learn differently from adults and, therefore, teaching/learning and research about the two should occupy different spaces. Only occasionally, such as in the classroom research of Duckworth (2006), or in the studies of mothers and daughters conducted by O'Reilly and Abbey (2000), do we read about adults and children engaged in the excitement of mutual learning. This stubborn division clings to the fortified silos – the institutions, departments within institutions, scholarly publications, workshops, conferences, and ever-increasing financial restrictions by funding bodies as to suitable topics of research – of higher education, adult education, and schools.

These dualisms of mind/body, high/low art, and adult/child learners, resisted by visionary men and women from the early twentieth century (Piaget, Steiner, Montesorri, Dewey, Kodály, Orff, Dalcroze), have been acted upon by second-wave feminist teachers (e.g., Duckworth on Piaget; Greene on Dewey). Often one hears comments that all this has been said before, that it is "just good teaching" (Ladson-Billings 1995). While the explicit charge of repetition is accurate, critics miss the implicit message that the "common sense" of arts-based, experiential, embodied, and discovery learning, directed toward all children – regardless of their home, ethnicity, social, and economic situations – is all too rarely practised in classrooms.

SUMMARY, AND A CLASSROOM SCENE TO CLOSE

This chapter addresses the long, painfully slow progress in society from knowing *what*, to knowing *how*. The opening quote, attributed to Confucius, points to this distinction: if I am told, I forget; if I am shown (as in much of our pedagogy in an age of constant visual stimulation), I remember; but if I am actively engaged, I will discover the purpose behind my action. This approach to teaching and learning, conjoining body and mind as "phonesis," has been long explored theoretically by philosophers and liberal theorists (Aristotle n.d.; Ryle 1990; Dewey 1980). It has been given new expression today by feminist teachers and researchers who employ the arts. As Glazer (1991) maintained almost three decades ago, feminism has questioned "a priori assumptions of the ways in which knowledge has been selected, constructed, distributed and legitimated," and thus has changed the lens through which we teach, learn, and conduct research (321). The feminist lens, in a postmodern setting, encompasses many peoples, cultures, and abilities. Moreover, it extends the dynamics of place to rural communities that have become marginalized in an urbanized world (Barter 2009; Butterwick and Selman 2003), and to post-secondary settings where international students struggle to find meaning (Etmanski 2007) in a market-driven economy. Ways of seeing and knowing (Berger 1972; Greene 1995) through the various languages of art, likewise, turn the lenses in imaginative directions for, as has been said about children, "if [they] don't shape images, images will shape them" (in Kibbey 2011, 50). I believe that a kaleidoscope of social, cultural, and political possibility is needed more urgently today, in this era of bottom-line accountancy, than at any previous period in world history.

The recent period of Canadian public policy has seen severe cuts to both feminist organizations and the arts, including arts education. Women's centres have been closed and arts funding greatly reduced across the country, and school programs in the arts dramatically scaled back. All of this – in keeping with financially imposed impediments to science research (Leung, 2014), foundational studies (deMarrais 2013), and citizen participation (Brodie 2009; Lewis 2014) – has been accomplished in the name of austerity, less government, and deficit reduction. The particular austerities, it would seem, are politically motivated to reduce critical commentary and action while government power has actually increased and deficits grown. In the face of this political atmosphere,[6] feminists have continued to fight back, as demonstrated here, using the arts to deliver their messages of resistance, hope, and resilience. I have tried to show that feminist messages have become, even in these difficult times, increasingly resistant (to the *status quo*), defiant (of programs that would divide people according to gender, class, and other markers of opportunity and oppression), and politically charged. I see those who work in ABE refusing to bow to the present neo-liberal order and, in many places, enabling the torch of possibility to burn brightly.

In ending, I return briefly to my own teaching, learning, and research as conducted in the all-grade school of Change Islands, NL. I do so for several reasons: because storylines provide a recognized tool for feminist pedagogy and research; because I realize that the feminist literature reviewed here, while rich in individual and collective adult learning, provides few school illustrations; and, finally, to invite others to share stories of arts-based pedagogy and research as feminist, embodied inquiry.

My research colleague and I are both "retired" from our professions, but still we write, conduct research, teach, and supervise graduate students and projects. Our feminist desire, in researching food practices in a remote site that was until fairly recently self-sufficient, is to explore with community members the oppressive manner in which food sovereignty has gradually, over several decades, been replaced by foreign ownership of fish plants, the demise of the fishery, and the importation of processed foods (Harris and Barter 2013, 2015). We see the marginalization of rurality as yet another form of oppression that deserves a place alongside existing feminist concerns for equity: gender, sexuality, class, age, race, ethnicity, and ability. Our research topic draws on women and men's knowledge of the home, garden, and community, men's sea-based experience, and children's eagerness to explore. Our teaching methods, therefore, are of discovery (following a pedagogy of questions) and our source of knowledge is experiential and place-based. Students, from grades 4–12, join us in the research of food practices, and community adults provide historical information. Together, we ask whose interests are being served –

or ignored – by present-day economic arrangements. Encompassing this pedagogy and research are music, games, poetry, and visual arts that open up a dimension inaccessible to the "established reality principle" of academic achievement. The new dimension is one in which "the estranging language and images" of art "make perceptible, visible, and audible that which is no longer, or not yet, perceived, said, and heard in everyday life" (Marcuse 1978, 72). Without these means of representation and expression, it is difficult to think how we – *every one of us* – would begin to see the world, not only as it is, but also as it was, and as it can become.

NOTES

1 Although the arts are often neglected, a contradiction in privilege appears as we examine the extensive involvement of middle-class children (including those of educational decision makers) in arts activities, whether in schools or private programs (Harris 1996b).
2 Further information about CASWE is available at the following URL: https://csse-scee.ca/associations/caswe-acefe/.
3 Welton (1995) refers to early Nova Scotian adult educators as "amateurs out to change the world."
4 CASWE page references are to the edited proceedings.
5 Website for the Transformational Learning Institute, http://www.transformationallearning.ca.
6 In October of 2015, Canada experienced a change of government. Although the new government promises to reverse certain austerity measures implemented by the previous regime, in 2018 neo-liberal policies concerning globalized trade and most social services remain intact.

REFERENCES

Abbey, S. 2002. "Ways of Knowing in and through the Body: Diverse Perspectives on Embodiment." In *Proceedings of the Fourth Biannual Summer Institute of the Canadian Association for the Study of Women in Education*. Toronto: Soleil Publishing.

Alghamdi, A. 2006. "Quilted Narratives of Arab Muslim Women's Tapestry: Intersecting Education, Experience and Gender Perceptions." Unpublished doctoral dissertation, Western University.

Aristotle. n.d. *Nicomachean Ethics, Book 6.* Retrieved from http://classics.mit.edu/Aristotle/nicomachaen.html.

Barter, B.G. 2009. "Urban Mindset, Rural Realities: Teaching on the Edge." In *Learning/Work: Turning Work and Lifelong Learning Inside Out*, ed. S. Walters and L. Cooper, 235–47. South Africa: HSRC Press.

Baskwill, J. 2008. "Stepping out of the Shadows and onto the Stage: Arts-Informed Research in Educational Administration as Activist Practice." *Journal of Educational Administration and Foundations* 19 (2): 37–55.

Bennett, J., ed. 2007. *Rene Descartes' Discourse on the Method of Rightly Conducting One's Reason and Seeking Truth in the Sciences.* http://www.earlymoderntexts.com/pdf/descdisc.pdf.

Berger, J. 1972. *Ways of Seeing.* London: BBC and Penguin Books.

Boal, A. 2002. *Games for Actors and Non-Actors.* 2nd ed. Translated by A. Jackson. New York: Routledge.

– 2006. *The Aesthetics of the Oppressed.* Translated by A. Jackson, New York: Routledge.

Bogdan, A. 2002. "Musical Performance as Embodied Listening." *Proceedings of the Fourth Biannual Canadian Association for the Study of Women and Education International Institute.* Toronto: OISE/University of Toronto.

Brodie, J. 2009. "From Social Security to Public Safety: Security Discourses and Canadian Citizenship." *University of Toronto Quarterly* 78 (3): 687–708. doi:10.3138/utq.78.2.687.

Brown, A., and A. Penniston. 2002. "Building a Community of Women through Dance." *Proceedings of the Fourth Biannual Canadian Association for the Study of Women and Education International Institute.* Toronto: OISE/University of Toronto.

Butterwick, S. 2002. "Your Story/My Story/Our Story: Performing Interpretation in Participatory Theatre." *Alberta Journal of Educational Research* 48:240–53.

Butterwick, S., and J. Dawson. 2006. "Adult Education and the Arts." In *Contexts of Adult Education: Canadian Perspectives*, ed. T. Fenwick, T. Nesbit, and B. Spencer, 281–9. Toronto: Thompson.

Butterwick, S., and J. Selman. 2003. "Deep Listening in a Feminist Popular Theatre Project: Upsetting the Position of Audience in Participatory Education." *Adult Education Quarterly* 54 (1): 7–22. doi:10.1177/0741713603257094.

Chadwick, W. 2007. *Women, Art, and Society.* 4th ed. London: Thames and Hudson.

Clover, D.E. 2005. "Sewing Stories and Acting Activism: Women's Leadership and Learning through Drama and Craft." *Ephemera: Theory and Politics in Organizations* 5:629–42.

– 2010. "A Contemporary Review of Feminist Aesthetic Practices in Selective Adult Education Journals and Conference Proceedings." *Adult Education Quarterly* 60 (3): 233–48. doi:10.1177/0741713609354119.

Clover, D.E., K. Sanford, and S. Butterwick, eds. 2013. *Aesthetic Practices and Adult Education*. London: Routledge.

Clover, D.E., and V. Smith, eds. 2010. "Connected Understandings: Women, Gender and Education." *Proceedings of the 2010 CASWE Institute*. Montreal: Concordia University.

Clover, D.E., and J. Stalker. 2005. "Guest Editorial: Social Justice, Arts and Adult Education." *Convergence* 38 (4): 3–7.

Collingwood, R.G. 1958. *The Principles of Art*. Oxford: Oxford University Press.

Cooley, M., R. Prescesky, and U. Walker. 1998. "The Messiness of Creativity." *Proceedings of the Second Biannual Canadian Association for the Study of Women and Education International Institute*. Ottawa: University of Ottawa.

Cooper, K., and M. Kooy. 2002. "Knowledge, Poetry and Action in the Classroom." *Proceedings of the Fourth Biannual Canadian Association for the Study of Women and Education International Institute*. Toronto: OISE/University of Toronto.

Coupal, L. 2002. "Learning from the Everyday: ICT and Gender in Secondary Schools." *Proceedings of the Fourth Biannual Canadian Association for the Study of Women and Education International Institute*. Toronto: OISE/University of Toronto.

Cranton, P. 2006. *Understanding and Promoting Transformative Learning: A Guide for Educators of Adults*. 2nd ed. San Francisco: John Wiley.

Darmaningsih, M. 2000. "Classical Javanese Dance and Teaching: Toward a New Dance of Freedom." *Proceedings of the Third Biannual Canadian Association for the Study of Women and Education International Institute*. Edmonton: University of Alberta.

deMarrais, K. 2013. "In Defense of Foundations: An Open Letter to Deans." *Critical Questions in Education* 4 (2): 118–29.

Desai, D., and E. Koch. 2012. "Educational Crisis: An Artistic Intervention." In *Art and Social Justice Education: Culture as Commons*, ed. T. Quinn, J. Ploof, and L. Hochtritt, 59–84. New York: Routledge.

Dewey, J. 1980. *Art as Experience*. New York: Perigee Books.

Dissanayake, E. 1992. *Homo Aestheticus: Where Art Comes from and Why*. Seattle: University of Washington.

– 2000. *Art and Intimacy: How the Arts Began*. Seattle: University of Washington.
Driscoll, H. 2013. "Power, Protest and Posters: Finding Spaces to Disrupt Dominant Discourses of School and Standardized Testing." *Our Schools/Our Selves* 22(3): 29–46.
Duckworth, E. 2006. *The Having of Wonderful Ideas: And Other Essays on Teaching and Learning*. 3rd ed. New York: Teachers College Press.
Dutton, D. 1994. "Bookmarks: Fire Is Hot. Hunger Is Bad. Babies Are Good." *Philosophy and Literature* 18: 199–210.
Eisner, E.W. 2002. *The Arts and the Creation of Mind*. New Haven: Yale University Press.
Epp, J.R., ed. 1998. *Centering on the Margins: The Evaded Curriculum: The Second Biannual CASWE International Institute Proceedings*. Ottawa, ON: University of Ottawa.
– 1999. "Where Are We Coming From? The Birth of the Canadian Association for the Study of Women and Education." In *A Challenge Met: The Definition and Recognition of the Field of Education*, ed. M. Allard, J. Cover, C. Dufresne-Tassé, A. Hildyard, and M. Jackson, 139–44. Ottawa: CSSE.
Etmanski, C. 2007. "Unsettled: Embodying Transformative Learning and Intersectionality in Higher Education: Popular Theatre as Research with International Graduate Students." PhD diss., University of Victoria, BC.
Ferguson, K.E. 1984. *The Feminist Case against Bureaucracy*. Philadelphia: Temple University Press.
Foucault, M. 1980. *Power/Knowledge: Selected Interviews and Other Writings*. New York: Pantheon.
Freire, P. 1986. *Pedagogy of the Oppressed*. New York: Continuum.
Gates, E. 2006a. "The Woman Composer Question: Philosophical and Historical Perspectives." *Kapralova Society Journal* 4 (2): 1–11.
– 2006b. "Damned if You Do, Damned if You Don't: Sexual Aesthetics and the Music of Dame Ethel Smyth." *Kapralova Society Journal* 4 (1): 1–5.
– 2007. "Fanny Mendelssohn Hensel: A Life of Music within Domestic Limits." *Kapralova Society Journal* 5 (2): 1–15.
Gilligan, C. 1982. *In a Different Voice: Psychological Theory and Women's Development*. Cambridge, MA: Harvard University Press.
Glazer, J.S. 1991. "Feminism and Professionalism in Teaching and Educational Administration." *Educational Administration Quarterly* 27 (3): 321–42. doi:10.1177/0013161X91027003005.
Glesne, C. 2010. "Disappearing into Another's Words through Poetry in Research and Education." *Learning Landscapes* 4 (1): 29–36.

Green, D.A., and W.C. Riddell. 2001. *Literacy, Numeracy and Labour Market Outcomes*. Ottawa: Statistics Canada, HRDC.

Greene, M. 1995. *Releasing the Imagination: Essays on Education, the Arts, and Social Change*. San Francisco: Jossey-Bass.

Guénette, J. 2002. "Reclaiming the Whole Self, Breaking Away from the Analytical: An Academic's Spiritual Journey." *Proceedings of the Fourth Biannual Canadian Association for the Study of Women and Education International Institute*. Toronto: OISE/University of Toronto.

Gustafson, D.L. 1999. "Embodied Learning: The Body as an Epistemological Site." In *Meeting the Challenge: Innovative Feminist Pedagogies in Action*, ed. M. Mayberry and E.C. Rose, 249–74. New York: Routledge.

– 1998. "Embodied Learning about Health and Healing: Involving the Body as Content and Pedagogy." *Canadian Woman Studies* 17 (4): 52–5.

Gustafson, D., and L. Goodyear. 2006. "Women, Health and Education: Promoting Health and Healthy Educational Communities." *Proceedings of the 6th Biannual International Institute of CASWE, York University, May 30–June 1*. St John's: Memorial University Press.

Hamdan, A. 2009. *Muslim Women Speak: A Tapestry of Lives and Dreams*. Toronto: Canadian Scholars' Press.

Harris, C.E. 1996a. "Aesthetic Imagination in the Literacy-Based Music Classroom: Implications for School Policy and Practice." *Canadian University Music Review* 16 (2): 100–15. doi:10.7202/1014427ar.

– 1996b. "Technology, Rationalities, and Experience in School Music Policy: Underlying Myths." *Arts Education Policy Review* 97 (6): 23–32. doi:10.1080/10632913.1996.9935082.

– 1998. *A Sense of Themselves: Elizabeth Murray's Leadership in School and Community*. Halifax: Fernwood.

– 2002. "A Sense of Themselves: Leadership, Communicative Learning, and Government Policy in the Service of Community Renewal." *Canadian Journal for the Study of Adult Education* 16 (2): 30–53.

– 2008. "Bourdieu's Distinctions of Taste, Talent and Power: Bridging Political Fields and Administrative Practice." In *Political Approaches to Educational Administration and Leadership*, ed. E.A. Samier, 89–108. London: Routledge.

Harris, C.E., and B.G. Barter. 2013. "Community Arts in Critical Research, Curriculum and Pedagogy: Understanding and Changing Food Practices as a Leadership Issue." *Journal of Educational Administration and Foundations* 24 (1): 27–47.

– 2015. "Pedagogies that Explore Food Practices: Resetting the Table for Improved Eco-Justice." *Australian Journal of Environmental Education*. Available on CJO 2015. doi:10.107/aee.2015.12.

Harris, C.E., and N. DePledge, eds. 1996. "Advancing the Agenda of Inclusive Education." *Proceedings of the CASWE Summer Institute, June 7–9*. St Catharines: Brock University.

Hayes, E. 2000. "Voice." In *Women as Learners: The Significance of Gender in Adult Learning*, ed. E. Hayes and D.D. Flannery, 79–109. San Francisco, CA: Jossey-Bass.

Heilbrun, C.G. 1993. *Toward a Recognition of Androgyny*. New York: W.W. Norton.

Karsemeyer, J., and Karsemeyer, J. 2002. "Choreography as Inquiry." *Proceedings of the Fourth Biannual Canadian Association for the Study of Women and Education International Institute*. Toronto: OISE/University of Toronto.

Kennelly, J. 2006. "'Acting Out' in the Public Sphere: Community Theatre and Citizenship Education." *Canadian Journal of Education* 29 (2): 541–62. doi:10.2307/20054176.

Kibbey, J.S. 2011. "Media Literacy and Social Justice in a Visual World." In *Activist Art in Social Justice Pedagogy: Engaging Students in Global Issues through the Arts*, ed. B. Beyerback and R.D. Davis, 50–61. New York: Peter Lang.

Korsmeyer, C. 2004. *Gender and Aesthetics: An Introduction*. London: Routledge.

Ladson-Billings, G. 1995. "But That's Just Good Teaching! The Case for Culturally Relevant Pedagogy." *Theory into Practice* 34 (3): 159–65. doi:10.1080/00405849509543675.

Lamb, R., D. Bates, and K. Frederickson. 1998. "Music on the Margins." *Proceedings of the Second Biannual Canadian Association for the Study of Women and Education International Institute*. Ottawa: University of Ottawa.

Lather, P. 1991. *Getting Smart: Feminist Research and Pedagogy with/in the Postmodern*. New York: Routledge.

Lennon, K. 2014. "Feminist Perspectives on the Body." In the *Stanford Encyclopedia of Philosophy*, Fall ed., ed. E.N. Zalta. http://plato.stanford.edu/archives/fall2014/entries/feminist-body.

Leung, M. 2014. "Hundreds of World's Scientists Urge Harper to End Funding Cuts." CTV News, 21 October. http://www.ctvnews.ca/politics/hundreds-of-world-s-scientists-urge-harper-to-end-funding-cuts-1.2063474#ixzz3KlvIpgPW.

Lewis, S. 2014. *2014 Symons Lecture. Confederation Centre of the Arts*. Charlottetown: Homburg Theatre. http://www.confederationcentre.com/en/symons-lecture-read-more.php?symons_lecture=14.

Lindsay, G. 2002. "Stories Bodies Tell: Reconstructing Experience in Liminal Space." *Proceedings of the Fourth Biannual Canadian Association for the Study of Women and Education International Institute.* Toronto: OISE/University of Toronto.

Mackie, J. 2002. "Reclaiming Voice through Embodied Singing." *Proceedings of the Fourth Biannual Canadian Association for the Study of Women and Education International Institute.* Toronto: OISE/University of Toronto.

Maddocks, F. 2013. "Marin Alsop, Conductor of Last Night of the Proms, on Sexism in Classical Music." *Guardian*, 6 September. http://www.theguardian.com/music/2013/sep/06/marin-alsop-proms-classical-sexist.

Manicom, A. 1992. "Feminist Pedagogy: Transformation, Standpoints, and Politics." *Canadian Journal of Education* 17 (3): 365–89. doi:10.2307/1495301.

Marcuse, H. 1978. *The Aesthetic Dimension: Toward a Critique of Marxist Aesthetics.* Boston: Beacon. doi:10.1007/978-1-349-04687-4.

Margolin, I. 2009. "Beyond Words: Girls' Bodyself." Unpublished doctoral dissertation, University of Toronto.

Martin, J. R. 1994. *Changing the Educational Landscape: Philosophy, Women, and Curriculum.* London: Routledge.

McGregor, C. 2012. "Art-Informed Pedagogy: Tools for Social Transformation." *International Journal of Lifelong Education* 31 (3): 309–24. doi:10.1080/02601370.2012.683612.

Meyer, M.J., and D. Young. 2013. "Tar (theatre as representation) as a Provocative Teaching Tool in School Administration: A Dramatized Inclusive Classroom Scenario." *Canadian Journal of Educational Administration and Policy* 142 (1): 69–89.

Naidus, B. 2007. "Profile: Beverly Naidus's Feminist Activist Art Pedagogy: Unleashed and Engaged." *NWSA Journal* 19 (1): 137–55. doi:10.2979/NWS.2007.19.1.137.

Neilson, A. 2002. "Dancing to Know, Knowing to Dance: Dance as Environmental Education." *Proceedings of the Fourth Biannual Canadian Association for the Study of Women and Education International Institute.* Toronto: OISE/University of Toronto.

O'Reilly, A., and S. Abbey, eds. 2000. *Mothers and Daughters: Connection, Empowerment and Transformation.* Lanham, MD: Rowman and Littlefield.

Patterson, P. 2006. "Body Sight/Site: A Performance." *Proceedings of the Sixth Annual Canadian Association for the Study of Women in Education International Institute.* Toronto: York University.

Peddigrew, B. 2002. "The Resonant Path: Poetry as Embodied Knowing." *Proceedings of the Fourth Biannual Canadian Association for the Study of Women and Education International Institute*. Toronto: OISE/University of Toronto.

Plato. 1987. *The Republic*. Trans. D. Lee. Harmondsworth, UK: Penguin Books.

Roy, C. 2012. "Why Don't They Show Those on TV? Documentary Film Festivals, Media and Community." *International Journal of Lifelong Learning* 31 (3): 293–307. doi:10.1080/02601370.2012.683610.

Ryle, G. 1990. *The Concept of Mind*. London: Penguin.

Sanford, K., H. Blair, and B. Schlender, eds. 2000. "Engendering Education." *Proceedings of the CASWE International Institute, May 27–28*. Edmonton, University of Alberta.

Smith, D.E. 1991. *The Everyday World as Problematic: A Feminist Sociology*. Toronto: University of Toronto Press.

Stalker, J. 1998. "Women in the History of Adult Education: Misogynist Responses to Our Participation." In *Learning for Life: Canadian Readings in Adult Education*, ed. S. Scott, B. Spencer, and A. Thomas, 238–49. Toronto: Thompson.

Sydie, R.A. 1994. *Natural Women, Cultured Men: A Feminist Perspective on Sociological Theory*. Vancouver: UBC Press.

Taber, N., and P.A. Guthro. 2006. "Women and Adult Education in Canadian Society." In *Contexts of Adult Education: Canadian Perspectives*, ed. T. Fenwick, T. Nesbit, and B. Spencer, 58–67. Toronto: Thompson.

Tisdell, E. 2000. "Feminist Pedagogies." In *Women as Learners: The Significance of Gender in Adult Learning*, ed. E. Hayes and D.D. Flannery, 155–83. San Francisco, CA: Jossey-Bass.

Wallin, D., S. MacPherson, and D.K. Liwiski, eds. 2004. "Sexism in the Academy? Ten Years Later." *Proceedings from CASWE's Tenth Anniversary Institute, June 1–2*. Winnipeg: University of Manitoba.

Weedon, C. 1997. *Feminist Practice and Poststructuralist Theory*. 2nd ed. Oxford: Blackwell.

Welton, M. 1995. "Amateurs out to Change the World: A Retrospective on Community Development." *Convergence* 28 (2): 49–62.

CONCLUSION

Moving On

An Invitation to Continue the Conversation

DAWN WALLIN AND JANICE WALLACE

In the introduction, we suggested that our intent was to explore the question, "What effect, if any, has feminism had on Canadian education, and to what end?" This chapter attempts to bring together some of the major themes of the text in order to draw conclusions on the extent to which feminism has affected Canadian education over time. We then turn to a discussion of future feminist contributions to educational thought and practice. We discuss three conclusions – the first two drawing extensively from the chapters in this book and the third exploring possibilities for the future of feminism and education: (1) feminism has had a muted but noticeable effect on Canadian education, albeit more slowly and conservatively than it has affected other academic disciplines and organizations over time; (2) feminist thought and/or agency is becoming more nuanced as Canadian education becomes more diverse, and as the complex social locations of women[1] necessitate greater consideration of the vast range of lived experience; and (3) the changing nature of social and political discourses will lead to a reconstitution of how we think about feminism and the complex spaces in which the feminist projects play themselves out.

THE EFFECTS OF FEMINISM ON CANADIAN EDUCATION

The chapters in this book demonstrate that feminism has had a muted but noticeable effect on Canadian education, although its effects have not been as radical, or as persistent, as many may have hoped. From a macro perspective, women and feminist theory have resisted dominant instrumental educational discourses and have sought a greater focus on equitable policy development; better access to educational services or programs for women and girls; stronger representation of women across organizational contexts and/or roles; growing pedagogical, curricular, and methodological diversity; and improved educational outcomes for a broader range of students (e.g., see Coulter 1996). From a micro perspective, feminist theory has provided educators with means to deal more openly and effectively with the diverse subjective identities represented in students, colleagues, work relationships, and themselves. These improved possibilities are largely due to broader aims of equity within educational environments, focused particularly on the ways in which power, hegemony, and discourse interact to perpetuate inequity in multiple and complex forms. While we celebrate these improvements, progress on the journey to equitable learning opportunities and results for all students as well as educators across all levels of education in Canada is still "three steps forward, two steps back."

As part 1 suggests, feminist movements in education were most often initiated as grassroots projects by teachers and/or community members who noticed firsthand how inequities within the education system differentially affected girls and women. Many of these individuals were also influenced by the political discourses of the civil rights movement in the United States and the activism of second-wave feminism in Canada arising from the report of the Royal Commission on the Status of Women in 1970. These individuals began to organize their local networks to develop political agency within unions, professional associations, and community groups to speak up about gender inequality in their classrooms and school systems and to mobilize change within local communities and educational institutions at all levels. As part 2 demonstrates, many of the women involved in these grassroots beginnings developed strong leadership skills and critical feminist understandings that eventually led them into leadership positions within schools and the academy. Though women in these leadership positions faced many trials and tensions, they worked within the system and spoke out with persistent courage to change institutional policy and practice.

As a kind of chronological mapping of the effects of feminism on education then, authors in parts 1 and 2 reveal the lived experiences of a history that began in the 1970s – an era of grassroots activism in

Canadian education related particularly to gender issues that led to changes in practice and policy, albeit more slowly than in other disciplines and/or organizations. The decade of the 1980s brought with it the *Charter of Rights and Freedoms* that embedded gender as a protected charter category, but it also precipitated an era of economic shrinkage and rationalization that greatly affected the education system and pushed feminist projects to the fringe. By the time the 1990s arrived, the growing diversity of populations in terms of gender, race, ability, ethnic origin, language, learning needs, sexual identity, and so on, led to broad discussions about social justice in educational organizations and the academy, but it also moved the gaze away from gender as a singular focus of discussion. As women – the majority of whom were white and middle class – achieved greater representation in educational milieus, it was assumed that women had "made it" and that gender issues were no longer as pressing as other equity concerns. This provided neo-liberal governments with the rationale to cut funding to feminist organizations and reconstitute professional committees premised on a more general discourse of "diversity" rather than particularist understanding of gender. The dearth of policy development that reaffirmed or focused on gender issues was almost immediate with the election of governments immersed in neo-liberal ideologies (Blackmore 2006).

In the 2000s, the effects of large immigration trends, the critique of colonialism from Indigenous and migrant communities, and social and political organization around LGBTQIA issues are three influences that decentred feminism's gaze on education. This phenomenon is reflected in part 3. The authors in part 3 demonstrate that feminist work over the last decade has been reorganized around anti-colonial and post-structural perspectives that critique earlier feminist understandings based on assumptions of white middle-class privilege and essentialized categories of gender. Instead, an intersectional feminism has emerged that takes into account race, ethnicity, language, class, sexual identity, and other markers of social/cultural positionality in relation to gender.

We propose that there has been growing evidence of social resistance and activism over the last decade, at least partly influenced by changing forms of digital media communication, and a growing polarization around economic position and privilege revealed in social and political discourses. For example, the Women's March following Trump's inauguration, which was referenced in this book's introduction, was a massive response by women and supporters to a Facebook page organized by Teresa Shook, a retired attorney from Hawaii.[2] Her tweet was taken up by others using social media and an international moment of resistance was born. In addition to a growing resistance to misogyny, racism, homophobia, Islamophobia, and other forms of intersectional gender oppression, we anticipate that feminist theorizing and activism will continue to develop complex understandings of gender, particularly as our national Canadian identity is troubled by our patriarchal colonial history, as evidenced by the report of the Truth and Reconciliation Commission of Canada.[3] We believe that we are in a time where feminism is going to (re)invent itself in response to unique challenges as our social and political fabric becomes more diverse. Early understandings of feminism may be threaded through these understandings, but feminist projects in education will be understood and argued on very different terms and grounds than they have in the past.

ACKNOWLEDGING THE DIASPORA

We predict this changing milieu for feminism will occur on the basis of challenges from feminists whose intersectionalities have positioned them on the margins of feminist discourses due to hegemonic privilege employed in the predominantly white, colonial narratives that have traditionally operated in Canada. Prime Minister Justin Trudeau gained international attention for using the phrase "because it is 2015" as his rationale for why he appointed an almost equal representation of men (sixteen) and women (fifteen) to cabinet in 2015. The overwhelming and mixed response to his action is as worrisome as it is praiseworthy. As authors have noted in this text, equal representation of men and women within any organization does not necessarily mean that a feminist agenda will be fostered. This belief hearkens back to liberal feminist pursuits and critiques of the 1970s. And yet, it is clear that the statement by the prime minister drew attention to a lack of representation that has existed throughout the history of our "progressive" nation. There is little doubt that the presence of women in decision-making circles inevitably changes an organizational and policy milieu, even if the women in those positions do not ascribe to feminism. However, as also evidenced by articles in this text is the idea that representation will itself become hegemonic unless it is representative of the diversity of the lived experiences of women.

The Canadian educational context may now have better gender representation, but those who identify as female teachers, administrators, and post-secondary faculty remain predominantly white, middle-class, heterosexual women. Such a reality creates its own hegemonic dominance in the discourse of feminism, and may push alternative understandings to the fringes of feminist thought. It may also have the effect of maintaining dominant forms of privilege in educational practice, thereby reifying the marginalization of women that feminism attempts to redress. Although intersectionality is actually not a new construct in feminist theorizing (see, discussion in Thompson 2002), its articulation and attempts to seriously address the effects of gender as it intersects with race, class, ability, sexuality, poverty, and other social locations has not been at the forefront of educational practice and policy development in the Canadian context. We would like to believe that all those ascribing to feminism would eventually deconstruct their own privilege and address this disconnect. Unfortunately, as with the critique of Justin Trudeau's comment, our educational systems are not much further ahead when we examine our own gendered milieus, even though "it is 2018."

In the case of educational systems, the wake-up calls for change have tended to come in reaction to issues that overwhelm the system. We argue that even though white Western feminists have influenced some changes in our education system over time, the next wave of feminist thought will likely occur due to the efforts of Indigenous women and women who represent the diaspora, whose views have not had the opportunity to influence systems in meaningful ways until now. Some examples are: the "demographic tsunami" of Indigenous children entering the school system as described by Helin (2006); the reaction to the final report of the Truth and Reconciliation Commission of Canada (2015) on the effects of residential schools on Indigenous peoples; and the waves of immigration to Canada, often precipitated by increasingly fractured alliances, wars, and famine. Each of these phenomena have intensified demands on provincial and federal governments and increased ethnic and linguistic diversity in a short period of time. As another example, the attention to LGBTQIA issues sweeping across educational systems in this country, especially evident in Ontario, Alberta, and Manitoba, are enabling school systems, and those who call themselves feminists, to rethink what is meant by feminist thought and praxis. Prior conceptualizations of best practices, equity, representation, and policy are being contested by those whose lived experiences fall outside of normative understandings of Western education and thought. As educators within traditionally conservative and slow-to-change educational institutions struggle with shifting categories of meaning, post-structural angst, and a multiplicity of perspectives, we will need to look to those who have been on the fringe to provide the feminist leadership necessary for new forms of educational equity.

FUTURE FEMINISM(S) AND THE FEMINIST PROJECT IN EDUCATION

Ultimately, we believe that patriarchy, hypermasculinity, and misogyny are alive and well in Canadian education; they reinvent themselves in nuanced ways as educational theory, discourse, policy, and practice shift. In response, new feminist theory will continue to be reinvented so that it can address not only new forms of patriarchy, but its own potential to become an essentializing discourse that excludes the experiences of the Other. As subsequent eras, differently positioned experiences, and alternate subjectivities arise over time, feminists will need to be as open to doing and thinking things differently as the first, second, third, and fourth waves of feminists challenged each other to be and do. In this sense, the feminist project has not changed significantly.

What has changed is the playing field. This field is perhaps more dangerous than it has ever been because it is often framed using the words espoused by feminists, but with the intent to divide and conquer feminist pursuits (Blackmore 2006), or to suggest that feminism is no longer necessary, or that its goals have been achieved. The influences of social media and alternative communication forms have affected the discourse and messaging of feminism and its critiques. Whoever controls and has access to these new communication tools and strategies has also engendered new forms of patriarchy. Ideas and alternate forms of persuasion via social media are more fully available to a general audience, which is as advantageous as it is potentially dangerous. The discourses of feminism will be shaped, resisted, and changed significantly by this influence, and by those who have never lived in a world where it did not exist.

We live in a world of growing social and political polarity. Neoliberal political ideology and global capitalism use technologies to confine perspective, reinforce patriarchy, and manufacture a false need for uniformity in order to serve capitalistic ends (e.g., Blackmore and Sachs 2007; Wilkins 2012). Juxtaposed to this are those who resist the effects of global capitalism and fight against it, often for the sake of environmental sustainability and/or diversity in all of its social forms. The result of this tension may lead to huge shifts in political thought and, arguably, to major policy shifts in Canadian federal politics in the future.

The evidence of growing social unrest on some fronts is added to political polarization and juxtaposed with greater social understanding on others, particularly as populations around the globe are more exposed to international perspectives. On the one hand, these developments have led to clashes of culture, religion, and territory that perpetuate instances of social unrest, prejudice, and conflict, often becoming public spectacles as media attention exacerbates tension rather than promotes understanding of difference. On the other hand, we also see instances of global solidarity and intercultural understanding, often led by youth, who demonstrate to us that our humanity has not been lost. We need to educate ourselves and learn from feminist theorists of the future so that we can understand and move through these complex times, and so that educational spaces do not become sites of ideological polarity, but rather sites of deeper understanding.

CONCLUSION

In the end, the lived experience of women in today's world, as with any historical period, is simply quite different than it has been in the past. Although enduring inequities remain for women and girls throughout the education system, we cannot simply assume that the ideas and practices that led to positive change in the past are those we need for the future. It will be essential, then, to ensure that students and educators are well versed in the history of Canadian feminist thought in K–12, adult, and post-secondary contexts, but we must also rethink our assumptions, let go of what no longer reflects lived realities, and be open to new ideas from innovative scholars and educators. We have observed a growing cadre of feminist scholars and practitioners who may recognize the important work of those who came before, but who have a shifting understanding of what the feminist project entails. These women, because of their multiplicity of perspectives, understanding, and experience, will be more than prepared to move forward with a sense of agency, criticality, and urgency as they insert themselves into feminist discourse, and will articulate new imaginaries for educational policy, practice, and pedagogy in our Canadian educational milieu.

NOTES

1 We recognize that the words woman/women encompass a whole range of social constructions, including cisgender and transgender women who experience and may take up feminism in diverse ways.
2 See Jia Tolentino, "The Somehow Controversial Women's March on Washington," *New Yorker*, 18 January 2017.
3 See "Honouring the Truth, Reconciling for the Future: Summary of the Final Report of the Truth and Reconciliation Commission of Canada," 2015, http://www.trc.ca/websites/trcinstitution/File/2015/Honouring _the_Truth_Reconciling_for_the_Future_July_23_2015.pdf.

REFERENCES

Blackmore, J. 2006. "Deconstructing Diversity Discourses in the Field of Educational Management and Leadership." *Educational Management Administration & Leadership* 34 (2): 181–99. doi:10.1177/1741143206062492.

Blackmore, J., and J. Sachs. 2007. *Performing and Reforming Leaders: Gender, Educational Restructuring and Organizational Change*. Albany, NY: SUNY Press.

Coulter, R. 1996. "Gender Equity and Schooling: Linking Research and Policy." *Canadian Journal of Education* 21 (4): 433–52. doi:10.2307/1494895.

Helin, C. 2006. *Dances with Dependency: Out of Poverty through Self-Reliance*. Warson Woods, MO: Ravencrest Publishing.

Thompson, B. 2002. "Multiracial Feminism: Recasting the Chronology of Second Wave Feminism." *Feminist Studies* 28 (2): 336–60. doi:10.2307/3178747.

Truth and Reconciliation Commission of Canada (TRC). 2015. *The Final Report of the Truth and Reconciliation Commission*. http://nctr.ca/reports2.php.

Wilkins, A. 2012. "Push and Pull in the Classroom: Competition, Gender, and the Neoliberal Subject." *Gender and Education* 24 (7): 765–81. doi:10.1080/09540253.2011.606207.

Contributors

SHARON ANNE COOK, PhD, is distinguished university professor and professor emerita at the University of Ottawa. Her most recent books are *A History of the Faculty of Education, University of Ottawa, 1875–2015* (2018) and *Sex, Lies and Cigarettes: Canadian Women, Smoking and Visual Culture, 1880–2008* (2012).

EVELYN HAMDON, PhD candidate, University of Alberta, author of *Islamophobia and the Question of Muslim Identity* and journal articles focusing on social exclusion at the nexus of gendered and racialized identities, is advisor in the Office of Safe Disclosure and Human Rights, University of Alberta.

CAROL E. HARRIS, EdD, is professor emerita at the University of Victoria and adjunct professor at Acadia University. A former music educator, she publishes nationally and internationally at the intersections of feminist leadership, aesthetics, and critical social theory.

JEAN HEWITT, PhD, held various senior administrative positions in education and committed herself for over fifty years to women's issues in education, increased awareness of the role of women in Canada's history, and the mentorship of women and girls through her active work with educational and community organizations.

ROSE FINE-MEYER, PhD, teaches in the Master of Teaching program at OISE, University of Toronto. Current publications include "Gaining Nationhood: A Comparative Analysis of Images Found in Ontario and Quebec History Textbooks, 1920 to 1948," *Historical Studies in Education* (Fall, 2017), with Catherine Duquette.

MARLENE E. MCKAY, PhD, is coordinator of field experience at the University of Saskatchewan. Her research interests include Indigenous feminisms, feminist epistemologies, Indigenous education, Aboriginal literacy, Indigenous language revitalization, and discourse analysis.

THASHIKA PILLAY is a PhD candidate in educational policy studies at the University of Alberta. Her scholarship focuses on the intersections of educational policy, migration studies, critical and anticolonial feminisms, and community engagement.

MELODY VICZKO is assistant professor in critical policy, equity, and leadership studies at Western University. Her research focuses on multiscalar governance and critical approaches to studying policy networks in education.

JANICE WALLACE is emerita professor at the Faculty of Education, University of Alberta. She has published in the areas of disability in the workplace, the experiences and contributions of the first female academics in educational administration programs in Canada, and women teachers in twentieth-century Ontario.

DAWN C. WALLIN, PhD, is professor and associate dean of undergraduate programs, partnerships and research in the College of Education, University of Saskatchewan. She specializes in educational administration and leadership. Areas of scholarship include educational leadership, rural education and governance, and gender issues in education.

Index

ableism, 111, 174; abled, 114, 175
Aboriginal feminism, 189, 195, 197–201, 206–7. *See also* Indigenous: and feminists
Aboriginal Women's Action Network, 195
Acker, S.: *Caring as Work for Women Educators*, 28, 31, 33, 34; *Chairing and Caring*, 92; *A Foot in the Revolving Door?*, 92
Actor-Network Theory (ANT), 145
actors: heterogeneous, 146; human and non-human, 146
Adamson, N., 46
adult education, 12, 124, 150, 153, 167; adult educators and community arts, 230–7; history of feminism in adult education, 179; intersectionality and adult education, 180–2. *See also* community: community arts
advocacy: advocacy groups, 42; feminist advocacy, 7, 18, 94, 106, 114; teachers' advocacy, 49, 91. *See also* resistance
AERA (American Educational Research Association), 36, 127

aesthetics, 11, 105, 227
affirmative action, 46, 48, 49, 50
Ambwani, V., 215
Andersen, M., 44
Anderson, H., 105; *The First Female Academics*, 106, 122
Angod, L., 9
Antigonish Movement, 179, 232
anti-oppression education, 167, 175, 178–81
anti-racism, 172, 181–2; anti-racist, 166
Antonelli, F., 236
Anzaldúa, G., 172
Arab/Muslim, 171, 173, 241
Archives of Ontario, 43
art-as-embodiment, 239
arts-based: education (ABE), 229; learning, 230, 248, 250; pedagogy, 228, 231, 248; research, 229, 230, 238
Asher, N., 124, 126, 128, 130, 136
assemblages, 146–7, 157, 159, 161. *See also* networks
Atkinson, M., 9
authenticity: as constructed within colonialism, 192, 202–5; in rela-

tion to Aboriginal feminism, 199, 203
autoethnography: feminist, 99; autoethnobiographical, 212, 213–14

Backhouse, C., 36
Ball, S., 128
Bannerji, H.: *The Dark Side of the Nation*, 112; *Thinking Through*, 172, 221; *Unsettling Relations*, 221
Barter, B.G.: *Community Arts in Critical Research*, 250
Bascia, N., 44
Battiste, M., 9
Belenky, M., 7, 8
Berger, M., 166, 45
Berkshire Conferences, 36
Bhabha, H., 112
Bill 8: A Bill to Repeal Job Quotas and Restore Merit-Based Employment in Ontario, 109
Bill 79: The Employment Equity Act, 109
binary: multiple forms of, 6, 44, 166, 168, 173–4, 176, 183
Blackmore, J.: *Deconstructing Diversity Discourses*, 120, 261, 264; *Educational Leadership and Nancy Fraser*, 4, 7; *Educational Leadership*, 108; *A Feminist Critical Perspective on Educational Leadership*, 111, 132, 137, 140, 145; *Leading as Emotional Management Work in High Risk Times*, 128, 134; *The "Other" Within*, 94, 108, 112–13, 114, 121, 123, 124, 130; *Performing and Reforming Leaders*, 37, 106, 145, 265; *Troubling Women*, 108
Boal, A., 243

Boalian theatre, 243
body awareness, 230
boundaries: breaking down, 124, 157; crossing, 124, 154, 157, 159; enacting, 159; exclusionary, 104, 154, 218; interdisciplinary, 130; objects, 147–8; political, 151; role, 136; shifting, 145–6, 147–8; working across, 218
Bourne, P., 45
Brah, A., 169
Briskin, L., 46
Brown, Y., 218
bureaucracy, 82; bureaucratic control, 32; educational, 20; educational administration and, 103, 104; women and bureaucracy, 80, 81
Butler, J.: *Gender Trouble*, 172, 214; *Giving an Account of Oneself*, 123
Butterwick, S.: *Adult Education and the Arts*, 230, 242, 246; *Class and Poverty Matters*, 179, 244; *Your Story/My Story/Our Story*, 243

Canadian Women's Movement Archives, 43
capitalism: colonial capitalism, 222; fraternal-patriarchal capitalism, 19; globalized capitalism, 110, 264; knowledge capitalism, 113; neo-liberal capitalism, 175; patriarchal capitalism, 167–8; resisting capitalism, 221, 222
Caplan, P.J., 23, 28, 32
Carastathis, A., 166
career, careers: academic women's careers, 105–6, 122, 132, 149, 153–4, 157–9; administrative ca-

reers, 127, 150; feminism and women's, 6, 17, 28, 34, 110, 135, 219; influences, 216, 220; limits/risks, 122, 132, 135–6; networks, 131; opportunities, 10, 110, 115; teaching career, 99, 100, 154, 195, 219; status, 10
Carr-Harris, S., 44
Carstairs, C., 46
CASEA (Canadian Association for the Study of Educational Administration), 127, 131–2, 133–4; critical examination of, 131
Casey, K., 50
CASWE (Canadian Association for the Study of Women in Education), 103, 126–31; CASWE Institutes, 237–241; compared to CCWH, 23, 26, 27–8, 36. *See also* CCWH
CAUT (Canadian Association of University Teachers), 23
Cavanagh, S., 85
CCWH (Canadian Committee on Women's History), 23–8, 36. *See also* CASWE
CHA (Canadian Historical Association), 26, 36
Charter of Rights and Freedoms, 261
chilly climate, 32, 92, 134
Chilly Collective, The, 32, 92
Cho, S., 183
Circular 14, 55
cisgender, 4, 20, 166
citizenship education, 10, 45
civil rights, 34, 37, 260
Clinchy, B., 7, 8
Clover, D.E., 242, 244, 247
colonialism, 9, 11, 110, 130, 168, 173, 174, 176, 177, 190; colonialism and education, 206, 221–2, 261; colonialism and patriarchy, 177, 198, 205; colonialism and violence, 202; Indigeneity and colonialism, 189, 191–2, 198, 200–1, 203–5; postcolonial, 6; post/anticolonial, 112, 176, 177
colonizer, colonized, 9, 169. *See also* decolonizing
community, 110, 189, 247; academic community, 94, 101; community advocacy, 42, 61, 243, 260; community arts, 234, 247–8; community-based education, 150, 230–2, 241; feminism and community, 36, 48, 80, 158, 241; Indigenous community, 201, 203–4, 217; schools as community centres, 23
Congress of the Humanities and Social Sciences (CHSS), 26
Connell, R.W., 6, 108
consciousness: consciousness-raising, 77, 110, 171, 231, 246; feminist consciousness, 17, 27, 33, 44, 125, 135; intersectional consciousness, 214; as scholar, 153
contradictions, 126, 130, 133, 192, 242. *See also* paradox
conventional: career routes, 150; male role models, 31; schooling practices, 35. *See also* unconventional
Cook, S.A.: *The Case for a Gender Issues Course in Teacher Education*, 29, 91; *A Case Study of Teacher Education*, 25, 91
corporate, 128, 136; corporatized, 128

Coulter, R.P.: *Doing Gender in Canadian Schools*, 91; *History Is Hers*, 32, 54, 91; *School Restructuring Ontario Style*, 5, 91, 111, 120, 260
Cree, 188–207, 217
Crenshaw, K., 166, 183
critical: conversation, 6, 10; critical analysis, 7, 82, 99, 105, 125; critical hermeneutic, 101–2; feminism, 4, 7, 8, 9, 83, 111, 260; theory/theories, 152, 156, 167, 176, 179, 180, 214
CSSE (Canadian Society for the Study of Education), 27, 126
curricular change, 42–62, 77, 81, 107, 180, 246; patriarchal, 23, 180; state expectations, 43; resistance to, 49; role of teachers in change, 20
curriculum, 50, 52; absence of Indigenous voice, 205; absence of women's voice, 81; commodification of, 113; exclusion, 218–19, 230–1, 238; formal, 18; inclusive, 18, 20, 35, 212; informal, 18; intersectional, 183, 217–18

Dawson, J.: *Adult Education and the Arts*, 230, 242, 246
decolonizing, 180, 205, 222; knowledge, 210; practices, 114, 198, 221
Deerchild, R., 194
democracy: democratic ideals, 152, 158; democratic possibilities in education, 228; social democracy, 232, 218
Dewey, J., 249
dichotomization of knowledge, 239
difference/s, 16, 32, 59, 77, 144, 147, 200; feminism and difference, 262, 265; gender differences, 108; identity and difference, 172, 197, 203; make a difference, 120, 128, 131, 145; pedagogy of difference, 181, 214; politics of difference, 176, 203, 215; theorizing difference, 167, 175, 176, 178, 182, 215
differently abled, 114, 175
disability, 4, 5, 6, 108, 178; disability studies, 178. *See also* ableism
disadvantage, 10, 23, 168, 215; structural disadvantage, 12, 83, 94, 110
discourse, 11, 73; equity, 111; exclusionary, 166, 168; knowledge-making and dominant educational, 214, 260; liberation, 78, 205; social construction of, 196–7, 217, 259; traditional and normative, 93, 112
discourse, feminist, 6, 8, 12, 72, 80; Aboriginal feminist, 197, 201, 202–5; dominant feminist, 172; gendered, 190; margins of feminist, 262, 263, 264
discourse, power and oppression, 9, 34, 111, 131, 139, 171; Aboriginal feminism, 189; colonial and imperial, 177; embodiment and body regimes, 24; historically produced, 191–2; political/policy, 48, 214, 260, 261; relations of, 196
discrimination: dismantling, 172; employment, 76, 77, 166; gender-based, 5, 72, 172; (non)-discriminatory practices, 18, 34, 73, 78; race, sexual identity, religious beliefs, ableness, Aboriginality, and other forms, 195, 215, 242

Donmoyer, R., 103
dualisms: challenging, 233; decentring, 169; mind/body, 227, 230, 248
Duckworth, E., 244
Dyke, L., 215

educational administration: canon of literature, 103–5; critiques of dominant theoretical perspectives, 92, 151, 158; experience of academic programs, 100–3; and feminism, 107–110; feminist scholarship, 92–4, 99–100, 105, 115; intersectionality, 110–14; women in educational administration, 33. *See also* leadership
education system: feminist critique of, 11, 260–1; formal, 10, 11; neoliberal, 46, 106; profoundly conservative, 46; and visible minorities, 213–221
Edwards, R., 146, 147, 148, 157
Eisner, E.W., 246–8
elementary education issues: curriculum, 18, 205; female administrators, 72, 80, 93, 109; female teachers, 23, 24, 33, 72; schools, 72
Elementary Teachers' Federation of Ontario, 83
emancipation, 37, 171, 173, 179, 180
embodiment: inquiry, 250; leadership, 124–5; learning, 230, 239, 240, 241, 244, 248; lives, 8; sexism, 122–3
emotional labour, 137
emotional management, 137
emotions, 105, 136, 234, 239

enactment, 7, 146, 204
Enslin, P., 18
entanglements, 94, 145–7, 161
Epstein, D., 88
equality: in educational organizations, 108, 140; gender equality, 4, 6, 22–3, 29, 45, 55, 59; structural equality, 52. *See also* inequality
equal opportunity, 10, 17, 18, 22, 28, 78
equity: educational administration, 92, 94; intersectional, 48; policy, 7, 17–19, 49, 50, 60, 101, 108–9
equity reform, 18, 20, 49, 152; of textbooks and curriculum, 52–5, 60; in working conditions, 78, 80–1
essentialism, 8, 155, 172, 180–1
Euro-American, 168, 212, 213, 216, 221, 235, 236
Euro-Canadian, 5, 120, 196, 202
Euro-Western, 174
exclusion, 6, 34, 52, 104, 136, 148, 152, 158; exclusion from arts, 166, 173, 206
exploitation, 215, 219, 220, 236

faculties: comparing rank of members, 23, 25–31, 33, 37; education, 30, 31, 32, 100, 106; engineering, 24; female faculty, 31, 93, 150, 230, 263; history, 23, 27, 29; humanities, 23, 24, 25; male faculty, 100; working relationships, 129, 132, 135, 144
Federation of Women Teachers' Association of Ontario. *See* FWTAO
feminism, 3, 27, 27, 29, 154; activism, 47, 48, 80; contention

across feminisms, 4, 5, 6–9, 10, 11, 174–5, 183; critical, 111, 227–8, 230; definition, 6–9, 22, 222–3; identification with, 47, 122, 125–30, 158–9; ideology, 46; impact on education, 6, 12, 19, 28, 46, 82, 115, 260; Indigenous/Aboriginal feminism, 112, 189, 197–205, 207; influence, 146, 149; intersectional, 83, 93, 110, 114, 167, 175–82; liberal feminism, 4, 7, 17, 20, 83, 110, 166, 175, 176, 177; postmodern/post-structural feminism, 8, 83, 111–12, 190, 213, 214–16, 233; professional practices, 28, 61, 71, 99, 100; queer feminism, 172; resistance to, 18, 29–36, 43, 109, 111, 135; scholars, 149, 160; scholarship, 105, 144–5, 151–2, 155; subaltern, 172; support of, 25. *See also* feminist waves; resistance

feminist waves: first wave, 22; second wave, 23, 44, 71, 83, 260, 261; third wave, 23; fourth wave, 23

Fenwick, T., 146, 147, 148, 157

Ferguson, K., 80, 84, 107, 233

film, 47, 56, 78, 241, 243–4

Fine-Meyer, R., 43, 44, 49

Fitzgerald, T., 108, 122, 130, 165

Foucault, M.: *Discipline and Punish*, 122; Foucauldian, 126, 143; governmentality, 137; *History of Sexuality*, 189, 191; power, 191–2, 194; *Power/Knowledge*, 219, 245

Francis, D., 206

Fraser, N.: *Fortunes of Feminism*, 174; *Who Counts?*, 175

Freire, P., 242

FWTAO (Federation of Women Teachers' Association of Ontario), 7, 11, 19, 47, 59, 71, 73, 108; advocacy and political action, 7, 59, 75, 78–9, 81

Gaetane, J.-M., 108

Gaskell, J., 5, 6, 18

gender: bifurcation, 233, 240; category of analysis, 27, 35, 37; cisgender, 4, 20, 165; and culture, 200–1, 203, 206; and curriculum, 43, 49, 81; equity, 10, 20, 47, 59, 73–4; equality, 29, 59; equitable, 43; hegemony, 7; in higher education, 45, 92, 103, 106–8, 144, 150–2; identity, 9, 12, 48, 168, 173, 261, 262, 263; oppression, 173, 175–8, 215–17, 241–2; organization of schools, 24, 33, 45, 50; performance, 8, 132–3; policy, 98, 102, 109, 261; in schooling, 5, 19, 29, 260; school texts, 52; stereotypes, 238, 261; social arrangements, 100, 191, 194, 198–201; solidarity, 59–60, 129–32; subjectivities, 8; work, 127, 140, 153, 172

Giddens, A., 111

Gidney, R.D., 60

Gidney, B., 30, 23

Gilligan, C., 7, 245

Giroux, H., 106

global capitalism, 264–5. *See also* capitalism

global north, 112, 114, 168

global south, 9, 110, 112, 114, 168, 216

Gluck, S., 45

Goldberger, N., 7, 8

Goodson, I., 44
graduate studies: doctoral, 24, 31, 102, 107, 154, 158, 168; master's, 152
grassroots: network, 43; projects, 260; work, 80
Green, J., 112, 197–201
Greene, M.: *The Dialectic of Freedom*, 98, 99; *Releasing the Imagination*, 99, 115, 232, 246, 249
Greenfield, T., 92, 101
Guidroz, K., 166

Haraway, D., 147
Harper, H.: *History Is Hers*, 32, 54, 91
Harris, C.E.: *Bourdieu's Distinctions of Taste, Talent and Power*, 230; *Community Arts in Critical Research*, 250; *A Sense of Themselves*, 231
Harris, Mike (premier), 60, 79; Harris government, 18, 19, 109
Heap, R., 23, 91
hegemony, 130, 260, 262; challenge to, 132, 140, 231; class, 212; discourses, 94; in educational administration, 133; Euro-American, 212, 216, 221; gender, 7; hegemonic forms of feminism, 213, 263; hegemonic masculinity, 9, 77, 92; histories, 215; knowledges, 212, 218, 221; privilege, 262; theories, 130
hermeneutic, 102; critical hermeneutic, 101, 102. *See also* critical
heteronormativity, 100, 110, 174
heterosexism, 32
heterosexuality, 9, 110, 111, 112, 263

hierarchy, 31, 44, 75, 79, 81, 103, 104, 124, 233
higher education, 10, 11, 92–3, 94, 106, 128, 179; corporatization of higher education, 128. *See also* post-secondary education
Hilda Neatby Prize, 26
Hill-Collins, P., 222
home-work balance, 34; household responsibilities, 75
hooks, b., 172, 174, 219, 220
Hoy, W.K., 124, 125, 155
human rights, 4, 48, 239

identity, 4, 9, 23, 112, 172, 173, 175, 178, 180–2, 190, 192; Aboriginal, 193, 197, 201, 203–4, 211, 214, 220; arts and identity, 238, 246, 247, 262; citizenship and identity, 218, 219; identity politics, 166, 173, 178, 222; as scholars, 138; as women, 215. *See also* identities
Imber, M., 103
inclusivity, 11, 12, 18, 57, 111, 166–7, 238, 244, 247; inclusion of women, 42, 45, 48, 49, 57, 79, 110, 144
Indigenous: authenticity, 203–5; education and educational leadership, 99, 130, 168, 218, 263; and feminists, 9, 112, 114, 168, 189, 201–2; peoples/communities, 34, 112, 113, 130, 168, 200, 203, 208; politics, 198; women, 5, 112, 168, 189, 192, 198, 219, 263; world view, 130, 189, 217, 219
Indigeneity, 108, 110, 111, 203, 204
inequality, 20, 23, 49, 99, 101; gender inequality, 43, 140, 260

inequity, 11, 20, 34, 37, 44, 46, 49, 61, 126, 183, 260
insider-outsider, 125. *See also* outsider
interdisciplinary, 130, 148
internationalization of education, 113
International Women's Year, 47, 78
intersectionality, 5, 11, 83, 93, 100, 108, 111, 112, 114, 165–7, 171–84, 210–23, 262; critique of, 166–7
Islamophobia, 173. *See also* Arab/Islam

Janovicek, N., 45, 246

Kealey, L., 36
Kehler, M., 9
knowledge, knowledges: base, 92, 94, 100, 103, 138, 149; boundaries of, 136, 146, 155–7, 159–61; dichotomized, 239–40, 247–9; Indigenous, 112–13, 194; kinesthetic/embodied, 241; place-based, 250–1; privileged, 9, 147–8, 181, 212, 216; production of, 48, 129, 130, 145, 151, 191, 214, 218, 221–2, 231; subjugated/colonized, 114, 144, 168, 212–14, 218–21; women's, 43, 104, 131, 137, 158, 220. *See also* power-knowledge
Kohli, W., 23, 43, 44, 62, 84
Kumashiro, K.: "Toward an Anti-Oppressive Theory of Asian-Americans and Pacific Islanders," 180; "Toward a Theory of Anti-Oppressive Education," 180

Labaree, D., 32
labour, 54–7, 204, 219, 220, 246

Lather, P., 8, 245
Latour, B., 145, 146, 157
Law, J., 147, 158
leadership, 7, 11, 25, 27, 31, 37, 53, 76–9. *See also* educational administration
lecturers, 25, 26, 31
legitimacy, 125, 193
Leiper, J.W., 23
LGBTQIA (lesbian, gay, bisexual, transgender, queer/questioning, intersex, asexual/ally), 12, 110, 114, 261, 263
liberal feminism. *See* feminism
liberation, 34, 78, 173, 176, 182, 198
lifelong learner, 244
liminal spaces, 12, 121, 131, 132, 139
Living and Learning (Hall-Dennis Report), 35
Llewellyn, K., 45
Lorber, J., 6, 22, 44, 83
Lorde, A., "The Master's Tools Will Never Dismantle the Master's House," 175, 176; *Sister Outsider*, 3
Loreto, N., 165
Lugg, C.A., 108

male: dominated, 32, 50, 73, 78, 103, 104, 112, 154, 240; oriented, 32, 79; privilege, 77
Manzer, R., 35
marginalization: Aboriginal women, 192, 196, 202, 206, 207; feminist scholars, 114; within patriarchy, 173; rural communities, 249, 250; in textbooks, 54; of women, 235, 263; in workplaces, 60, 83

margins, 130, 131, 171, 172, 176, 207, 262
Marsden, L., 47
Marshall, C., 7, 84
Martin, J.R., 133
masculinization, 121, 149
master teachers, 31, 32, 37
McCall, L., 183
McIntosh, P., 204
McLaren, A.T., 5, 6, 18
McPhail, M., 46
Millar, W.P.J., 23
Minh Ha, T., 172, 175
ministries of education, 20, 49–50, 52, 55, 77, 81
minority sexual identity, 108, 110, 111
Miskel, C.G., 124, 125, 155
misogyny, 4, 168, 200, 207, 235, 247, 262, 264
Miss G Project, 81
Mitchinson, W., 36
Mohanty, C.T.: *Feminism without Borders*, 167, 172, 174, 177, 182, 183, 215, 221; *Under Western Eyes*, 202, 203
Munro, A., 22
Muslim. *See* Arab/Muslim

NAC (National Action Committee on the Status of Women), 47
Neatby, N., 23
neo-liberal society, 120
networks, 22, 47, 53, 58, 61, 94, 109, 131, 260; feminist networks, 27, 43, 50, 59, 79, 131; networks/assemblages, 146; women's networks, 46, 61–2
newsletters, 27, 43, 47, 53, 55

Noddings, N., 7
normal schools, 24, 32

O'Brien, M., 9, 46
Odora Hoppers, C., 221, 223
OISE/UT (Ontario Institute for the Study of Education/University of Toronto), 35, 49
omission, 43, 45, 50, 52
oppression, 7, 123, 132, 168, 171–3, 181, 192, 193, 219, 241, 242; and gender, 173, 175, 182, 201, 206; in Indigenous communities, 112; intersectionality and, 166–7, 178, 187, 198, 262; normalized, 202; and power, 9, 112, 222, 250; systems and sources of, 80, 166, 167, 173, 180–1, 198, 211. *See also* anti-oppression education
oral history, 43, 45, 61
Osborne, K., 52
Ottawa Teachers' College, 31
outsider, 105, 131, 133, 201, 211, 215, 216, 241
OWHN (Ontario Women's History Network), 26, 47

paradox, 9, 46, 126, 132, 133
part-time, 33, 219
Patai, D., 45
Pateman, C., 19, 109
paternalism, 75, 78, 135, 136, 203, 247
patriarchy, 109, 171–84, 210–23; discipline, 126; ideology, 193; patriarchal capitalism, 19, 167–8, 168, 175; patriarchal colonialism, 198, 200–1, 202, 205, 207, 262; patriarchal culture/norms, 8, 112, 133,

177; patriarchal state, 4, 7, 195; systems, 177, 183, 192, 205; violence, 200
pedagogy/pedagogical, 20, 42, 61; approaches, 43; arts-based, 228, 229, 230–1, 248; decisions, 42; disruptive, 180, 181, 214; feminist, 8, 11, 28, 43, 180, 237, 244, 245, 250–1; practices, 42, 43, 183, 217, 249
Peden, S., 9, 130
performativity, 128–9, 146, 147, 160
phallocentrism, 173, 183
philosophy, 61, 152, 153, 231
Phoenix, A., 7, 8
politics: of difference, 176; feminist, 23, 172, 233, 236; Indigenous, 199, 204, 222; macropolitics, 167; micropolitics, 167; ontological politics, 161; populist, 3; practical, 4. *See also* identity: identity politics
Pollock, K., 213
popular theatre, 241, 242, 243
positionality, 112, 113, 168, 245, 261
positivism, 92, 101
post/anticolonial feminism, 9, 112
post-secondary education, 19, 22, 34, 35, 150, 179, 202, 206. *See also* higher education
poverty, 34, 59, 243, 263
power, 4, 9, 10, 19, 29, 31–3, 80, 83; distribution of power, 93, 112, 132, 203, 205, 260; intersectional power relations, 216, 217; political power, 71, 75, 79, 109, 138, 250; power relations, 53, 78–80, 103, 104, 105, 158, 181, 190, 233, 244

power-knowledge, 8, 108, 110, 122–3, 178, 189, 191, 222
pregnancy, 74, 75
Prentice, A.: *The History of Women and Education in Canada*, 45, 46; *The Feminization of Teaching in British North America and Canada*, 23, 35, 91, 213; *Women Who Taught*, 91, 107
principal: certification, 58, 72; female principals, 72, 78, 80, 108–9; gender distribution, 24; interview process, 76; resistance of, 75, 80
privilege: discursive, 93, 114, 165, 216; in faculties of education, 19; male, 7, 92, 109, 197; positional, 77, 120, 123, 132, 261, 262; signifier of, 113, 230; systemic, 177; unexamined, 122, 123, 204; white females, 94, 110, 112, 150
productivity, 34
professional: activism, 129, 261; appearance, 74; aspirations, 11, 149; associations, 260; communities, 49, 80, 130; development, 32, 56, 104; practice, 31, 46; professionalism, 48; programs, 23, 30, 78, 93, 112; status, 25, 30, 195
professor, 25, 31, 33, 51, 100, 103, 111, 152; professoriate, 25, 28, 34
promotion, 25, 26, 34, 72, 126; bias, 74, 75, 76; promotional interviews, 75
protests, 34, 44, 74, 75, 237
psychoanalytic, 6, 101

queer, 8, 12, 174, 175, 180. *See also* feminism: queer feminism quilt: metaphor of resistance, 236–7; quilted narratives, 241

race, 212, 242; racialization, 4, 5, 6, 9, 32, 34, 171, 175, 177, 194, 197, 215, 218, 222
radicalism, 34, 35
Razack, S.: *Geopolitics, Culture Clash and Gender after September 11*, 167, 174; *Looking White People in the Eye*, 214
REAL Women, 197
"relations of ruling," 99
Report of the Royal Commission of Inquiry on Education in the Province of Quebec, 35
Report of the Royal Commission on the Status of Women in Canada, 4, 6, 10, 17, 35, 46, 48, 72, 73, 260
representation: Aboriginal, 206; arts, 230; female, 25, 32, 33, 260; gender, 262, 263; organizational, 73, 79, 91, 92, 261; programmatic, 92; under-representation, 10, 37
reproduction, 114, 234
reproductive rights, 193
residential schools, 201, 205, 263
resistance: arts as, 250, 261; feminist, 82, 167, 221; gendered, 122; institutional, 134, 135, 191; male, 109, 122, 262; pedagogical, 46; of state, 18; resistor, 120
Reynolds, C.: *Women and Educational Leadership*, 33, 99, 101
Ribbins, P., 92, 101
Richards, H., 221, 223
rights: civil, 34, 37; economic, 22, 46; human, 4, 48, 239; political, 260; rights denied, 193; rights

feminism, 108, 111; women's, 10, 18, 79, 81, 83, 109, 200, 203. See also *Charter of Rights and Freedoms*; reproductive rights
Riley, J.: *The Case for a Gender Issues Course in Teacher Education*, 29, 91
risk, 3, 126, 133–6, 139, 203, 244, 247, 248
Rochdale College, 34
Rottmann, C., 8
Royal Commission on the Status of Women (RCSW), 4, 6, 10, 17, 46, 48, 72–3, 260
rural education, 127, 129–30, 227
Ryan, J., 213

Sachs, J.: *Performing and Reforming Leaders*, 37, 106, 145, 265
Said, E., 112, 171
Scheurich, J.J., 103
Schick, C., 181
self-reflection, 77
self-reflexivity, 124
settler society, 198
sexism, 79, 81, 109, 122–3, 172, 195, 198–9, 214, 240
sex-role stereotyping, 5, 18, 49, 77
sexual harassment, 53, 81, 107, 115, 122–3
sexual minority, 4, 5, 6, 110
Shakeshaft, C., 100
Sherman, S., 108
Shields, C., 138
silence, 122, 135, 189, 192, 221, 245; "quiet work," 127, 135, 140; silenced, 122, 133, 140, 171, 202, 204, 207
Sinner, A., 121
sixties scoop, 201

Smith, D.: *The Everyday World as Problematic*, 236, 245; *Institutional Ethnography*, 99
Smyth, E., 45
social: benefits, 99; change, 9, 37, 46, 54, 124, 137, 214; history, 54; justice, 53, 57, 104, 124, 130, 152, 231, 261; media, 23, 166, 262, 264; processes, 190–1, 196; reality, 7, 196; transformation, 46, 130, 140, 218
society: societal changes, 43
socio-political, 172, 174, 178, 183, 200
speaking ourselves into existence, 192
Spivak, G., 172
Status of Women Canada, 27, 28
Status of Women Committee, 53, 73, 74–5, 77, 91
status quo, 43, 46, 47, 124, 130, 158, 231, 244
St Denis, V., 197, 199, 200, 201, 206
St Pierre, E., 123, 140, 189, 190, 223
structural-functionalism, 156, 158
students: female students, 23, 24–5, 33, 58, 81, 144, 154; student learning, 42
subjectivity/subjectivities, 94, 121, 260; Aboriginal, 192; gendered, 8, 154; intersectional, 190, 264; scholarly, 160
subjects, 5, 23, 93, 123, 140, 167, 172, 175–6, 180, 182, 191, 236
subjugation, 171, 189, 195, 199, 222; of women, 230, 235
suffrage, 54, 57, 78
systems, 19, 29, 37, 49, 60, 212, 216

Tarule, J., 7, 8
teacher: activism, 7, 72, 78; certification, 24; female teacher dress code, 74, 80; male, 7, 24, 44, 59, 74, 78, 83; strike, 75
tenure, 23, 33, 34, 37, 106, 128, 132; tenure track, 28, 36, 92; untenured, 26, 126
textbooks, 50, 51–2, 54–5, 72, 77
Theobald, M.R.: *Women Who Taught*, 91, 107
Tilly, C.: *Durable Inequalities*, 99, 116, 119
Tong, R., 18
Tooms, A.K., 108
Toronto Board of Education, 42–62
Toronto District School Board Archives, 43, 53
transformative learning, 239, 242, 243, 245
Truth and Reconciliation Commission of Canada (TRC), 262, 263, 266
Tuhiwai Smith, L., 9

unconventional, 125, 150, 154
university: courses, 45; structure, 19, 30; University of Alberta, 30, 91, 150; University of Calgary, 30; University of Ottawa, 31, 43; University of Toronto, 51; University of Toronto archives, 43. *See also* faculties

Viczko, M.: *The First Female Academics*, 105, 106, 122
visible minority, 210–23
visual artists, 242, 247

visual arts, 235, 238, 239, 243, 251
voice, 4, 7, 10, 11, 12, 18, 20, 44, 56, 61, 75
Voice of Women (VOW), 49, 71

Wallace, J.: *The First Female Academics*, 105, 106, 122; *The Voice Inside Herself*, 105
Wallin, D.: *The First Female Academics*, 105, 106, 122; *The Voice Inside Herself*, 105
Wane, N., 218, 221
Wa Thiongo, N., 169
Weedon, C., 189, 190, 191, 233, 236, 245
Weiler, K., 213
wellness, 7, 135, 139
Western, 30, 48, 82, 113, 165, 173–7, 192, 200; non-Western, 174
whiteness: unproblematized whiteness, 113; white default, 165; whiteness as privileged signifier, 113
Wilkins, A., 265
Williams, V., 108

women: women's history, 23, 26, 27, 36, 43, 44, 47, 52, 54, 57, 58; women's issues, 27, 48, 54, 93, 190, 202; women's movement, 43, 44, 46, 47, 51, 59, 125; women's narratives, 42, 52, 56, 60; women's studies, 44, 50, 57, 58, 79
Women's Education Resource Centre (WERC), 47, 49
Women's March (2017), 3, 4, 261
working class, 179
workshops, 7, 47, 53, 77, 81, 109, 239, 248
world view, 120, 153, 168, 213, 217, 218, 219, 220
Worth Report, 35
writing myself into being, 124, 134, 144, 156, 160

Young, B.: "An Other Perspective," 91–2, 144; *Women and Educational Leadership*, 33, 99, 101
youth culture, 34

Zurzolo, C., 44